T5-AMZ-574

COURAGE

COURAGE

True Stories of American Sports Heroes

MIKE CELIZIC

A Gallen / Golenbock Book

Carroll & Graf Publishers, Inc.
New York

First Carroll & Graf edition 1991

Carroll & Graf Publishers, Inc.
260 Fifth Avenue
New York, NY 10001

Library of Congress Cataloging-in-Publication Data

Celizic, Mike.
Courage : true stories of American sports heroes / by Mike Celizic. —1st Carroll & Graf ed.
p. cm.
"A Gallen/Golenbock book."
ISBN 0-88184-687-2 : $19.95
1. Athletes—United States—Biography. 2. Courage—United States. I. Title.
GV967.A1C42 1991
796'.092—dc20 91-12764
[B] CIP

Manufactured in the United States of America

For my parents, Carl and Louise M. Celizic, who showed me first—and best—what courage is made of.

Contents

Acknowledgments

Without Margaret Sinnott, this book would not exist. She never complained about all the work I didn't get done around the house, about my bizarre schedule, about never getting a day off. She got me through the bad times. She's a great woman and a great wife. Thanks, Margaret. I love you.

Among the others I owe thanks are: Peter Golenbock and Richard Gallen for commissioning this work and for their support; Kent Carroll for his patience and editing skills; Herman Graf for helping me deal with reality; Laura Langlie for putting up with all of us.

Also: The National Baseball Library in Cooperstown; Lew Freedman, sports editor of the *Anchorage Daily News;* John Heisler, sports information director at the University of Notre Dame; Bill Pennington, my comrade-in-columns at *The Record;* Jim Wright for unswerving moral support; Gabe Buonauro, sports editor of *The Record,* and his faithful sidekick, Rob Tanenbaum, for putting up with me; *The Record*'s photo editor, Rich Gigli, for tracking down the art; Martin Lader of United Press International; and the wonderful ladies at the Albert Wisner Public Library in Warwick, New York.

Finally: Carl, Jim, Jane, and the Zack-man for forgiving me the time I missed with them. I couldn't ask for four finer children.

Introduction

Before I could write about courage, I had to decide what it was. The dictionary was not much help. It equated courage with bravery, bravery with courage, and both with fearlessness. Many of us do the same.

But if that's all courage is—bravery—then it's not that big a deal, for bravery is momentary. It's running into a wall to catch a fly ball. It's climbing on a roller coaster. At its noblest, it's charging into battle knowing that any moment might bring death.

It is possible to be brave without being courageous and to be courageous without being brave. Some of the most courageous people in the world never risk their lives. And they're certainly not fearless. We see such people every day. They are the wage earners who keep punching the time clock and doing their best because to do less would be to give up. They are the single parents who work two jobs to provide better lives for their children. They are all the people who don't quit when life mixes in a curve ball.

They have fears. Everyone but the foolhardy does. But they overcome those fears, sometimes every day of their lives.

And that's what courage is. It's overcoming the obstacles that life keeps throwing at us. It's not giving up, even when there seems to be no chance of success. It's facing overwhelming odds and continuing anyway. It's picking yourself up after defeat and trying again. It's refusing to say to life, "I quit."

The people in these pages have done that. They've persevered. They haven't always won, but they never give up. They are not all perceived as nice guys, but they have all been true. They have arrived where they are by deciding what they needed to do and then doing it. And as much as they've gotten from their triumphs, they've given back.

With sports pages filled with tales of failure, complaint, and greed, one tends to ask, "Where have all the heroes gone?"

They haven't gone anywhere. They're here, real heroes with real courage, the role models who didn't go away.

Mike Celizic
July 1991

It's Not Over Till the Fat Man Swings

The hardest thing to do is to dare to compete.

Big George Foreman, all 257 glistening pounds of him, is leaning on the top rope of a boxing ring set up in a ballroom at the Trump Plaza Hotel and Casino in Atlantic City. Moments ago, he was waltzing around the ring with a succession of sparring partners, practicing pratfalls and engaging in pitty-pat exchanges of punches. His great shaved head and broad, cherubic face were covered by a red leather sparring helmet with a pointed prow and two big holes for his eyes so that he looked like a vintage DeSoto out for a Sunday drive.

Now the workout—such as it was—is over. An assistant pulls off his headgear and helps him unlace his gloves. He steps out of the big protective cup that boxers wear outside their trunks when sparring. He throws a towel over his shoulders and now, dressed in an old pair of workout trunks and a black sweatshirt with the sleeves torn off, with sweat running freely off his boulder of a skull, he is ready to entertain his fans.

More than three hundred people have paid a buck each to see his show. The money goes to a charity. Ever since Foreman arrived in Atlantic City, they have been coming by the hundreds to catch a glimpse of the old man who would be champ, or—as his promoter, Bob Arum, says in his old-time New York accent—"champeen." The undisputed heavyweight champion, Evander Holyfield, is also training at the hotel and also invites visitors. But Foreman's workouts always attract far more people.

Holyfield doesn't mind. He knows that Big George, the born-again, cheeseburgertarian, round mound of pound, is the showman. Holyfield, a man as quiet as Foreman is voluble, is content with just being champion. If people don't want to see him force his sculpted body through a grueling workout, that's up to them. If they'd rather watch Big George waltz with his partners and stick around to listen to his fat-old-man schtick, he can understand that, because Holyfield enjoys Big George Foreman as much as the rest of America. "I love the guy," he admits. Not that his affection will stop him from trying to separate Foreman from his senses when the proper time arrives.

It will arrive soon. In just two days—on Friday, April 19, 1991—Big George will fight for the heavyweight championship of the world in the great, arched-roof cavern that is the Atlantic City Convention Hall (the same building that hosts the annual Miss America Pageant).

Two days before a fight, Foreman should not even be in the ring. But Foreman hasn't whipped up a soufflé of publicity for himself across the nation by doing what he's supposed to do. If he had done that, he'd still be at home on his ranch in Marshall, Texas, living his version of the good life. So while Evander Holyfield is lying low in a Trump Plaza hotel room, watching "Sesame Street" (honest), playing cards, and waiting for the interminable minutes to tick by, Foreman gives his fans one last show.

They come to Atlantic City from Philadelphia on the Atlantic City Expressway, from New York on the Garden State Parkway, from Baltimore on the New Jersey Turnpike. Most ride the big day-trip buses run by the casinos. It's virtually a free trip—at least until you step inside the gambling halls: all passengers get lunch tickets and a roll of quarters on their way off the bus. Many are senior citizens. They come to Atlantic City for the day, feed their quarters to the clanking ranks of one-armed bandits, have a complimentary drink or two, then go home to nurture their dreams and count their woulda-coulda-shouldas until the next trip.

They have simple hopes, these bus people. They dream of hitting the big one, the one that makes the red light flash and the bells ring and the sirens whoop. On the way into town, the billboards sprouting out of the salt marshes that line the highways scream out in neon colors the names of the lucky jackpot winners. That's the dream: win a million dollars and see your name in paint.

The dream is just the other side of impossible, of course. The odds of winning the big one are about the same as getting run down by a rogue elephant ridden by an Albanian dwarf in Ames, Iowa. But dreams aren't supposed to be easy.

Big George Foreman could identify with these people. Forced to be serious he would say, "If you don't dream, you may as well be dead." And dead is one thing Big George isn't. Reasonable, sober people told him how silly his dream was, just as they are more than willing to tell Atlantic City's bus people how vain their quests are. Foreman listened to the skeptics politely—he had become a polite man over the years—then he used their mockery of him to stoke his legend.

"People say I'm a fat, old man," he tells the audience. "But they're just saying that because it's true."

That one always gets a laugh. The people who adopted Foreman as one of their own were soaked every day of their lives in a deluge of electronic images telling them that the worst things to be in America are fat and aging. They are told every day about the horrors of hair loss. They heard so much about oat bran, many of them had actually tried to eat the stuff.

And then along came Foreman—three months past his forty-second birthday and about to fight for the heavyweight championship of the world. He was gloriously plump, as bald as a cue ball, and he wouldn't apologize for any of it.

When someone in one of his audiences insisted on continuing to ask about those liabilities, Foreman responded, "You can't go through life dwelling on the negative. If you do, then you're one of the many. Just don't pull me down in the mud with you. I've been a winner. I've been a loser. But here I is."

Repeating another story he never tires of, he said, "I've always been big. When I was born, the doctor looked at me"—and here he held up his hand, pantomiming a doctor holding a newborn by the ankles —"and said, 'Yes, he's big.' " The crowd laughed again, and as they did Big George smiled his Santa Claus smile. They liked him, and he liked them. Life was good.

It wasn't always that way. There was another George Foreman who lived a long time ago—one who didn't tell jokes, who didn't like crowds, and who wasn't liked in return. That George Foreman was also big, but only in the conventional sense of being six-foot-four and 220 pounds, with huge arms and shoulders and chest—and a belly so hard you could strike a match on it. He was nowhere near the size of the current edition of George Foreman.

Both George Foremans come from the same place—the Fifth Ward of Houston, Texas, which is not the sort of place anyone would choose to grow up. He was one of seven children, always big for his age, and always strong—which was a good thing, because you had to be strong to survive.

At first Foreman fought to protect himself, then he fought for fun. Although he reads a lot now, in those days he had little use for school. What good would it do him anyway? There seemed to be no way out of that place and that life. One of his cousins, an older girl, told him as much one day when she caught him playing hookey. She didn't scold him because, as she put it, "No one from around here becomes anything anyway."

At fifteen he dropped out of school—not that he went much anyway. He had made it to the ninth grade, but all he had learned was how to be another tough kid on the street. He and a couple of friends went into the mugging business together. They'd get hold of some cheap wine or liquor, get fired up, and do some damage. It was fun beating people up, and profitable too.

"I was the biggest," Foreman once told Lew Freedman of the Anchorage *Daily News*. "I'd hold the guys, and the others would take money out of their pockets." It was after one such mugging that he realized that the steel doors were going to clang shut on him sooner or later.

He had run and hidden under a house, trying to make himself invisible while the police searched the streets for him. He remembered what his cousin had said about no one from the Fifth Ward ever amounting to anything. "If I get out of here," he promised himself, "I'm going to be something."

But what? The answer came a few days later when he was watching television. An ad came on for President Lyndon Johnson's Job Corps. Two sports stars, Jim Brown and Johnny Unitas, were touting the program as a way out. Foreman had always liked Jim Brown—his quiet toughness and strength—so he listened to the ad. "It seemed that he was speaking specifically to me," Foreman says. So he signed up.

It was 1965. George Foreman was sixteen years old. He was sent to a place called Grants Pass, Oregon, where there were trees and flowers instead of trash and dirt. You could ride horses up there, just like John Wayne, another of his heroes. He had a job. He had freedom. But he also had an attitude.

He kept getting into fights and picking on other kids in the program. It was what he knew best, being a bully. Finally, the people who ran the program sent him to another Job Corps site in Pleasanton, California, where there was a counselor named Doc Broadus who might be able to do something with the kid.

Broadus told Foreman that if he wanted to fight so much, he ought to come to the program's gym and put on the gloves. Foreman accepted the challenge, and after a week of learning the basics he had his first amateur fight. The kid he fought knew something about not getting hit.

"I swung at him with my left," Foreman recalls. "*Whoosh.* I threw a right. *Whoosh.* I ran at him and tried to hit him in the belly with my shoulder. I missed that too, and I fell down."

He was so disgusted and embarrassed that he took the gloves off and walked out. It was five months before he came back. But he did come back, and in February 1967, he started boxing in earnest. He doesn't really know why. He remembers only that as a child, "My father would come up to me and rub my head and say, 'Here's the next heavyweight champion of the world.' I was so young, I didn't know what boxing was. But that might have planted the seed." It didn't take long for the seed to grow.

He had a talent for fighting. He was already a heavyweight at the age of seventeen, and he packed a terrifying wallop in his fists. His rise was meteoric. In little more than a year, he went from raw beginner to being a member of the U.S. Olympic team that would compete in the 1968 Mexico City Summer Games. When he left for the games, he had fought eighteen amateur fights, was nineteen years old, and weighed almost 210 pounds.

Foreman had taken such delight in just being an amateur fighter competing in Golden Glove competitions that he would scan the newspapers for the listings of each night's amateur bouts. The bouts were printed in tiny type, but Foreman would find his name, cut out the tiny line of type, and save it. And now he was on the Olympic team.

The 1968 Olympics were among the most memorable ever, and George Foreman played a part. The big news had been coming from the track and field venues, where the thin air of Mexico City was coughing up phenomenal performances. Bob Beamon leaped more than a foot past the long jump record to set a standard that still stands. Tommie Smith set a record in the men's 200-meter dash, and James Hines set another in the 100.

But the incident that touched off a firestorm had nothing to do with running and jumping. It had to do with the rising anger of black athletes toward the racism they faced every day of their lives. Tommie Smith and John Carlos (who finished third in the 200) had been human rights activists before the games. When it came time to stand on the medal platform, they demonstrated their convictions by mounting the platform barefooted. They explained later that their bare feet were meant to symbolize the poverty that blacks endured in the United States. When "The Star-Spangled Banner" played, they bowed their heads and thrust black-gloved fists into the air—the black power salute. The Olympic establishment was shocked by the display. Within two days, Smith and Carlos were sent home, where columnists and commentators ate them alive.

If ignorance is bliss, then George Foreman was in heaven. "I was too young to be original enough to think of that," Foreman responds when asked whether he'd thought of joining Carlos and Smith in their protest. "I didn't even know there was anything to be mad about."

For Foreman, there was just the other guy they kept sending out in the ring. Whoever it was, and from whatever corner of the world, Foreman didn't care—he beat them all. And when he had beaten the Soviet, Ionas Chepulis, in two rounds in the final, he was on top of the world. He stood in the center of the ring, reached inside his robe, pulled out a tiny American flag, and waved it proudly.

The picture was everywhere. Foreman, the media declared, had restored the dignity that Carlos and Smith had destroyed. It was a spontaneous thing, his way of showing his joy. It made him a hero.

To George Foreman, though, winning the gold medal was the main thing, not the little number with the flag. "The greatest achievement I had as an athlete was winning that gold medal," he says. The medal now resides in a place of honor in the Marshall (Texas) Historical Society Museum. The bad kid had turned good. A professional career—the same route taken by earlier Olympic champions Muhammad Ali and George Frazier—beckoned.

Foreman's first professional job was as a sparring partner for Sonny Liston, who had been heavyweight champion of the world before losing the title to Muhammad Ali. Liston was as bad as they come, a scowling, churlish man who seemed to always be in trouble. Liston was also the first man Foreman met in a ring who wasn't afraid of him. "Since I'd come into the ring in 1966, everybody had to be careful with me," he says. "But Sonny Liston was the only guy who didn't. *I* had to be careful with *him*."

Foreman traveled with Liston and learned from him. "That's where I picked up the bad attitude," Foreman confesses—from Liston. Foreman says that when they were at a fight site, and Foreman was talking to reporters all nice and sociable, Liston would walk in, and "everybody would leave me and go to him. And he'd be growling and grunting and cursing, so I said to myself, 'I guess I got to be mean so they'll come to me.' "

Foreman grew a mustache and an Afro. He practiced for years to perfect a John Wayne swagger in his walk. One night at dinner Liston told him what being champ meant. "When I was champ, a lot of people acted like they didn't want me to be champ," Liston told him. "A senator said, 'He's bad, he's no good, he's dirty.' And then I fight Clay,"—Liston always called Ali Cassius Clay—" 'and everybody tells me, 'You shoulda beat him.' "

One day Liston asked Foreman if he wanted to be champ. Foreman said he did. "And Liston said, 'You get to be champ of the world, and you spit on the sidewalk, and they write about it in the newspaper.' I kept waiting for more. And then he said, 'All I care about is the do-re-mi.' "

Foreman knew there was more to being champ than the do-re-mi, and he knew that Liston "was doing more than just spitting on the sidewalk." Still, Liston was his role model, so Foreman practiced being mean, and in time he became extremely good at it. "Before a fight, I'd say, 'I'm gonna kill him.' " Foreman doesn't blame Liston (who died young—apparently from a heroin overdose). Liston was his friend. "He gave me lots of good advice. He told me terrible stories about people who messed with dope." Some of the advice stuck, because of all the trouble Foreman would eventually get himself into, none ever involved drugs or alcohol. He had quit smoking cigarettes and drinking when he became a boxer, and he never went back.

George Foreman fought his first pro fight on June 23, 1969, on an undercard in New York City. Don Waldheim was the victim by knockout in the third round. The following week he knocked out Fred Askew in the first round. Two weeks later Sylvester Dullaire went down in one. By the end of the year, Foreman had fought thirteen fights in just over six months, and he had thirteen victories, all but two by knockout. In 1970 he fought and won twelve fights, all but one by knockout. Over the next two years he fought twelve more times and knocked every opponent out. He had become the Mike Tyson of his day—young and strong and merciless.

He trained by chopping wood, pushing wheelbarrows filled with rocks, and running uphill in combat boots. Dick Sadler, his trainer, said of his power: "Anywhere George would hit you, he'd hurt you. Joe Louis was a great finisher, but George dropped people with his jab. George was raw power."

With each fight he got closer to the most glamorous title in sports—heavyweight champion of the world. His shot at the title came on January 22, 1973, in Kingston, Jamaica. His opponent was Joe Frazier, the reigning champion. The previous year Frazier had beaten Ali in fifteen spectacular rounds in Madison Square Garden. He had knocked Ali down and almost out. He was a relentless attacker who took two of your best shots and gave you a ferocious left hook in return. He was like Rocky Marciano, always coming at you, always throwing punches. He had almost destroyed Ali, and no one gave this Foreman kid a chance against him.

But Frazier didn't take the bout seriously. When he should have been sleeping, he was up dancing and singing in Kingston nightclubs. And he didn't listen to his trainer, Eddie Futch, who had told him to stay away from Foreman for the first five rounds, and then—when Foreman was tired—to take him out. But Frazier, who was built without a reverse gear, came straight at Foreman. And he went straight to the canvas.

Foreman put Frazier down three times in the first round and three more in the second before the referee decided that Smokin' Joe had taken enough. One of Foreman's punches, an uppercut of terrifying power, had lifted Frazier clean off the canvas. When it was all over, the world had a new champion.

Foreman took to the wealth and fame of the championship like a baby to cotton candy. He discovered how easy it was to get women and how many ways there were to spend an evening. He also discovered lawyers. "Within a couple months of winning the title, I got my first divorce," George remembers. "That's one thing that happens. Everybody wants to sue you."

But nobody really wanted to fight him. After what he had done to Frazier, there was no questioning the power of George Foreman, although his stamina might be questioned, and often was. He had, after all, never fought longer than ten rounds—and he'd only gone that far three times in his career. The last time had been in 1971, when it took him that long to knock out Gregorio Peralta. Since that bout he had not had to fight longer than four rounds.

There seemed to be no way to test Foreman's stamina: he only had to hit you once and it was over. His first title defense, on September 1, 1973, was in Tokyo, and he dispatched Jose Roman in one round. Then he defended against Ken Norton on March 26, 1974, in Caracas, Venezuela. Norton could punch with the best of them. In March 1973, he had broken Muhammad Ali's jaw, and although he had lost a rematch to Ali in September, his reputation as a hard hitter was undiminished.

Foreman took Norton out in two.

Life was good, very good, but Foreman had no idea how to handle it. "It changed my personality," he now says. "Who can tell you anything? Nobody. You get to be heavyweight champion of the world, and you start thinking, 'Hey, I can buy this car with cash.' You see a young lady and you have someone say, 'Hey, that's George Foreman.' You start thinking that you're better than anyone. There's no way to prepare a guy for a position like heavyweight champion of the world."

So he bought cars and houses as the whim struck him. He wore full-length fur coats and tore up a hotel room in New York. He listened to no one. "I thought and acted like a thug," he says. "I had Sonny Liston as my model, and I thought that's how you were supposed to act as world champ."

He even went out and got a gun—another thing tough guys were supposed to do—but here the real George Foreman won out over the one he had manufactured. "I shot it once," he says. "The explosion so scared me that I had to get rid of it."

Even without the shooting iron, he had once again become the bully he had been as a kid, taking whatever he wanted, surrounded by toadies eager to win his favor—and his money. No one could tell him anything because he was the king of the world. He was the champ.

But the day comes when every bully runs into someone who isn't paralyzed by fear, someone who takes his best punch and punches back. The bully never knows when that day will come because he doesn't know that day *can* come. And so the bully loses his edge. He figures that all he has to do is show up and act mean. And that's fine—until the day it doesn't work. That's when first confusion and then darkness close in and swallow him.

After detaching Norton from his senses, Foreman signed to fight Muhammad Ali in Kinshasa, Zaire. The fight was billed as "The Rumble in the Jungle," and no one gave Ali a chance. As good as Ali was, he had lost to Frazier—and Frazier had been smashed to pieces by Foreman. What's more, Ali couldn't even hit like Frazier. He couldn't knock you out with one punch, and if he couldn't do that, how could he stop Foreman?

Foreman subscribed to that analysis completely. "I thought Muhammad Ali would be the easiest fight I ever had," he says. "I was overconfident. I beat the guys who whipped him, so certainly I was going to whip him."

The fight was scheduled for September 25, but during a sparring session nine days before the fight, Foreman got cut above his right eye. The cut was bad enough to need stitches, and the fight was postponed until October 30.

Foreman wasn't having fun in Zaire. He wanted to leave while the cut healed, but the government, afraid that he might not come back, wouldn't let him. Ali took advantage of the extra five weeks to get in better shape. Foreman moved from the army camp where he and Ali were training back to the city where there was more excitement, which meant that he had a long commute every day.

Just the same, the odds against Ali were long. His trainer, Angelo Dundee, kept telling him to keep away from Foreman, to use his speed to keep turning Foreman around and take away his punching angles. Like everyone else, Dundee was terrified about what would happen if Ali got hit flush.

The fight was scheduled to begin shortly after 4 A.M. so that it could be seen live on closed circuit television at 10 P.M. eastern standard time. It was a hot and humid predawn, and as the fighters came into the ring in the outdoor stadium, the crowd chanted "Ali Bumaye"—"Ali, Kill Him."

Dundee set up shop in Ali's corner, worried about the condition of the ring. The previous afternoon he had discovered that the ring was tilted on its foundation, and the ropes were fearfully loose. He and Bobby Goodman worked alone leveling the ring and tightening the ropes, but the top rope was still too loose for Dundee's tastes, and he wanted Ali to stay away from the ropes. He didn't want Foreman to be able to tee off on Ali. He wanted Ali to move.

Almost from the beginning, though, Ali went to those ropes. He found that he could lean far back against the top rope, cover up, and let Foreman hack at him. And hack Foreman did, as if his hands were axes and Ali was an oak tree to be splintered into kindling. Dundee was horrified, and so were millions of fans around the world. Ali was covering up and slipping punches as only he could, but he couldn't avoid every blow.

If Ali wanted to get hit, Foreman was more than willing to oblige. He rained his bludgeon-like fists on Ali, and he didn't worry about getting tired, because the fight wasn't going to last long enough for that.

"I had that Muhammad Ali whipped," Foreman says years later. "I had him out a few times, and then the bell would ring and he'd go to his corner and come back the next round as fresh as a daisy."

Foreman didn't realize it at the time, but he had finally met the man who wasn't afraid of him, wasn't afraid of his punches, wasn't afraid of losing. And on top of that, Ali had the strongest chin in the business. As the rounds went by and Foreman continued to swing, confusion closed in, and the strength leaked out of his massive muscles.

Part of Foreman's problem was that he never ate anything or drank any liquids for a day or two before a fight. It's an old bodybuilder's trick: when the body is drained of fluids, the muscles stand out beneath the skin.

"I wanted to look good," Foreman told boxing writer Mark Di Ionno. "I was very, very vain. I wanted to impress people with my physique. So I would get down as low as I could. I would dehydrate myself. People would look and say, 'Man, look at the body on that guy!' "

But a body without fluids is an engine without oil. It wears down quickly, parts start to grind, fatigue sets in, and finally it stops. By the fifth round Foreman was near empty. By the sixth he could barely lift his arms. On into the seventh and eighth rounds, he continued to be sucked into the black hole of Ali's improvised strategy.

The end came in the eighth round. Years later, when asked what he remembers of the moment, he says, "Horrible memories. I remember being hit with a left, another left, a right, a left—*da-da-da-da-da.* It sounded like an auctioneer."

A final right sent Foreman to the unfamiliar territory of the canvas.

He had never been floored before. As he struggled to regain his senses, he remembered having been told to stay down until the count of eight, which was supposed to give a hurt fighter a chance to clear his head. "I was confused," he says. "By the time I heard the referee count eight, it was too late."

Foreman now says that if a fighter is knocked down, he should get up as soon as possible. "That way, you can regain your balance and clear your head," he says. The referee will count eight anyway. Better to get up while you can.

But he didn't get up in Zaire, even though he says he could have. And that's what really hurt—not being beaten, but knowing that he could have gotten up.

"Why was I staying down there?" he asked himself when he realized it was over. "I'm still alive, so I must not have given it all I have."

The darkness was total. Foreman couldn't live with the defeat. He refused to be consoled and took out his rage at himself in a fury of spending. He had a different woman every night, and bought himself pet lions and tigers. He tried to prove his manhood, to rescue his shattered ego, by destroying his sparring partners and sneering at anyone who tried to talk to him.

The fact that Muhammad Ali was the darling of the media and the public further enraged him. Determined to show that he could put on an exhibition as well as Ali, on April 26, 1975, he took on five opponents in Toronto—one after the other, three rounds each. The last three he knocked out.

Instead of bringing him respect, his stunt brought derision. When he fought two more exhibitions later in the year, the barbs got even sharper. Now, his critics said, he was afraid to fight.

Finally, on January 24, 1976—more than a year after his loss to Ali—Foreman fought for real again. His opponent was Ron Lyle, a hard-hitting heavyweight. The site was Las Vegas.

The moment of truth came early in the fight: Lyle caught Foreman with a mighty blow, and Foreman went down. But this time he didn't stay on the canvas. He got up and in the fourth round he returned the favor. Lyle didn't get up.

"When I fought Lyle," Foreman says, "I said to myself, 'He's going to have to kill me.' When I got up off the canvas I proved to myself I wasn't a quitter. From that point on, I could have quit boxing at any time because I was at peace with myself."

George Foreman didn't become a nice guy overnight, but he stopped being a bully, and he learned the difference between losing and being beaten. "Defeat is to go out and not give your best," he says. "It bothered me a long time when I lost to Muhammad Ali, because I didn't give it my best."

Against Lyle he gave his best. He followed that win with four more knockout victories including another thrashing of Frazier, and he felt good again. He felt powerful. And he felt that the heavyweight championship was again within reach.

He signed to fight Jimmy Young, a slick boxer, in San Juan, Puerto Rico on March 17, 1977. In Dave Anderson's book, *In the Corner,* Foreman's trainer, Gil Clancy, recalls telling Foreman, "Puerto Rico is a different climate. I want you down there at least three weeks before the fight to get used to the heat."

Foreman didn't come down until eight days before the fight, and Clancy knew that something was wrong. George wouldn't listen to instructions, his sparring partners were beating him up, and some people close to him had convinced him that someone was trying to poison him. He was just paranoid enough to believe it.

The fight was in Roberto Clemente Coliseum, and it was hot. Clancy says that as soon as Foreman got in his dressing room, he had one of his cornermen tape all the doors and vents shut: "George thought someone was going to pump in poison gas. Now there's no oxygen in the room. None. I was dying. Every once in a while I'd open the door, look around the hall like somebody was out there, and yell, 'What was it you wanted?' Anything to bring a little air into that dressing room."

As usual, Foreman had not had any water for two days and hadn't eaten. Stir in the searing heat, and the brew was deadly. As it turned out, the someone who was poisoning Foreman—at least figuratively —was himself.

Even so, Foreman had Young in trouble by the seventh round and very nearly took him out, but he couldn't quite finish the job. Worse, his gas tank was empty. Although he survived the last five rounds, the decision went against him.

"Losing that fight didn't bother me," he says. "I knew I had given it everything I had."

He had given it more than he had. After the fight, he stripped down and hauled himself into the shower. Suddenly, he came out of the shower screaming, "There's water all around me. There's water all around me. I see God. I see God." He was stark naked, and it was all his handlers could do to keep him from running into the corridor and wrestle him down onto a rubbing table.

It was there, Foreman says, that he died. It's a story he likes to tell when he's preaching. The doctors were working over him, treating him for dehydration—heat prostration—and he was no longer there in that wonderful body. He was bargaining with the Lord, offering him money in return for his life.

Foreman says, "The Lord told me, 'I don't want your money. I want you.' I got scared. I never heard no one turn down money."

Foreman was allowed to rejoin the living, and he awoke screaming, "Jesus Christ is coming alive in me!"

Just like that, he quit boxing, went back to Texas, and decided to work the fields of the Lord. He scowled no more, thought of killing his opponents no more. He did, however, think of cheeseburgers.

His love affair with cheeseburgers goes back to his youth, but he had forgotten just how much food meant to him until after he lost to Ali and couldn't drag himself out of his deep depression.

"I looked around at what boxing had given me, all the cars, the houses and all the money, and I was depressed because it seemed like there was something else I should be happy about, but I couldn't figure out what it was," Foreman once told boxing writer Earl Gutskey. "Well, it was cheeseburgers. When I was a kid in Houston, we were so poor we couldn't afford the last two letters, so we called ourselves 'po.' There was a Dairy Queen two blocks from my house where a burger was twenty-nine cents. To me, that Dairy Queen was luxury, but I could afford only one a week. I was sixteen when I joined the Job Corps and left Houston. My goal that day was to come back rich enough to walk up to that Dairy Queen and order five burgers. Really, that's what money represented to me then—lunch and dinner. When you walk around hungry, food is important. And you never forget."

Then, after his loss to Ali, he was driving aimlessly when, he says, "I drove to a Jack-In-The-Box, drove through in my Rolls-Royce, and bought a burger. I drove home and ate it, and it hit me. I suddenly remembered what I'd dreamed of that day when I'd left Houston—the ability to buy all the burgers I wanted. So I went right back to that Jack-In-The-Box and bought another one."

His love of burgers is so genuine and so pure that once, when he was in Los Angeles to appear on "The Tonight Show," some NBC big shots invited him to dinner. His hosts planned to go to one of Tinsel Town's fashionable restaurants, but Foreman insisted on going to a Fatburger franchise. So they had their chauffeurs drive the limousines to the humble eatery, and all of them piled out in their expensive suits to talk dinner over a pile of Fatburgers. When Foreman's cheeseburger addiction became public knowledge, he was swamped with offers to do commercials for various burger chains, but he turned them all down. "I like them all," he explains. "How would it look if I was doing commercials for Burger King, and someone saw me in a McDonald's or Wendy's? I couldn't do that and sleep at night."

This revelation came the afternoon before the Holyfield fight. Foreman strolled into the press room of the Trump Plaza and stayed for two hours, just as he had done twice the day before and the day before that. He didn't seem the least bit nervous. Rather, he was smiling. Why is he so happy, someone asked.

"Because I have enough to eat," he replied.

If eating was Foreman's avocation after he left the ring in 1977, preaching was his vocation. Convinced that his vision in the San Juan dressing room was real, he turned to the pulpit. He didn't go to school for it, and he is not ordained by any religious group. But he reads the Bible, and he talks about what he knows to be right.

He started on a street corner in Shreveport, Louisiana—not far from his ranch in east Texas. The man who had feared nothing in the boxing ring found himself barely able to hold the microphone of the portable sound system that he and his companions were using. When he was a fighter, tens of thousands of people paid to see him live and millions more watched on television. But on that street corner, it was as if he were invisible.

"No one would pay attention to me," he says. "One of the other guys I was preaching with said, 'Tell them you're George Foreman, the former heavyweight champion of the world.' So I said, 'Yes, I'm George Foreman,' and suddenly people are listening. I got them now."

As word spread of Preacher George, demand for him grew. He was invited to speak at the Crystal Cathedral in California—another high-anxiety performance. He started his own church, the Church of the Lord Jesus Christ, in a run-down section of Houston. That's when he realized that the preaching business was more than simply opening the doors and passing around the collection plate.

"At first, they would come in droves to see the ex-boxer," he says. "But after a while I had to think of something to say. That's the hardest thing in the world—thinking of something to say."

He's not a fire-and-brimstone kind of guy. His message is inspirational, about what a person can do if only he will try. It's about being a winner and not a loser. It's about overcoming life's obstacles. He's the Norman Vincent Peale of the flannel shirt and work boot set.

The ways of the world were no longer for him, he decided. He got rid of every television set in his house and started traveling the country to spread his message. His newfound zeal, good will, and asceticism (except, of course, for cheeseburgers) didn't agree with his fourth wife. She had come aboard when he was a different sort of man, and one day she simply took their two children and went home to the island of Saint Lucia.

Foreman was devastated. With the help of friends, bribes, and some cloak-and-dagger moves straight out of spy films, he went to the Caribbean island and brought his children back. He has since married for the fifth time, and this one seems set to last. He and his wife-to-be, Joan, were looking at a house together when he says he decided he had to marry her. "I don't like mice," Foreman confesses. "That's what brought me to my wife. We were looking at this house and we opened a closet. Inside it was a whole nest of mice. She started catching the mice. She rescued me, and I knew then I could never live without her."

In January 1991 she gave birth to his fourth son (and ninth child). The family got together to name the child. His other three sons are all named George, and the family decided it was a tradition too sacred to break. Welcome to the world, George V.

As the years of Foreman's retirement slipped past, he slipped further and further into obscurity. He was still traveling the country, still meeting thousands of people, but as a preacher, and a preacher talking to fifty or a hundred people in a humble church doesn't make the network news. But that didn't bother Foreman. He was doing what he wanted to do. He was at peace.

He hadn't spent all the money he earned during his boxing career, as many other champions, including Sonny Liston and Joe Louis, had. "I learned a long time ago you got four pockets in your pants," he explains. "From the first three pockets, you spend for the things you want. But what's in the fourth pocket you save for the future."

He dipped into that money not for himself but for his church and for the George Foreman Youth Center in Houston. After awhile, he says, "The pocket that paid for it was getting empty. There's a lot of good to do in the world, and most of it takes money."

That's when he got the idea of a comeback to make money for his youth center. He truly believed he could be heavyweight champion of the world again. It was late in 1986 when he made the announcement. He weighed 315 pounds and was nearing his thirty-eighth birthday. No one took him seriously.

He went back into training on his own. "I got one of those scales that talks to you," he says. "I got on it, and it said, 'You weigh three hundred fifteen pounds.' " He went out and chopped wood, ran, beat the heavy bag, and wore himself out for a week. When he got back on the scale, "it said, 'You weigh three hundred fifteen pounds.' I said, 'You lie,' and took it back to the store."

Foreman hadn't watched television for ten years, and he had no idea who the reigning champion was. He had never heard of Mike Tyson, but he wasn't concerned about who was on top right then. He hadn't returned to boxing for a big payday. "If I wanted the money, I would have fought for the title two years ago," he said on the eve of the Holyfield fight. He truly wanted to win the title, and he treated himself as a rookie whose career was just beginning.

He knew he wasn't the same man he had been a decade earlier, and he wouldn't be the same fighter. For one thing, he was going to be bigger than his old fighting weight of 220. Much bigger.

"When I decided to make a comeback, I looked in the mirror and said, 'I am a big man.' I had actually grown since I quit the ring. I grew an inch in height, and my feet got bigger. So I looked in that mirror and thought, 'I may not look good, but I'm going to do good.' "

When anyone asked him about the comeback, he told them, "I don't like to call it a comeback. I like to call it a resurrection."

His first opponent was one Steve Zouskie. The fight was scheduled for Sacramento on March 9, 1987. Foreman tilted (and bent) the scales at 267 pounds. He looked slow and rusty, but he dispatched Zouskie in four rounds. Foreman said that the hardest part of the fight, "was just getting in the ring." He wasn't afraid of Zouskie, though. What bothered him was that "no one had seen me with my shirt off in ten years. I was a preacher, and you just don't do things like that."

But he got used to being bare-chested in public, and although his performance didn't receive rave reviews, he wasn't discouraged. He was, after all, 1-0 in his new career.

The next opponent to fall, on July 9 in Oakland, was Charles Hostetter. Foreman took him out in three. Then came Bobby Crabtree in Springfield, Missouri, on September 15.

"That's the one time I was discouraged," Foreman says. "Everybody said Crabtree was made to order for me. They said he comes straight at you. Then, the day before the fight, somebody said, 'I hate to say this, but he's a southpaw.' " Okay. Foreman could deal with a lefthander. But when he got in the ring, Crabtree didn't come right at him. He moved around "like a young Muhammad Ali."

Crabtree danced and stuck while Foreman plodded after him. Finally, in the fourth round, Crabtree's manager started yelling at his fighter, "Go after him. His legs are dead." As Foreman tells the story, he looks down at his legs and says, "What's he talking about? My legs look all right to me."

Crabtree took his cue and swarmed over Foreman. "Boom! Boom! Boom!" Foreman says. "I'm saying, 'Oh, Lord, I've had a good life. Why is this happening to me?' "

So what did George do?

"I had to fight him off of me."

Then what?

"I knocked him down."

Score another KO for Big George.

And so it went, in small towns and big cities all over the country. George Foreman fought five times in 1987, nine times in 1988, and five times in 1989. All but one fight ended in a knockout. The public was getting hooked, turning out in bigger numbers. The critics, however, weren't sold.

"They say all I've done is beat up on a bunch of tomato cans," Foreman says, using the ring term for a pug who gets hit a lot. "But they're just saying that because it's true."

At other times, he says, "They say I won't fight anybody unless he's on a respirator. That's not true. He has to be off the respirator at least eight days before I'll fight him."

And then there's his old standby: "They say I'm old. I'm slow. And I'm fat. But here I is."

On January 15, 1990, in the twentieth fight of his second incarnation, Foreman climbed in the ring with Gerry Cooney, the last great white hope whose career had been ended first by Larry Holmes and then by Michael Spinks. Cooney hadn't fought since Spinks knocked him out in five rounds two years earlier. He had a left hook, one of the best in the business, but he didn't have much else. The fight was held at Caesars Palace in Atlantic City, and the pundits quickly dubbed the collision "Two Geezers at Caesars."

The fight writers were laughing, but television personalities such as David Letterman, Arsenio Hall, and Johnny Carson were mentioning Foreman regularly in their monologues. And Foreman was encouraging them by giving them new jokes to pass on to the world.

This sort of behavior was unheard of in the ego-driven sport of boxing. One thing most fighters are incapable of is laughing at themselves, but Foreman had a doctorate in self-deprecation. Even writers who thought little of his skills found that they truly liked this overgrown child who was having so much fun at his own expense.

Cooney caught Foreman early with one of his vicious left hooks. The blow had Foreman virtually out on his feet. But Foreman retained enough of his senses to keep coming at Cooney as if the punch hadn't fazed him. Cooney, who fought as if he thought a combination was something you used to open a bicycle lock, didn't follow up. Foreman quickly cleared his head and sent Cooney to never-never land.

There was no stopping him now. The public wanted to know what Foreman could do against Tyson, the undisputed champion, but the following month Tyson got knocked out in Tokyo by Buster Douglas. Evander Holyfield was in line to fight Douglas for the title, and Foreman didn't want to fight Tyson unless it was for the championship, so he fought four more fights in 1990—and he knocked everyone out.

Late in the year Foreman signed to fight Holyfield, who had since beaten Douglas for the title. The fight was announced in a packed ballroom at the Grand Hyatt Hotel in New York. It would be held on April 19, 1991, in Atlantic City. The tone of the promotion was set when a group of elderly people led Foreman into the ballroom to the tune of "Happy Days are Here Again." When it came time for Foreman to stand up at the microphone and give his spiel, he was interrupted by two waiters pushing serving carts on which were giant, silver-domed serving trays.

"Room service for Mister George Foreman!" the waiters called out, rolling their carts up to the dais. The crowd roared with laughter, and the waiters lifted the silver domes to unveil a roast turkey with all the trimming and a giant platter of cheeseburgers. As a score of photographers started burning film at a frightening rate, Foreman ripped a leg off the turkey with one hand and grabbed a cheeseburger with the other. Even Holyfield—a quiet, poker-faced man not given to public displays of emotion—had to laugh.

The scene, with variations, was repeated across the country on a twelve-city publicity tour, and Foreman never tired of the act. "I'm going to have a big buffet table when I train," he'd tell his audiences. "As I walk by, I'll grab a leg of chicken, a roast of beef, porks of chops." And then he'd smile, showing off a set of teeth that is remarkably small for such a large man. Invariably, he'd be asked to talk more about food. What did he eat for breakfast?

"Normally, I'll have a package of bacon and a dozen eggs," he'd say. "But when I'm training, I'll only have eleven eggs."

He'd talk about his age. "When I win the championship, I'll go home and stand by the mailbox wearing my championship belt and wait for my Social Security check."

Until Foreman came along, big fights were always sold by having the two fighters insult each other or talk about how they were going to tear each other limb from limb. By contrast, the television ads for Foreman-Holyfield featured Foreman sitting in a rocking chair and talking about how he was going to put the championship belt around his arm—because his waist was too big. Bugs Bunny, Bart Simpson, and Billy Crystal all played roles in the publicity. "Evander," Crystal warned, "forget about it. You've never had to fight a man with prostate problems."

It was a great show, but it was also for a purpose. Foreman encouraged all the jokes about his being old and fat, hoping that it would lull Holyfield into a false sense of security. When he went home to train, Foreman was a different man. He harnessed himself to a pickup truck, loaded the kids in the back, and pulled the truck around his two-hundred-acre spread. He'd run fifteen miles on flat land, then go into the hills and run for two or three hours in heavy work boots. In the gym, he'd throw hundreds of punches at the heavy bag without stopping. But when it was time for dinner, he didn't wolf down cheeseburgers. Instead he ate piles of vegetables and lots of chicken (no skin) and fish.

The promotion might have been a joke, but the fight wasn't going to be—not if Foreman had anything to do with it. One thing he remembered from his failures in the ring was that a fighter who didn't take his opponent seriously was in trouble. He hoped that Holyfield would not take him seriously.

In the days before the fight, Foreman spent hours talking to the media while Holyfield holed up in his hotel room. Foreman would talk about anything, and the story usually ended with a joke.

How did he intend to beat Holyfield?

"If I miss him with my left, I'll hit him with my right. If I miss with my right, I'll hit him with my belly."

He was determined to have fun right up until he went into the ring. To do otherwise, he felt, was foolish. He'd tried it the other way—sitting in his room—and it was nerve-racking. This time he was going to enjoy himself. "You work hard to get to a certain position, you get there and you don't enjoy it, you're a fool," he explained.

When people weren't asking him about his girth, they were asking about his age. "I've prayed and hoped for a lot of things," he told them, "but I never prayed to be young. I really like my age. I enjoy getting older. Every year I get wiser, I get more respect. I look forward to getting older and enjoying life. I'm not trying to recapture my youth. I'm trying to be the heavyweight champion of the world."

When he was asked if he was a brave man, he said he thought he was. When he was asked whether being brave meant climbing into a boxing ring, he said it didn't. "Anybody can get in a boxing ring. You don't have to be brave to do that. Bravery is standing up. Most of the time it's standing up by yourself when you believe in something. That's bravery. The hardest thing to do is to dare to compete."

Foreman dared, and as the fight drew closer more and more people found themselves seeing ways that Foreman could win. Maybe it was partly that they wanted him to win—wanted him to strike his blow for middle age and bulging waistlines, wanted him to prove, as he said he was going to, that "turning forty isn't a death sentence."

He nearly pulled it off. In the second round, he clubbed Holyfield with combinations and had the champion staggering backward. In the fifth and seventh rounds, he had Holyfield in trouble again. And each time one of his mighty punches cut through the air like a cannonball, the crowd in the Convention Center (and millions who were watching on pay TV) roared with delight.

Holyfield, who weighed 208 pounds, looked like a middleweight next to Foreman's 257. But if he wasn't as big in body, Holyfield was every bit as big as Big George where it counted—in the heart.

In the third round, just before the bell, Holyfield unleashed a barrage of punches that nearly dropped Foreman—and would have if he had had ten or twenty more seconds. In the seventh, Holyfield responded to Foreman's clubbing blows with an eighteen-punch volley that again rocked Foreman. And again in the ninth, as the bell rang, Holyfield had Foreman turned around on the ropes, within a whisker of unconsciousness.

But Holyfield, who had knocked out twenty-one of twenty-five opponents, including all seven he had fought as a heavyweight, couldn't put Foreman down. Foreman, in the end, was a bit too slow—a bit too old—to win the fight on points, but he wasn't too tired. At the end, the man they said couldn't go the distance actually looked fresher than Holyfield, the man who trains harder than anyone in sports. Foreman never sat down between rounds. And in the last couple of rounds, it was Holyfield, not Foreman, who was clutching and holding, trying to get a breather.

By the twelfth and final round, Foreman knew that unless he knocked out Holyfield, his dream was over. As the two fighters touched gloves to begin the final round, Foreman showed how much he'd grown since his days as a bully. He leaned over to Holyfield and whispered in his ear, "Thanks for the opportunity."

He had his chance, and he made the most of it. He walked out of the ring with his first defeat in the twenty-five fights since his comeback. He also had a welt the size of an apple on his cheek and lumps and bumps all over his broad, shaved head.

"He earned a lot of respect," an admiring Holyfield said after his win by unanimous decision. "He proved that, at forty-two, he had a good chin. He hit me with some good shots. He pressured me almost the whole twelve rounds. He made me do things I didn't want to do. I wasn't able to get him off balance. He forced me to take punches I didn't want to take." It had been Holyfield's longest twelve rounds. It had not been a farce.

Bob Arum, Foreman's promoter, said that Big George "showed all the athletes who act like punks that that's not the way to do it." He showed that dignity, grace, charity, and good humor were not antithetical to boxing.

It took Foreman a long time to get to the interview room after the fight, but when he got there his sense of humor was intact. Unlike the debacle against Ali, in this fight he had done everything he could.

He joked that he lost because of Lou Duva, Holyfield's co-trainer. "I had that fight won," Foreman said, "then Lou Duva slipped a mule in the ring, and that bugger hit me good. I would hit him and he'd be actually out. I'd go in to finish him off, and the next thing I knew he was finishing me off. I had no idea that guy could give that much and take that much.

"I came within inches of being the heavyweight champion of the world," he went on. "The only thing that stopped me was the chin of Evander Holyfield. There's no dignity lost. He kept on coming. The boy's a fine champion. I told him after the fight, 'Man, you're one heck of a champion.' "

Foreman did not rule out fighting again, but he wasn't going to stay in Atlantic City. "I got to get out of here so I can get to my Sunday school class," he said.

It was early Saturday morning, and the next day he would be at that class, talking not about losing a fight, but about living life, about daring to compete.

"He scored the points, but I made a point," Foreman concluded. "If you can live, you can dream."

The Last Shall Be First

Yo, home girl! Do it!

On the afternoon of April 24, 1991, Zoe Koplowitz walks into the grand ballroom of Manhattan's Marriott Marquis hotel. She is alone in the big hangar of a room, and she looks across a sea of fifteen hundred table settings. In the middle of that ocean of crystal and silver and spotless napery, under a sky of chandeliers, is the place where Zoe will sit in a few hours with her friends and family. She makes her way to that table.

Her progress is slow, but that's nothing new. She has multiple sclerosis, a disease that attacks the central nervous system, forming scar tissue on the nerves and blocking the transmission of such basic information from brain to limbs as left foot, right foot, left foot, right. She navigates with the aid of two metal crutches that clamp around her forearms.

This evening she will have to walk some thirty yards from her table to a dais at the front of the room. There's no getting around it. She is the guest of honor. This is a scouting mission, a rehearsal.

On the dais is a lectern stage left. On the back wall of the big room are four enormous pictures. One is of Yogi Berra, former baseball player and quotesmith. Another is a montage of the Super Bowl champion New York Giants. The third is of Julie Krone, the most successful woman jockey in history. And the last is of a woman in running clothes leaning on two metal crutches.

I look like the attack of the fifty-foot woman, Zoe thinks as she looks at her picture. But it's not a depressing thought. Zoe Koplowitz is a large woman, and that's all right. She knows it and accepts it the same way she accepts the disease she was diagnosed with seventeen years ago when she was twenty-five and just starting to make her own way in the city of her birth. That diagnosis had started her on a journey that would end this evening on the dais that looks so far away, under the picture that looks so huge. Zoe Koplowitz doesn't want to crash at the finish line.

All those people, she thinks as she looks at the tables which will be occupied by women in gowns and jewelry and men in black ties and rented shoes. *All taking time out in the middle of the week to see me. They could have sent a check and been done with it. Another tax write-off. They have jobs and appointments tomorrow morning. But they're coming anyway.*

Yes, they would come, fifteen hundred people who had paid five hundred dollars each for the privilege of attending Zoe Koplowitz's night of nights. The occasion is the nineteenth annual Multiple Sclerosis Dinner of Champions, and the theme of the evening is "The Will to Win." Few embody that will like the woman who is making her way alone between the tables and up to the dais, practicing how she will move.

She makes it to the dais, mounts the steps, walks to the lectern, and looks out, imagining what it will be like. "I wanted to see if I could get up five steps without falling on my face," she will say later in explaining why she had gone to the ballroom early. She was only half kidding.

And that's why she is being honored as the recipient of the MS Society's Special Achievement Award. She has to practice going up a flight of stairs, but this same woman had the previous November completed her third consecutive New York Marathon. As a symbol of her speed, she carries a stuffed animal, "Flash, the Miracle Racing Turtle," around her neck when she runs. It took her twenty-one hours and thirty-five minutes to complete the marathon. She traversed the Bronx and Harlem in darkness, passing drug dealers and muggers. During her second marathon, she was accosted by a man with a gun in his pocket. She and her running companions—her pit crew, as it were—continued on and finished in the scary darkness of Central Park at five minutes to four in the morning. For that she earned a line in the record books of the New York Road Runners Club, the marathon's sanctioning body. She is the slowest woman ever to complete the run.

Zoe laughs about that, as she laughs about most things in life. "It sounds like I'm being honored for being slow," she says, her electric blue eyes sparkling beneath a startling set of red curls that make her look like an oversized edition of Orphan Annie.

The resemblence, if accidental, is nonetheless significant. "For years, my theme song was 'Tomorrow' from the musical *Annie,*" she says.

For fourteen years, to be exact. That was how much time elapsed between the day she was told that she has MS and January 8, 1988—the day Zoe Koplowitz, Marathon Woman, was born.

Not that Zoe was beaten down by MS. She's not the sort of person to be beaten down by anything. She's a New Yorker of the best sort—tough and mouthy on the outside, mushy on the inside, and in tune with a drummer who could never play anywhere else. She's a resident of the East Village, the neighborhood where people go who want to be different. She lived there long before it was discovered by the sort who are formula different. She was there when the place was populated by originals. She has survived a mugging and an attempted rape. She has kicked drug dealers out of her building and fought to keep her neighborhood decent. Through it all, she has remained an original.

"I've never seen myself as a victim of MS," she will tell the dinner crowd. "But I made a conscious, deliberate choice to focus on the cerebral and spiritual aspects of my life. And I have a good life, one filled with good friends, good times, and good jobs."

And then came January 8, 1988. The day was like any other spent running Smart Moves Trucking, the moving company that she and a friend had founded. Those with MS suffer excessively from colds, so —just as she did every day—Zoe popped a big vitamin C tablet.

The pill didn't go down. It caught in her throat, and there, in her office, Zoe struggled to breathe as the world went black. "I was gone," she says. "I was turning blue."

Just in time, her business partner saw what had happened. He executed a Heimlich maneuver, and the pill flew out. Zoe was alive.

"That day changed my life," she says. "When I came to, I thought it was such an insult that I wasn't going to die from MS but was going to choke to death on a vitamin C pill.

"I decided that my near-death experience necessitated a commitment to the quality of my life. I wanted back everything I had surrendered to this disease over the years. I wanted back my mobility. I wanted back the use of my left leg, which dragged along behind me. I wanted it more than I had ever wanted anything in my life."

She tells the audience in the ballroom these things, and they listen, struck through to the soul by this remarkable woman's story.

"I decided I needed to have a dream," she says. "A dream that would ask for everything I was and still demand something more. I decided that I needed to do the most outrageous thing that I could imagine doing."

It didn't take her long to figure out what that was. She was a New Yorker, and the craziest thing New Yorkers do to prove themselves is run the New York Marathon, so the marathon it would be.

There was only one problem: Zoe didn't know how to run. She was more than sixty pounds overweight, and thanks to MS she had difficulty just walking down the street with the aid of her crutches. How was she going to run 26.2 miles?

She didn't know how. She just knew she would. "I tried to run and I kept falling down," she says. "I had to wear knee pads and elbow pads to train." That's when someone told her about the Achilles Track Club, a special club founded and run by a man just as remarkable as she—Dick Traum.

Like Zoe, Dick Traum was in his thirties when his life changed. The year of Traum's epiphany was 1975. Traum (also a native New Yorker) owned a computer-related business called Personnelmetrics. He was doing well, traveling around the country and watching his business grow. His main form of exercise was hauling his carry-on baggage from the curb to the gate in airports.

He had once been an athlete, had been on the wrestling team as an undergraduate at NYU. But in 1965, just as he was finishing work on his doctorate, he was standing behind his car at a gas station when another car hit him from behind, crushing him between the bumpers.

The doctors did what they could, but his right leg was history and had to be amputated above the knee. The resilient Traum wasn't devastated by the loss, though. "It's like getting in a fight and having a pair of teeth knocked out," he says, "You get replacements."

That's what he did. Six months later he was fitted with an artificial leg, and two days later he was at a party. "I was probably on the dance floor," he says.

How did he dance?

"Lousy," he says. "But then I was a lousy dancer on two legs."

He got on with life. The loss of a leg is "an inconvenience," he says. "And it looks much worse than it is. It's nothing that has tremendous consequences, particularly if you're working as a business professional. In college I had a job driving a soda truck and carrying cases of bottles. If that were my career, I would have had to change jobs."

In 1975, Traum thought that life couldn't get much better. Then suddenly, one day a friend and business associate dropped dead of a heart attack. Just like that. He was thirty-five years old, just like Traum. He had been a Type A personality, a real go-getter. Just like Traum.

Another friend suggested that maybe Traum ought to think about exercising—you know, get the old ticker in shape. The friend had noticed that Traum tended to limp and thought it was because he had gotten so out of shape. Traum didn't tell him the reason he limped, but he agreed to go to an exercise class at the West Side YMCA.

The class was the usual hour of calisthenics, but the last ten minutes were devoted to running, and Traum didn't know if he could run on an artificial leg. To tell the truth, few others knew either. It just wasn't done.

Traum gave it a go and found that he could do it. Achiever that he was, he decided to see if he could do more. "I started doing a mile in fifteen minutes," he says. "I was proud of myself. Then I got caught up in it. If I could do one mile, was it possible to complete two?"

He fell in with a group of runners, a breed still on the fringes of respectability in those days, and ended up on the board of directors of the New York Road Runners Club, the sanctioning body of more than a hundred races a year, including the New York City Marathon, which claims to be the world's greatest mass-participation sporting event.

By May 1976 Traum felt so good that he entered his first real race, a five-miler. He had never run outdoors. Before the race, he asked his running coach, Bob Glover, to watch him jog. "I asked him how I compared to other amputee runners," Traum says. "He said I looked good, but then again, he had never seen an amputee runner before."

By October Traum was ready for something longer—the marathon. He wasn't trying to break ground. He didn't even know that an amputee running a marathon was unheard of. He just did it. "I got caught up in the excitement," he says. And Fred Lebow, president of Road Runners, wasn't the sort to tell anyone he couldn't run.

Traum finished in 7:24—a respectable time, everything considered. The photographers spotted him, and his picture and story ended up in *Runners World* magazine.

Five months later, an eighteen-year-old man named Terry Fox was lying in a hospital bed in Canada, waiting for the next morning, when his leg would be amputated. He had cancer. In an effort to be upbeat, someone showed him the picture of Traum finishing the marathon on his artificial leg. Inspired by Traum's story, Fox resolved to run across Canada when he recovered from his treatments. He would use the publicity to raise funds for cancer research. Fox ran a marathon a day and called his long and grueling run "The Marathon of Hope." His story touched millions, and his life became the subject of a motion picture. After Fox's death, Traum went to Canada to help continue the fundraising efforts Fox had begun. By 1991 more than eighty million dollars had been raised.

There's something about running that gets to the core of human effort and will. There are more stories of courage to be found among runners than anywhere else. Perhaps that's because the activity is so basic, so primal. The wolves are back there. You're here. Can you make it to that tree before they catch you? That's where it started.

Running was the first sport at the Olympics of ancient Greece. Our word *stadium* comes from the Greek *stade,* that original race of about two hundred meters.

You don't need any equipment to run. You don't need any special skill. You don't even need two legs. You just need the will to get to the finish line.

By finding that will in himself, Traum awakened it in others who, like him, were disabled. Traum got the idea of forming a club for disabled runners in 1982, the year after Terry Fox died. The club would offer support, training, and technical expertise. It would give disabled people a chance to compete with able-bodied people and, by doing so, help the newly traumatized rejoin the mainstream of life. Traum took his idea to Lebow. The track club would be called Achilles, Traum told him, as a reminder that all the members were lacking one thing. Lebow said, "Do it."

"There wasn't tremendous enthusiasm at the beginning," Traum remembers. "Fred said that if three disabled people showed up for the first workout it would be a success. We got two disabled runners. Fred said, 'Well, it's a success anyway.' "

Traum began to recruit members wherever he could find them. "A friend saw a man on crutches selling marijuana in a park," Traum says. "He asked him if he was in the Achilles Track Club. He joined and eventually ran the marathon. But he was still selling grass, and then he moved up to cocaine. One day when he couldn't pay his suppliers, he moved to Miami, and that's how the Achilles Track Club of Miami got started."

True story.

By 1991 Traum was devoting most of his time to Achilles. He had a list of corporate sponsors. He had some forty chapters in seventeen countries with more than two thousand runners. There are Achilles chapters in Mongolia, China, Poland, and Moscow (one of the biggest). In 1990 nearly one hundred disabled runners finished the New York Marathon. Among them were a Polish woman who ran on two artificial legs, an American woman who is a triple amputee (two legs and an arm) and races in a wheelchair, an American man severely afflicted with cerebral palsy who pushes his wheelchair backward with his feet. "This guy can't even scratch his nose, but he can run a marathon," says Traum. And he does it in just over seven hours, faster than Traum's first effort.

"We've got every brand of disability there is," Traum continues.

"Cystic fibrosis, cerebral palsy, blind, heart by-passes, polio, quadriplegics, paraplegics, multiple sclerosis, and single, double, and triple amputees."

In addition to helping members run, Traum helps them get better. For example, he arranged for Mongolian, Polish, and Soviet runners to get state-of-the-art prostheses free of charge. He arranged for a cornea transplant for another Mongolian, and for a Trinidadian. The transplants were done after the races, and the recipients later returned as sighted running guides for other blind runners. He obtained sports wheelchairs for Achilles members from the U.S.S.R., Poland, Colombia, Morocco, and the Dominican Republic.

One Achilles chapter is headquartered at Gaylord Rehabilitation Center in Connecticut, a hospital/halfway house. In 1990 one of the center's patients was the young woman who was viciously beaten and raped in Central Park and became known as the "Central Park Jogger." Through Achilles, she started running again—a slow and deliberate quarter mile at first, with each stride a conscious effort of will and determination. Eventually, she was running several miles at a time, and continued running after her discharge and return to work.

"Running is a sport disabled people can really compete in," Traum says. Sometimes they compete so well that they raise the hackles of able-bodied runners who are too self-consumed to recognize the courage of the disabled. One year an Achilles member, Pat Griskus, finished a New York Marathon in 3:33—an excellent time for anyone. As he crossed the line an able-bodied runner who had finished just behind him tried to force his way past Griskus. "No cripple is going to beat me!" the man was screaming.

That's an exception, though. Most people recognize how special these runners are, although not always in ways one might expect. Traum says that one man noticed several disabled runners in a race for the general public and was overheard wondering aloud, "Gee, this must be a dangerous sport."

Traum—his name in German means "dream"—says that he and other disabled runners are trying to make up for their handicap. "Terry Fox did that. He had a dream that he ran across Canada. He was compensating for losing a leg," Traum says. But, he adds, "What's wrong with that?"

What's wrong with challenging the conventional wisdom that says you can't do something? It may turn out that you can't, but you won't know unless you try. And so the runners of Achilles try with all their might. They gather every week in cities around the world to work out together and give each other strength. Zoe Koplowitz walked into one of those meetings in early 1988.

"I can still remember my first night at Achilles," she says. "I was horrified when I walked into the room. There were blind people, people in wheelchairs, amputees, people who had had strokes—a veritable cornucopia of disabilities. For one terrifying moment, I imagined that all the people in that room had multiple sclerosis—just like me. I was paralyzed by my fear of becoming just like them—vision-impaired or wheelchair-bound. It was a direct and painful confrontation with the fact that I was not able-bodied."

But it was also an opportunity to begin to break the shackles of a disease that had bound her too closely to the ground for fourteen years. Support groups for disabled athletes bubble over with a merry froth of humor and laughter. The athletes have their own shorthand slang for their disabilities. A person who introduces herself as a "left BK," for example, is saying she's a left leg below-the-knee amputee. They do not refer to themselves as "disabled," "handicapped," "differently abled," or any of the other politically correct euphemisms. They call themselves "gimps." The able-bodied are "normies"—normal people.

The optimism and humor are infectious. "In the weeks and months that followed my first meeting," Zoe says, "I began to build friendships with other Achilles members. Not tenuous relationships based on mutual frailties or vulnerabilities, but strong, life-affirming friendships filled with humor, hope, strength, and inspiration."

Among the people Zoe met was a woman from Bayonne, New Jersey—Hester Sutherland—whose daughter is a victim of sickle-cell anemia. The girl, Maude, was just entering her teens at the time. Because of the hereditary disease, she is a quadruple amputee. But neither Hester nor Maude is defeated by that. Maude races in her wheelchair internationally and Hester is a volunteer helper for Achilles. Zoe calls Hester "my spunky buddy." Hester calls Zoe amazing.

When she met Zoe, Hester says, "We hit it off immediately. We understand each other. We know why we're there—to finish, to meet that challenge."

To reclaim control of her body, Zoe took martial arts classes for balance, African dance classes for movement, and played pinball for hand-eye coordination. With daily workouts she lost fifty pounds and no longer had to wear protective gear when she trained. She felt more physically alive than she had in years.

"Zoe is a true spirit," says Traum. "I once ran a hundred-kilometer [62-mile] ultra-marathon, and it took me about as long as she takes to finish the New York Marathon. I empathize with her. She's making a statement."

And what is that statement?

"Don't let the bastards wear you down," Traum says. "I have problems, but that doesn't mean I can't do what others do. That's the statement. She's celebrating life. What can be nicer than that?"

In the abstract, he's right. But on the streets of New York, nice isn't the word to describe Zoe's three marathons, each taking longer than the one before. At times they have been shot through with pain and punctuated with periods of sheer terror.

The wear and tear on Zoe's body is enormous. The very best women marathoners—runners like Grete Waitz, Ingrid Kristiansen, and Joan Benoit Samuelson—finish a race in less than two and one-half hours. Zoe takes ten times as long. That means her body is working hard for ten times as long as an elite runner's. In marathoning, slower isn't easier.

Zoe starts alone at sunrise, more than four hours before the 10:45 A.M. official start time. Some nine miles into her race, the lead runners catch up to her and flash past. Then the rest of the thundering herd—twenty-four thousand five hundred runners—follows. Finally, she and Hester, her running companion, are alone again in the dark —and in the nastiest parts of the city.

"A lot of people are out there all day in pain, but if they had the opportunity to relive one day of their lives, they'd relive the marathon," says Traum. "They'd tell you it's painful, but there is a joy in using all their senses."

Zoe exudes joy. She dresses for her long day in running shoes, tights and a jersey. Around her neck she wears her stuffed turtle. Around her shoulders she wears a shawl with I'M NOT GRETE inscribed on the back, a reference to perennial New York Marathon champion Grete Waitz. To complete the ensemble, she wears big rhinestone earrings that she found in a junk shop. During one of her runs, some gang members asked her if the earrings were real. "As real as you can get for seven dollars and fifty cents," she told them.

"Hester and I are thinking about making a Zoe doll," she says. "Wind it up and it staggers across the finish line in twenty-eight hours."

What makes it so funny is that it's true. But the point is, she *does* make it to the finish line. She doesn't quit.

"When all is said and done, for me the New York Marathon is purely and simply a matter of magic and miracles," Zoe once wrote.

It begins in the solitary splendor of the sunrise, with the mighty Verazzano Narrows Bridge, which takes up the first mile of the race, all hers and Hester's. She makes friends along the way, explaining to people what she's doing. Some already know her from having seen her on television.

When the lead pack catches up to her, she steps onto the sidewalk and watches them pass. "I am in awe of their beauty and grace," she has written. "Could it be that their feet never touch the ground. . . ? I see the winning moment in their faces just as I will recognize that moment in my own face, many miles and many hours down the road. And right now . . . the only real difference between us is one of pace and stride.

"With a conscious act of choice, I bridge that difference. I close that gap. I let my heart and imagination run with the pack.

"I am wild and free."

Once the lead pack passes, Zoe rejoins the race. She loves Brooklyn the best, the borough in which nearly half of the marathon is run, and the borough she sees in the light of day. "It is a borough of hugs and handshakes," she says. People invite her into their houses for food and drink. They offer the use of their facilities. They ask if she's married, and if not, would she like to meet their brothers.

During her first marathon, in one of Brooklyn's poorest neighborhoods, she was stopped by a man who was probably about her age, but who looked ancient. Years of drink and despair had eroded and shrunk him, and as Zoe passed, he reached out and touched her. "When you cross that finish line, think of me," he said, with tears cutting furrows through the grime on his face. "Cross that line for me, too, because you're all I got."

Zoe has looked for him along the route in the years since, but she has never seen him again.

From Brooklyn, she crosses into Queens, then Manhattan, then the Bronx. It's dark by the time she gets there, and it's not a place most New Yorkers would visit at any time of the day. An alternate route for late finishers bypasses these neighborhoods, but Zoe won't detour from the official route marked on the pavement by a painted blue line. "Wherever the blue line goes, I go," she says. It's a matter of principle.

It's also an affirmation that the streets of the city—all the streets—are, or should be, everyone's streets. It is her way of reclaiming them, if only for the time that she passes through them.

Her passage, however, has not always been pleasant. In 1989, she, Hester, and two other friends were approached by two men, one of whom had his hand around a gun that was clearly visible through his jacket pocket. For a frozen moment, the men stared at her in her running outfit with the big runner's number pinned to the front. They passed by, shaking their heads in amazement.

Later, their route took them by a teen gang. Zoe boldly announced to the youths that she was running the marathon and had less than seven miles to go. One of the kids had seen her story on television, and soon they were all fast friends. The gang members escorted her to the border of their territory, where they handed her off to another gang—and so she made it through the Bronx. As she left them behind, they shouted after her: "Yo! Home girl! Do it!"

In Harlem that same year, she and her companions stumbled into an outdoor drug supermarket, where a man in a beat-up sedan told them that they were taking their lives into their hands. He identified with them because he, too, had run a marathon. He sent them to an all-night fast-food joint that was protected from the thugs by thick sheets of bulletproof glass. While Zoe and her friends waited, the man negotiated safe passage for them with the drug dealers in the street.

"My life flashed before my eyes," Zoe says. "Those few blocks seemed to take longer than the whole marathon." She remembers thinking, *God, I don't want to die.*

"And I didn't want my friends to be maimed or injured either. Where do you take a stand in this life? What distinguishes a life-affirming choice from a willful act of self-destruction? I honestly didn't know."

Later, she would write: "I know there are no easy or magic solutions for drugs and homelessness. But I'm beginning to understand what it would take on a spiritual and emotional level.

"How many more blocks, how many more miles, and how many more neighborhoods will I quietly surrender in the name of common sense and self-preservation? How many more activities will I eliminate from my life simply because they are not safe to do any more?"

It's the litany of anyone who lives in any big city. Certain things you don't do—such as wandering around certain neighborhoods after dark, and even before dark. But Zoe was determined to finish the marathon, no matter what, and her companions agreed with her.

"This is my life," she says. "I want it back. I have a right to be on those streets. I have a right to run the marathon. I will not go away, I will not quit, I will not alter my course. If I give up once, then I will have lost something very special."

It's a gesture. Except for marathon days, Zoe's not about to spend her nights wandering the streets of the Bronx. But it's an important gesture. After her second marathon, she was urged not to go through the same neighborhoods again in 1990, but she was determined to follow the blue line.

In 1990 the Guardian Angels, the controversial civilian patrol group founded by Curtis and Lisa Sliwa, volunteered to escort her. Escorted by three large young men trained in the martial arts and equipped with walkie-talkies, that marathon went more smoothly. She still saw drug deals and ran past people stripping cars, but the thugs took one look at the Angels and decided not to hassle the lady with the crutches.

"You would not mess with these guys on a bet," Zoe says. "The ones who went with me through the worst parts are the Angels' heavy hitters. There were three guys, a guy named Strong Belt, one named G-Man, and one named Bart. When Bart took his beret off, he had a Bart Simpson haircut.

"It was tough for the Angels going with me. Any other night, seeing these crack deals and cars being stripped, they would have been running after the crooks, not by them. But they were there as escorts, and the primary thing was safety. Strong Belt kept shaking his head ruefully. One of the other guys told him not to worry: they'd come back. Those three guys put their lives on the line for us," Zoe says.

"At one point, one of the Angels turned to me and said, 'This isn't about a race. This is about life.' He got it."

Finally, she reached the entrance to Central Park and the last couple of miles. The park was so dark they needed flashlights to find their way.

By then, some twenty hours into her race, Zoe was physically wasted but emotionally euphoric. She warned her companions that, as time went on and she reached her limits (and exceeded them), a number of things could happen, none of them pretty. Her speech could slur, her vision could blur, she could lose her coordination. By then her left leg wasn't working, and she had to drag it along behind her.

"It's not a big deal," she says. "I start to stagger toward the end because that's what happens with MS. And my left arm did become quite spastic. But my speech was intact, and my vision was okay."

It's her runner's "wall," the barrier that lies at the limits of the body's resources. "For me, 'hitting the wall' is an opportunity to see what's on the other side of where I usually give up in life," Zoe says. "It's a chance to go deep inside myself for a few moments and really appreciate all that I usually take for granted. I store up the people and memories during the day, and then when I need them toward the end, I begin to draw on them for strength. When I do, I acknowledge that portion of me that can pursue a dream beyond the boundaries of reality. That's what the marathon is. It's above and beyond anything that makes any kind of logical sense."

In her first two marathons, when Zoe got to the finish line behind the Tavern on the Green, even the squirrels were gone. There was no time clock, no timekeeper, no officials of any kind. She crossed alone and phoned in her time.

She thought it would be the same in 1990. The race had taken her more than twenty-one hours, and it was nearly four in the morning. But this time, six more Guardian Angels were waiting for her along with some race officials. They had a medal for her, the same medal every finisher gets. And they had a single red rose, the traditional favor for every woman finisher. She was official.

"I do not need spectators," she says. "I do not need medals. The day has been my gift. My heart is full and, for now, it is more than enough. Perhaps it is more than most people could ever hope for in a lifetime. It is an eternity of emotion compressed into a single moment in time." Still, she appreciated that people were there. That in itself was as incredible as the rest of the day.

Zoe doesn't barge across the finish line. Before she crosses, she stops. In her mind, the tune of Whitney Houston's song, "One Moment in Time," plays. This is her moment in time. After more than twenty-one hours, why rush it?

"I stop and let the day catch up with me," Zoe says. "I think of all the hundreds of people who have touched my life with their kindness and generosity. I remember their faces, their handshakes, and their boundless goodwill. And I let it all in. They're a part of me now, and as I cross the line I cross it with their dreams as well as my own.

"And as I cross the line, at the top of my lungs, I shout 'Yes!' to the morning sky."

She didn't set out to be famous. She set out to run the marathon. But after three marathons, people started to notice. After the 1990 marathon, she was on "The Joan Rivers Show," and Rivers—who had invited her with the intention of having some fun at the expense of the world's slowest woman—was so overcome by Zoe's story that she promised to run with her in 1991. The Multiple Sclerosis Society chose her as an ambassador to promote its annual Super Cities Walk fundraiser. In that role, she spent a morning with Willard Scott on "The Today Show." Finally, she was invited to the Marriott Marquis, to the grand ballroom where she would be honored with a special achievement award.

The guest list that night was loaded with the Big Apple's most prominent movers and shakers. When the presentations began, they applauded for Yogi Berra and Julie Krone and the Giants. But they stood up and cheered when Zoe was called to the front of the room to receive her award, and they remained standing for the duration of her stately walk to the dais.

Diane Dixon, one of the world's fastest woman over 400 meters, presented the award. Then Zoe spoke to the crowd. She told them the story of her quest, of nearly choking to death, and of her decision to run the marathon. She told them of the gangs who had accosted her and of the hundreds of wonderful people who had helped her.

"Tonight is truly for me one moment in time," she told them. "Right here, on this stage, I'm completing the longest run of my lifetime. I was diagnosed in 1974. For all intents and purposes, it's taken me seventeen years to make the journey from that table to this podium."

She told them how much it meant to her that they had come. "You need to know how very much you matter," she said, her voice choking. "You need to know what a difference you make. You've made me bigger, braver, and stronger than I ever dreamed I could be. And from the bottom of my heart, I bless you and I thank you."

Then she walked back to her table. The crowd stood again and applauded. There wasn't a dry eye in the house.

A Winning Hand

I don't think of myself as different.
I don't think of myself as courageous.

By the start of spring training in 1989, it seemed that even Tibetan monks had to have heard about Jim Abbott's right hand. He had talked about it with Phil Donahue for the benefit of that part of America that found itself housebound in the late morning and on after-midnight sports programs for the benefit of insomniacs. It had been the subject of articles, both short—in *USA Today*—and long—in *Sports Illustrated.* No question about it, no right hand from Jack Dempsey's to Rocky Marciano's was more famous than the right hand of Jim Abbott.

Which is pretty strange when you think about it, because Jim Abbott doesn't have a right hand—at least not much of one. It's more of a genetic afterthought, a palm stuck on the end of a right arm that is almost a foot shorter than his left arm. Growing from the palm is one rudimentary finger that isn't really long enough to do anything with.

But the reporters still asked him about it.

"What about the hand, Jim?"

"Don't have one, guys. Born that way."

Abbott would rather have talked about something else—his pitching, his feelings about being in a major league camp, what he had eaten for breakfast, how many Angels could dance on the head of a Louisville Slugger—anything but another round of questions about the hand that wasn't there.

He was twenty-one years old, attending his first major league spring training camp. He wore the uniform of the California Angels, who, on the strength of his left arm, had made him their first pick in the 1989 baseball draft (the eighth player in the nation to be picked). The number on his uniform was 60. A number that high identified him as a player the team planned to assign to the minor leagues once the season began. In fact, the Angels had projected him to begin his professional life in Class AA, the second-highest level of the minor leagues, in the Texas League.

Kids with numbers in the 60s in spring training usually do not rate so much as a "Good morning" from the baseball writers. But Abbott, a strapping six-foot-three blond kid from Michigan, was different. During his amateur career, with the University of Michigan and the U.S. National Team, he had collected more awards than a twelve-year-old tennis prodigy. He had been the first American pitcher to beat the Cuban national team in twenty-five years. He had pitched the gold-medal victory against Japan in the 1988 Seoul Olympics. He had won the Sullivan Award as the nation's top amateur athlete and the Golden Spikes Award as the nation's top amateur baseball player. He had done a hundred or more things worthy of lengthy articles fairly bursting with overripe prose. But none of that brought the relays of reporters to Mesa, Arizona. Nope. It was the hand they came to talk about.

"I didn't know the questions about the hand would be such a blatant issue," Abbott said during his third week of daily sessions with the notepads and microphones. Normal attendance at one of those sessions was a half-dozen people, and in Abbott's first three weeks as an Angels prospect he went through at least twenty-five such sessions and filled more notebooks than Reggie Jackson did in three seasons.

Abbott usually conducted his interviews in a temporary office set up in a trailer next to the clubhouse at the Angels' spring training complex in sun-kissed Mesa. He was less likely to bother his teammates that way. But just getting the few yards from the clubhouse to the trailer could take him more than ten minutes because of all the fans with baseball cards and cameras who wanted autographs and pictures to take home. He never turned down a request for an autograph, never snapped at anyone who shoved a scrap of paper at him and barked, "Sign this!"

Once he had walked the gauntlet of fans, he climbed up the three steps to the trailer and exchanged introductions with that day's panel of inquisitors, shaking hands with each of them. He shook with his left hand. Then he sat down to explain once again what it was like to have been born with only one hand and then to have grown up aspiring to be a major league ballplayer.

On this particular day, Abbott came in, met everyone, and sat down in the open end of a horseshoe of reporters. The writers had heard that he was a good guy, but they knew that this sort of constant attention could wear on anyone. They had all approached players who got tired of answering the same question the second time it was asked, and downright ornery at the third mention.

But Abbott set everyone at ease with a bright smile and an introductory comment: "I don't mind hearing the same old questions if you don't mind getting the same old answers."

This particular group of reporters started the session without even mentioning the hand. So Abbott did it for them, taking them through the basics of playing baseball with only one complete hand, but also talking about how intrusive the questions had become. Someone asked him why he went out of his way to satisfy all the writers and fans and didn't simply tell them all to go to a place considerably warmer than Mesa, Arizona.

Abbott responded by telling a story about Don Sutton, a pitcher who had a long and illustrious career. One day Abbott had seen Sutton patiently signing countless autographs when he would rather have been somewhere else. Abbott asked Sutton why he was so giving of his time. "It's a reasonable rent to pay for the space I get to occupy," Sutton had responded.

"I try to keep that in mind," Abbott told the reporters.

It was an amazing bit of insight for such a young ballplayer. Many athletes never stop to think that it is the fans who make the game so profitable for them.

So Abbott paid his rent, and talking about his right hand—with dignity and humor—was one of the ways he did so. That willingness was one of the reasons the Angels took him with their first draft pick of 1988.

"The thing with Jim Abbott was that we felt this kid had an unbelievable makeup," says Bob Fontaine, one of several Angel scouts who had watched Abbott mature through three years of college and two seasons of international play. The first time Fontaine saw Abbott, the young pitcher was warming up to start a game for the Wolverines.

"I went to the bullpen to watch him throw," Fontaine remembers. "Every time I turned around, there was a camera in his face." But Abbott never complained, and that amazed Fontaine. "He is the only kid I've ever signed that I was one hundred percent sure what kind of makeup he had," the scout said.

James Anthony Abbott was undoubtedly born with some of that makeup. He came into the world on September 19, 1967, in Flint, Michigan, a no-nonsense, sports-crazy city where automobiles were the foundation of the economy.

His parents, Mike and Kathy Abbott, got married young and had Jim, the first of two sons, when both were only eighteen. Although they were short on experience, they were blessed with determination. Mike worked himself up to an account executive position with a beverage distributor, and Kathy became a lawyer. In a way, being young was an advantage to the new parents. They didn't set limits on themselves, and they didn't set any on Jim, either.

Only once did Jim's parents try to deal with his birth defect by artificial means. When Jim was four, they had him fitted with a prosthetic arm that fit over his right forearm. The arm had a hook on the end. Jim put up with the prosthesis until he was five, then he threw it in the garbage.

"I hated that hand," he says. "It limited the things I could do. It didn't help me do anything. It was ugly. It drew attention to me. I threw it out." Jim didn't feel then and doesn't feel now that he had any limits. Ask him what he can't do and he replies, "Button my left sleeve."

He was sports-minded from the start, and if the other kids were playing something, he wanted to join them. His parents never said he couldn't.

"We didn't want him not to be involved because of his hand," his father says.

"We raised him by instinct," says his mother. "I don't know if we deserve that much credit. There was never anything he couldn't do."

That isn't to say he didn't field his share of childhood cruelty.

There were kids who called him "stub" and every other name their nimble minds could think of. Sometimes he came home crying, but not often. "We'd just send him right back out the door," his father says. "We would try to encourage him."

"They put me right in the mainstream and let me do it," says Abbott of his parents. "Nobody ever told me I couldn't do anything." That was vital, and it's something other parents could learn from Mike and Kathy Abbott. They never thought of reasons why their son couldn't do something.

"The only thing that would have been a handicap is if anyone had ever been negative around me," Abbott said. "If anyone had said, 'You can't do this,' or 'How do you expect to do that with one hand?' I probably wouldn't be playing ball now. But nobody ever said I shouldn't play. My mom and dad and coaches and teammates always said, 'Go do it.' So I've played."

Abbott's dad helped him work out a way to manage a baseball glove with his one hand. Alone in the backyard, Jim spent countless hours throwing a ball against a wall and catching the rebounds to perfect the art.

He manages by resting the pocket of his glove on his right hand. Then, when he throws the ball, he slips his left hand into the glove as he follows through. After a catch, he tucks the glove under his right arm, deftly catches the ball as it drops out of the pocket, and is ready to throw again.

It sounds complicated, but he does it all so smoothly that if you didn't know he was doing it, you could watch him for quite some time before realizing that his right hand isn't all there.

He learned to bat by holding the bat with his left hand and supporting it with his right. During World War II, there had been a one-armed outfielder, Pete Gray, who played for the St. Louis Browns (the team that became the Baltimore Orioles). Gray had lost his arm in a childhood accident, and he went through life bitter at what he thought was the unfairness of it. As a hitter he was pretty amazing, but even against the depleted pitching of the war years, he managed only a .218 batting average in his one year of service. He played in 61 games in 1945, getting to bat 234 times. Of his 51 hits, six were doubles, two triples, and none were home runs.

Of course, well-meaning people told Abbott about Gray, but Abbott made it clear that he had other role models. His senior year in high school, he hit .427 with seven home runs. He also had hits in his only two college at-bats. And in spring training in 1991, when he came to the plate for the first time as a major leaguer, with the outfield pulled tauntingly close, he ripped a triple off the wall, four hundred feet from home plate.

"I didn't want to be like Pete Gray," Abbott told anyone who asked. "I wanted to be like Nolan Ryan."

That was his childhood ambition, and with no one to tell him it was impossible, he pursued it. Years later, when he was on the verge of realizing his goal, he realized how grandiose that goal had been.

"I always thought I would play pro ball," he said that first spring in Mesa. "I didn't think about anything holding me back. I grew up playing baseball with one hand, and I just figured I'd play until someone told me I wasn't good enough. I never thought how outlandish that was. Looking back, I realize it's really an unusual situation—me having just one hand—and I guess if I had any common sense, I would have given up long ago." But he didn't have that common sense that tells people they can't do certain things. All along, Abbott's sense was as uncommon as the talent in his left arm.

As a kid, Abbott thrived not on the sufferance of other children, but because he was good enough to compete with them and beat them. He played basketball and football as well as baseball. That's what kids did in Flint—played ball—summer, fall, winter, and spring. "There's an unbelievable athletic spirit in Flint." Abbott says. "Everybody plays ball in Flint.

"Sports was always a buffering agent between myself and my peers," he says. "Kids don't make fun of you if you play just as well as they do. I'm not sure how it would have been if I didn't play sports."

He probably would have done just fine. But he did better than fine, because when a kid can blow away opposing hitters and hit balls over the fence, other kids suddenly stop caring about how many hands he has. They just want him on their team.

Flint is home to just over a hundred and fifty thousand people, but its sports obsession has produced pro football players Reggie Williams, Carl Banks, Jim Morrisey, Lonnie Young, and Mark Ingram. Pro basketball players Trent Tucker and Jeff Grayer are also from Flint, as are baseball players Jeff Hamilton and Rick Leach. And those are just the ones who preceded Abbott.

Going through high school in Flint at the same time as Abbott were basketball stars Glen Rice, who led Michigan to its first National Collegiate Athletic Association championship; Terence Greene, who played at DePaul; and Roy Marble, who played at Iowa. Star pro football player Andre Rison also graduated with Abbott.

Abbott first met the glare of the spotlight when he joined Flint's twelve-and-under Greater Flint Youth Baseball Program. The motto of the league was, and still is, *Every kid can play.* Once again, Abbott met with no barriers, no one telling him, "You can't do this, kid."

The Flint Journal heard about Abbott, not only because he had one hand, but also because at eleven years of age, he led his team in batting and was unbeaten as a pitcher. Recognizing a good story when it saw one, the paper worked up a feature, and for the first time knowledge about Jim Abbott spread beyond his immediate friends and acquaintances.

When Abbott was growing up, Flint had two major high schools, Flint Central and Flint Northern. Abbott went to Central, and he made the baseball team as a freshman. In the first game he pitched, the opposing coach took one look at him and was overcome with a vision of brilliant strategy.

You can imagine the wheels turning in that coach's head: *The kid ain't got no right hand. We'll bunt that sucker to death. Yeah, bunt him to death.* You can imagine him gathering his team around him before the game and relaying this incredibly clever strategy to them. So the first kid goes up, bunts, and gets on first base when Abbott doesn't handle the ball.

Now the genius coach is convinced he's got this kid's number. So he gives the bunt sign to his number-two hitter. The kid bunts, Abbott fields it cleanly and throws him out. Number three then bunts with the same result. Same with the cleanup hitter, and the inning is over.

The next inning, the crafty coach tries it again. Three batters, three bunts, three outs. In the third inning, the coach tries again with his eighth hitter. Bunt it to the pitcher. The kid does, and Abbott throws him out. That's eight straight bunts and seven straight outs. Finally convinced that the one-handed kid can field his position as well as anyone, the coach gives up and lets his team swing away. Abbott doesn't care. He beats them that way, too.

That kind of stuff lasted clear through to the majors. Opposing managers would look at the glove perched on Abbott's right hand and figure they could bunt on him. As soon as Abbott threw a couple of them out (on quick plays he fielded the balls bare-handed) they gave up. He'll probably never be a Gold Glove fielder, but he handles his position as well as most and better than many.

Someone once asked him, "Sure, but what do you do if the batter hits a line drive right at you?"

"I do what everybody else does," he answered with a laugh. "I duck."

He didn't limit himself to baseball. He also played basketball in high school, and by his senior year he was the starting quarterback on a football team that went 10-2 and almost won the state championship.

In his first game as a quarterback, he threw four touchdown passes. But he most enjoys telling the story of the day his Flint Central team was scheduled to play its big grudge game against Flint Northern.

The two schools had a program in which some students switched schools for certain classes. Abbott was one of those students. As luck would have it, the day of the big game was one of the days he went to Northern for afternoon classes. Since everyone at Northern knew he was the quarterback for Central, he expected to hear about the game. What he didn't expect was for most of the students at Northern to come to school with socks over their right hands just to rattle him.

So then what happened?

"We beat them forty-nine to fourteen," Abbott says, still grinning years later at the sweet taste of revenge.

By the spring of his senior year, major league scouts were making the trip to Flint to see the big kid with the ninety-plus mile-per-hour fastball who would finish the high school season with a 10-3 record, a 0.76 earned run average, and 148 strikeouts in 73 innings. Among them were scouts from the Toronto Blue Jays, who liked what they saw so much that they drafted Abbott out of high school in the thirty-sixth round of the 1985 amateur draft.

Don Welke, one of the Blue Jay scouts, had reservations going up to see Abbott. Then he watched him pitch. "After watching him pitch," Welke says, "I didn't think of the right hand at all. For me, he was just another outstanding prospect."

The Blue Jays offered him fifty thousand dollars to sign, and Abbott says he was tempted. At the same time, some people who had only heard about Abbott but had never seen or met him started to talk about how the Blue Jays had only drafted the one-handed pitcher as a publicity stunt. It wasn't true, of course, but the same charge would later be leveled against the Angels.

Abbott had another offer, from the University of Michigan. Growing up in Flint, he had always dreamed about playing for the Wolverines. "I think I can have both my dreams," he said. "I can play college ball and have pro ball still waiting for me down the road."

He picked up his freshman year at Michigan where he had left off in high school. He finished the season at 6-2 with a 4.11 earned run average. He was ESPN's Amateur Athlete of the Week after a 1-0 shutout of Western Michigan and was named to the Big Ten Playoffs All-Tournament Team after beating Minnesota in the league championship game.

In 1985 the March of Dimes had named Abbott its Athlete of the Year, and in 1986 the Philadelphia Sportswriters Association named him its Most Courageous Athlete.

In 1987, his junior year, he won eleven games, including a streak of nine straight wins and thirty-one scoreless innings. He also led the team to a second straight Big Ten title and was named a third-team All-American.

Iowa coach Duane Banks was moved to comment: "I don't think Jim Abbott knows he has a handicap. If nobody tells him, he may never know."

After the college season, Abbott was invited to try out for the U.S. National Team that would play a summer schedule that included five games in Cuba and culminated in the Pan Am Games in Indianapolis.

Ron Fraser, the University of Miami baseball coach, was the coach of the National Team. He admits that he didn't expect Abbott to make the team. "When I brought him to the trials, it was more curiosity than anything," Fraser says. "I knew the competition would be the best in the world, better than college teams." When Abbott pitched, Fraser, like so many coaches before him, ordered the hitters to bunt at Abbott to see if he could handle it. He could. "He proved me wrong," says Fraser.

Abbott was spectacular that summer. During the team's warmup tour, he was 8-1 with a 1.70 earned run average and 51 strikeouts in 47.2 innings. Then it was time to take on the Cubans.

By 1987, the United States—the country that took pride in having invented baseball and in playing the game professionally better than any other country in the world—had a bit of a credibility problem on the amateur level. The chief cause of that problem was Cuba. Although Americans had not been allowed to travel to Cuba since Fidel Castro had turned the country communist in the early 1960s, the two countries had managed to get in some baseball now and then, particularly at the quadrennial Pan Am Games, which Cuba always seemed to win. It had been, in fact, twenty-five years and thirty-one games since the United States had beaten Cuba in a game of baseball. That fact rankled American baseball fans almost as much as it delighted El Presidente Castro, a former pitcher who once had entertained delusions of playing in *las ligas grandes.*

The Americans and Cubans would meet later that summer in the Pan Am Games in Indianapolis, but first they would meet on Castro's turf—in Havana.

American amateur baseball had improved considerably over the years. All of the top prospects no longer went straight from high school into the minor leagues, where they were ineligible to play as amateurs. Many, like Abbott, now went to college before turning pro.

So the Americans were brimming with confidence when they took the field for the first game of the series against the Cuban National Team. But the Cubans quickly deflated the Americans' hopes. They won the first and second games, running their winning streak against *los gringos* to thirty-three.

With the good guys down 0-2 in games, Fraser handed the ball to Abbott. To say that Havana's stadium was packed for the Cuban debut of the kid with one hand is like saying that New York City subways get a little bit crowded during rush hour. Castro himself was there, along with fifty-six thousand other Cuban fans—several thousand more than the stadium had room for.

The idea of someone trying to play ball with only one hand was preposterous to the Cubans. If a one-handed kid had come to one of their country's state-run programs and asked to play, he would have been summarily dismissed. The Cubans had already chalked this one up in their win column. They just wanted to see how ugly it would get.

One of the first Cuban hitters, a speedburner named Victor Mesa, hit a hard chopper right back at Abbott. As the crowd gaped, Abbott—using the skills he had honed in those endless hours in his backyard—slid his hand into his glove, snared the ball, slipped the glove under his right arm, dropped the ball into his left hand, and nailed the runner at first. It takes more time to explain than it did to perform—a little more than three seconds from bat to glove to first base.

"It was a real bang-bang play," Abbott says. And when he handled it so slickly, "the Cubans went crazy. They had a ball with it. They thought it was the nuttiest thing they had ever seen. I got a standing ovation and they were on our side after that."

It was a good side to be on that night, for Abbott pitched a complete-game, 8-3 victory, the first over the Cubans in twenty-five years. If there was any question of his talent going in, there was none coming out.

"He was no longer a freak," says Fraser. "He was a pitcher."

Castro himself was so impressed that he sought out Abbott,

clapped him on the back, and congratulated him. Two years later, when Abbott made the big leagues, Castro didn't forget. He had his people make some phone calls, and one day in Mesa in the spring of 1989, an Angels press secretary brought a baseball to Abbott with the request that it be autographed to Fidel Castro.

When reporters asked Abbott after the game about the bang-bang play in the first inning, he told them, "I do the same thing now I did the very first day I went outside with my father as a kid. He thought it up. It wasn't designed to beat the world." But it was designed to handle the necessities of playing baseball, and now it had beaten the Cubans.

At the Pan Am Games, Abbott was chosen by his fellow athletes to carry the U.S. flag during the opening ceremonies. During the baseball tournament, he was perfect—winning two games and giving up not a single earned run. Fraser worked the rotation so that Abbott would pitch the gold-medal game against Cuba. Again he started and again he gave up no earned runs, but after he left the game the Cubans won the gold medal. The Americans settled for silver.

After that summer of 1987, Abbott had grown to a national figure. He was awarded the Golden Spikes Award, given each year to the nation's best amateur baseball player, and he won the Award for Courage at the Academy Awards of Sports.

He went back to school that fall, and in the spring he led the Michigan baseball team in starts, complete games, and innings pitched while leading his team to the Central Regional round of the NCAA College World Series. It would be his last year of college ball, and for his first three years he had a cumulative record of 26-8 with a 3.03 ERA and six career shutouts. He was named Most Valuable Pitcher by his Wolverine teammates, Big Ten Conference Player of the Year, First Team All-Big Ten, and a *Sporting News* All-American. And he was chosen for the 1988 U.S. Olympic Team, this time not out of curiosity.

If the United States had a problem with Cuba, it also had one with the Olympics, which had taken on baseball as a demonstration sport in Los Angeles in 1984 and would entertain an encore in 1988 in Seoul. In Los Angeles, even with the Cubans absent by reason of the

Soviet-led boycott, the U.S. team had lost the gold medal to Japan. In Seoul, the Cubans again would be absent, but Japan would be there, and the U.S. team wanted revenge.

Abbott excelled during the team's summer tour, going 8-1 with a 2.55 ERA and being named to the All-Tournament team at the World Baseball Championships in Parma, Italy. Now it was time for the Olympics.

In Korea, Abbott was swamped by the curious. Like Cuba, Korea is not a place where a one-handed boy would be allowed to play baseball, so when the Koreans read about Abbott, they had to see him for themselves. That's when Abbott really showed what he has inside.

The first time he came out of the locker room at the Olympics, he was met by a crowd of Koreans. They were shy yet forward at the same time, pushing close to him, reaching out as if they wanted to touch his hand. Abbott didn't need a translator. "Go ahead," he said, holding out his right hand. "You can touch it." Then he stood there patiently as the crowd pressed forward to gently stroke and feel his right hand.

As in the Pan Am Games, Abbott was named to start the gold-medal Olympic game. The opponents were the Japanese, who had denied the U.S. team the medal in 1984. But they would not deny Abbott. He pitched a complete-game victory, holding Japan to three runs on seven hits in a 5-3 win.

When the last out was recorded, Abbott's teammates rushed the mound and darn near killed him with gratitude.

"My face was being crushed into the mound, and my arms and legs were pinned," he said the next day. "It was the greatest feeling in the world. I'm sore all over, but it was worth it. I'd do it a thousand times over. I loved it." And when they unpiled everyone and lined them up on the victory stand to hang gold-plated medals around their sweaty necks, "It was incredible," he said.

Now the honors really poured in. He had already been drafted in the first round by the Angels. Then came the Tanqueray Achievement Award in Amateur Sports, the Big Ten–Jesse Owens Male Athlete of the Year award, and finally—the biggest one of all—the Sullivan

Award, given annually to the nation's best amateur athlete. Until Abbott came along, no baseball player had ever won it.

When Abbott arrived at the Angels' camp with a minor-league contract, he figured he had at least proved he could pitch. The status of his right hand should no longer be an issue.

Instead, it became a bigger issue than ever.

"I really don't know why it is," he said. "It's just the hand. The questions don't seem to go beyond that. I knew there would be a lot of press this spring, but there's a different line of questioning for professional athletes than there is for amateur athletes. The questions are almost antagonistic. It's like I'm more public property now as a professional."

It was as if the questioners wanted to know: *How dare he attempt to play this game without a full complement of extremities? Who does he think he is?*

What few seemed to understand was that not having a right hand was no big deal to Abbott. He had, after all, been born without it. It wasn't as if he'd had a hand for a number of years and then lost it in an accident. It's a lot easier to get by without something you never had. He had set out early in life to be a professional ballplayer, and that's what he was. What was the all the excitement about?

"Whether you're rich or poor or one-handed or whatever, your own childhood just seems natural because it's the only one you know," he once told an interviewer for *Parade* magazine.

His life may have seemed natural to him, but most of the world can't play baseball—not on the very highest levels, at any rate—with two hands. And if you were a person who had tried to play it as a kid and eventually hit your level of incompetence using all the body parts nature provides, it might be unsettling to watch this kid with only one hand not only succeed, but make it look easy.

So people came from all over and asked insensitive questions, and Abbott, to their amazement, answered them with good cheer—the same way he signed the autographs and posed for the pictures—because that was his job.

Even people who had been around baseball all their lives were amazed at his bottomless well of aplomb. "He is very mature for his age, a classy young man," observed Marcel Lachemann, the Angels' pitching coach, after watching Abbott for just two weeks.

"He's a wonderful man, a tremendous human being in every way," said Doug Rader, his manager. "He's very patient, very mature. He has all the emotional attributes you'd love to see in everybody. To be able to deal with the constant attention the way he has, it's absolutely amazing to me."

Abbott pitched beyond expectations early in spring training, and the Angels' intentions of starting him out in Class AA were soon upgraded to starting him in Class AAA. In his first outing as a professional, in a "B" game against San Diego, he pitched three scoreless innings. In his next outing, he was thrown in against the American League champion Oakland A's for two innings. He got through those two, giving up one run and one hit and striking out Jose Canseco.

Angels catcher Lance Parrish said that Abbott's fastball was in the same league as that of Ron Guidry, who had turned in a 25-3 year for the Yankees in 1978. Joe Coleman, the team's bullpen coach, said Abbott had a smooth motion that reminded him of Steve Carlton, baseball's leading all-time left-handed strikeout artist.

Before long, the Angels' weren't talking even about Class AAA, but about the major leagues for their prize rookie. That was a step—going straight to the majors from college—that only fourteen pitchers had taken in the era of the draft. When Dan Petry, the Angels' fifth starter, was injured and pitched ineffectively, the decision was made to start Abbott in the majors.

The Angels were accused of wanting to bring him up just to sell tickets. Abbott responded to the charges not with anger but with logic: "If I was 0-5 in the minor leagues, and the Angels were dead last in July, I might think it was a publicity stunt. But I feel I earned my place on the team, and if somebody watched me pitch in spring training and thinks I didn't, I think they're wrong."

Another distraction that Abbott had to deal with going into that season was his instant popularity with what seemed like every charity on the face of the planet, every one of which absolutely needed him to help their cause. "I'm trying to make a career of something and all of a sudden people see me as a beacon," he said. "It's not something I want to run away from, but at the same time, it's not something I want to promote. You make the team, and there are one hundred different charities saying, 'Now you owe this to us.' I just try to keep my time as much as I can to myself. Maybe when I get a little more established, I'll be able to make some commitments."

The baseball season started on April 4. Five days later—April 8, 1989—it was Abbott's turn to pitch. The opponents were the Seattle Mariners.

The event drew a hundred and fifty reporters and five Japanese television crews to Anaheim Stadium. (After beating Japan in the Olympics, Abbott had become something of a hero in that country and had made an antidrug commercial aimed at Japanese youth.) It also drew a crowd of 46,847—more than opening day and about fifteen thousand more than the team's average attendance.

The storybook version of Jim Abbott's life would have him throwing a shutout in that first game, but real life is not so kind. After the first two Mariner batters singled off him, he knew he was in for a long day.

He lasted four and two-thirds innings, allowing six hits, all singles, and six runs. Only three of them were earned. He didn't strike out anyone.

But the crowd had been with him on every pitch, clapping and cheering not because the scoreboard told them to but because they wanted him to win. When he left the game, they gave him a standing ovation. He waved back.

Afterward, he admitted that "maybe I was unnerved in my first start. I didn't throw real well, and that took some of the sweetness out of it. But I don't think the world will end tomorrow."

He was asked again about the odds he had overcome to get where he was, and with his mother and father looking on, he answered. "I don't think there is anything special about me being in the major leagues," he again insisted. "What I've done is not any more triumphant than anyone else's effort. I'm not special. It's not like I'm going to be bitter tonight because I have only one hand."

Five days later, he tried it again, this time against Oakland. He recorded his first of the 115 strikeouts he would ring up that year (against Dave Parker), but he also lost as the Angels were shut out for his second straight start.

He had to wait eleven days for his next start, against Baltimore in Anaheim. This time he pitched six innings, allowing four hits and two runs. He left with a 3-2 lead, and the bullpen, after a few tight moments, held onto it for his first major league win. The date was April 24, 1989.

"Now I feel like I belong," Abbott said.

"It's a feeling of relief," said Doug Rader, his manager. "It was vitally important to get Jim off the charge of never having been a winner in the majors."

He won two of his next three decisions. One of them, on May 17 against Boston, was his first career shutout, and the man he beat was Roger Clemens, possibly the best pitcher in baseball.

A week after beating Clemens, he made his first trip to New York. After his rocky start, his record was now 3-3, and his earned run average was a respectable 3.56. He was proving himself as a major-league pitcher, but when he got to the visitor's locker room in Yankee Stadium, another crowd of writers was waiting for him, and they didn't want to know about pitching. They still wanted to know about his hand.

He would go through similar sessions every time he visited a new city. The television crews, in particular, hounded him. Most major-league cities send writers to spring training, so they had already eaten at Abbott's trough. But television stations don't always do the same, and now their cameras followed him, zeroing in for a closeup of his hand.

Abbott admitted that it was starting to get to him. "The only part of this whole media crush that's made me sad is that there was never a point before when I tried to duck it," he said. "But now there are times when I see a microphone across the room, and I try to shrink away from it." When the microphone was followed by a camera, he found himself draping a towel across his right hand, a small declaration of privacy.

But he put up with the monotonous thud-thud-thud of questions. And every time he opened a newspaper, the stories about him mentioned somewhere early on that he was a "one-handed pitcher." That he could accept. What bothered him was that *USA Today* continued to refer to him as a one-armed pitcher, as if the story would be better if they took away another body part.

The other bothersome line of questioning was the one about being handicapped. Again, Abbott had to explain, "I don't particularly like that word. A handicap is a limitation, and I've never felt limited in what I can do."

He knew the questions weren't going to go away. That first year, his job description might well have been pitcher/professional human-interest story. Even so, he longed for the day when he would only have to answer questions about his pitching.

"I don't think anyone gets much out of it," Abbott said. "I would like to be more my normal self." His normal self was like any other well-adjusted twenty-one-year-old, a self that wanted to savor the joy of a first season in the big leagues. "I just want to pitch," he said. "I don't try to be inspirational or anything."

He didn't think the way he was born mattered any more than the color of Jackie Robinson's skin mattered when he stepped to the plate to hit. And that was precisely the point: it didn't matter to his performance.

That's why all those writers and broadcasters had to talk about it. Because here was something that the world had thought was a handicap, and look, everybody—it's not. His hand may have been insignificant to him, but it wasn't to people who saw him: it helped to lift another limit that had existed only in our minds.

One of the reasons Abbott put up with all the intrusions and insensitive questions was because he really did understand that, even though breaking new ground was not what he had set out to do. "I pitch to win, not to be courageous," he said. "But I've grown up enough to know that being called a one-handed pitcher is not an insult. If it helps a kid or the parents of a kid in a similar situation, then I guess that makes my playing even more worthwhile. That goes beyond baseball."

But baseball was his profession, and if he was an inspiration, it was only because he succeeded.

He started twenty-nine games that first season and finished with a 12-12 record. In his twelve losses, the Angels scored only twenty-three runs. In six of them, the team scored either one or no runs. His earned run average was 3.92.

They weren't Hall of Fame numbers, but of the fourteen pitchers who had gone directly from amateur ball to the major leagues before him, none had won more than six games in his rookie year and only one—Dick Ruthven of Philadelphia in 1973—had won that many.

His sophomore season went the way of many sophomore seasons—10-14 and a 4.51 ERA. But he showed that he deserved a place on a pitching staff. And slowly the world started to let him be what he was, a young left-handed pitcher who threw hard and was battling to make his place in the game.

In 1991, his third season, several things happened that illustrated just how much he had accomplished. Early in the year, a paragraph about him in a suburban New Jersey newspaper observed that Abbott, who had come on strong after a poor start, was no longer being judged by the number of hands he had, but by how he pitched.

And during his first visit of the year to New York, no one wrote a gushy feature about him. However, he was spotted signing a baseball for a young fan after a game at Yankee Stadium. When he had signed it, he rolled it across the dugout roof to a small boy who wore a smile as wide as the stadium as he caught it with his left hand—the only hand he had.

Then there was the note in a newsletter published by the office of the commissioner of baseball. It was just a paragraph in an article about the nominees for the Clemente Award, which is given annually to one player who contributes significantly to the community. The Angels' nominee was Jim Abbott. The citation said that he hosts a celebrity golf tournament for an organization called *Amigos de los Ninos* (Friends of the Children), of which he is chairman. He had also met privately with more than five hundred handicapped adults and children during the previous year and had been named Sportsman of the Year by the Children's Hospital of Orange County, California.

Three years earlier he had said he didn't set out to be an inspiration, but that when the initial hoopla about his career died down, he would do his part. And now, without the microphones and notepads taking down every word and gesture, he was doing that.

Finally, there's the story told by Abbott's father, Mike. It seems that one day in Jim's old neighborhood in Flint, some boys—maybe eight or nine years old—were playing catch. One of the boys would catch the ball, put the glove under his arm, take his hand out, grab the ball, and throw it back with the same hand he had used to catch it. Then he'd put his hand back in the glove and do it again.

The boy's father asked him what he was doing.

"Playing catch," the boy said.

"Why are you only using one hand?" the father asked.

"That's the way Jim Abbott does it," said the boy, as if anyone who would do it differently didn't know how to play baseball.

The Pacesetter

I like the challenge.

Once, she had authored what has been called the greatest individual marathon ever run by a woman, but that was a long time ago. She was Joan Benoit back then in early May of 1984, at the U.S. Olympic marathon trials, a waif-like figure in baggy shorts whose legs looked too short and whose gait too awkward to hold up for twenty-six miles.

All she could do was run, not with blazing speed, but with the dogged determination it takes to grab hold of a pace and not let go. She won the marathon trials on a right knee that had been operated on seventeen days earlier and a left hamstring that had been pulled so badly only a week earlier that she could barely make it up a steep flight of steps. And then she ran into America's heart in the Los Angeles Olympics, beating the best women runners in the world and winning the first Olympic women's marathon.

Now it is late spring 1991. Seven years have passed since her moment of incandescent glory, and she is now Joan Samuelson, the mother of two children. For nearly three years she has been hobbled by an obstreperous nerve in her right leg. The nerve was insulted during the birth of her first child, and ever since it has been refusing to transfer the orders of her brain to the muscles of her leg. Sometimes she has to drag the leg behind her, unable to feel it, able only by sheer force of will to make it chase her left leg across the miles.

She is thirty-four years old, and her dark hair, bobbed sensibly short, is graying at the temples. She is still five feet three inches and 105 pounds, but she appears more wiry than she did in Los Angeles. Earlier in the spring, she finished fourth in the Boston Marathon, her first good marathon in—what was it, six years?

It is shortly after nine in the morning on June 1. The place is Central Park in New York City. Samuelson and forty-five hundred other women have gathered a couple hundred yards south of the Tavern on the Green to run a ten-kilometer road race. The runners in such races are given numbers that correspond to their ranking in the field. The fastest runner gets No. 1, the second fastest No. 2, and so on. Samuelson is wearing No. 21 today.

It is already eighty degrees when the marshals herd the women behind the starting line. Someone gives last-minute instructions on the public address system, mainly practical advice about what to do if you feel like croaking halfway through the race, and about the importance of taking advantage of the water stations along the route. Then they introduce the top runners—Liz McColgan of Scotland, Wanda Panfil of Poland, Delillah Asiago of Kenya, Aurora Cunha of Portugal, Uta Pippig of Germany, and so on down the list. Finally, the announcer pronounces the name of Joan Benoit Samuelson. There have been murmurs of applause for the other women, but now the entire field—all forty-five hundred women—cheers and applauds with gusto. She isn't the fastest anymore, and she isn't the favorite in the race, but she is still Joan, the woman who won the big one. No one will ever forget that.

At the gun, she leaps into the lead like a spooked rabbit. It's what she's always done and what she always will do. She and the forty-five hundred women behind her charge up a slight incline that leads under the race's finish line, a point to which they will return in slightly more than half an hour. As they run under a gay arch of balloons, a truck carrying photographers and reporters just ahead of the leaders downshifts and accelerates, spewing a toxic cloud of diesel exhaust directly into Samuelson's face. "That finished me," she would say later.

She managed to hang onto the pace through a 5:02 first mile, and then she faded as 19-year-old Delillah Asiago ran away from everyone and won the race. Samuelson finished ninth. "The first American," she says with a hint of sarcasm and a roll of her steel-gray eyes.

Her time was 33:56—not blazing, but not bad. It was, in fact, less than a minute slower than her best time. Considering that she had gotten to New York late after attending an aunt's funeral the day before, and considering the dose of exhaust fumes, it was not bad at all.

But Asiago had won in 32:24. She had simply taken off and run away, not pausing to worry whether she was going too fast or where the rest of the pack was. "I think she doesn't know any better," Samuelson said of the winner's lack of tactics. "It's new to her."

"You used to run that way," someone said, recalling how she had won the marathon trials, the Olympic marathon, and all her other races.

"I don't any more," she replied. Then she walked to the elite runners' changing area—a lone PortoSan toilet just past the finish line in an area roped off by orange tape tied around some trees. She collected her things and walked to the Tavern on the Green, where an interview room was set up. As she walked, her right leg dragged slightly.

"It's a problem," she said of the leg. "It's not an excuse. It's a problem. I'm not feeling really fluid, but I'm feeling better and better."

She submits to interviews as most people submit to dentistry: it's necessary. She accepts it, but she doesn't enjoy it. She likes to keep her thoughts to herself. "People from Maine are reticent," she once said. "It's a nice quality. They say what they need to and that's it."

Ever since she ripped off a then-world-record 2:21 in the 1985 Chicago Marathon, she has talked about becoming the first woman to run faster than 2:20 for a marathon. It's been the long-range goal that has pulled her through the injuries, pain, and bad times of the past three years when doctor after doctor has inspected her and poked and probed and pondered what to do. Some say surgery. Some say exercise. Some say no exercise. There are as many opinions as doctors.

Finally, she has gone with her own opinion, and that is to keep running—to ignore the leg when it goes dead and simply will it to keep moving. She does stretching and strengthening exercises as well, but mainly she just keeps running.

She figures she'll give it until she turns thirty-five in 1992. After that, even if she were completely healthy, the odds of her running a record marathon will diminish because of her age. But she isn't letting go until then. "It's what keeps me going," she says of the marathon record.

A fine time to set the record, many have told her, would be the 1992 Summer Games in Barcelona. It would be eight years since her triumph in Los Angeles. It would be the world's biggest stage.

She knows that, and she's not sure she'll even try to make the Olympic team in the marathon. "Right now," she says, "I'm toying with the idea of trying to make the Olympic team in 10,000 meters. I have an outside shot."

Her reasons are simple. First, she would have to move to a warm climate during the winter to train for the marathon trials, which would mean spending Christmas in Florida or Texas instead of in her 150-year-old house in Freeport, Maine, with her two children playing in front of the big stone fireplace. "I'm not sure I want to do that," she says. Besides, "It would be more of a challenge, more of a thrill, to make the team in the 10,000. It would be a huge personal achievement. And I could never match what I did in Los Angeles in the marathon."

Joan Benoit didn't set out to be a runner. As a girl growing up in Maine, she wanted to be a skier. Her father had learned to ski as a member of the 10th Mountain Division in the U.S. Army. When he had children of his own, he put them on the slopes, too. Joan liked the sport and did well in it until she crashed and broke a leg.

To rehabilitate the leg, she took up running. Back in those days, the idea of running for the health of it hadn't yet taken hold of the national consciousness. People in cars were apt to stare at runners and maybe shout a few insults out the window. And people certainly didn't go to parties and tell other people that they liked to run.

When Joan Benoit started running, she stopped every time she heard a car coming and stooped down by the side of the road, pretending to be looking at wildflowers. After a while she didn't stop anymore. And after a longer while everyone was out running with her. "I felt I was joining a parade," she says.

She started running to get in shape for skiing, but she found that she loved to run—loved the solitude, the effort, the challenge.

She ran the mile in high school, turning in a best time of 5:20. After high school, she enrolled at Bowdoin College, a small, Division III school in Maine. She didn't go on an athletic scholarship. She didn't even know there was such a thing, but she joined the track team because she loved running.

She now believes that she was lucky she didn't go to college on a track scholarship. Scholarship athletes, she says, are under pressure to race all the time. There's cross country in the fall, indoor track in the winter, and outdoor track in the spring. "Long-distance runners are really expected to compete three seasons a year," she says. "One season of that is enough to knock anybody for a loop, let alone four years. At the end of four years, they're pretty much burned out."

It's a big part of the reason, she says, that the United States has a hard time turning out top distance runners. The other part is that after a runner graduates, he or she discovers that there's money to be won by running races. In the early 1980s, a whole generation of male American marathoners burned themselves out running too many races in an effort to collect big money. Even today, there are 10K races for good money nearly every weekend of the year. "They start to chase the money, and they live from race to race," she says.

She didn't have to run three seasons a year in college, and there wasn't that much money to be made professionally. She ran because she wanted to, not because she had to.

She got steadily better until, by the time she was a senior, she was a national collegiate champion at 10,000 meters.

She didn't know it when she entered the 1979 Boston Marathon, but she would soon become famous. She was not quite twenty-two years old when stardom grabbed her, and it was very nearly too much for her. She won the Boston Marathon that year, her first big victory, and New England loved her immediately.

She was cute in a waiflike way. Small and shy, she had run wearing a Boston Red Sox cap. The crowd and the press were captivated by this woman who didn't look to be constructed for long-distance running. Her legs were too short, her feet splayed out, and she didn't have the gaunt and stringy look of a marathoner.

She wasn't the first to appear ill-suited for her sport. Sonny Jurgenson was too fat to be a quarterback in the National Football League. Jack Dempsey was too small to be heavyweight champion. Cal Ripken Jr. was too big to be a shortstop. Magic Johnson was too tall to be a point guard. Rocky Bleier was too slow to be a halfback. Still, they all did pretty well.

So it was with Joan Benoit. Maybe she didn't have the ideal body for long-distance running, and maybe her gait wasn't going to get her in the touring company of the Bolshoi, but she could move those too-short legs faster and longer than anyone else out there. And she could run harder than anyone else cared to. And she could win.

That's all she wanted—to run faster for longer than any woman had ever run. She hadn't reckoned with what would happen when she won America's most venerable marathon. She hadn't figured that winning a footrace would make her a celebrity. She had won plenty of races at Bowdoin College, and no one had noticed then. Why now?

Appearing on talk shows wasn't what she had in mind when she ran all those miles in Maine preparing herself for the race. Endorsing products wasn't on her list of career goals. She didn't like to say more than she absolutely had to. And she had no desire to see if every hotel room in every city in America really did look like every other hotel room in every other city.

"Everyone wanted another piece of me," she says of the experience. "If I didn't give it to them, I was terrible."

She once swore she would never get an agent, but she wound up having to hire an attorney to fend off the hordes who wanted to know her innermost thoughts on any and every subject and the corporate agents who wanted her to drink this liquid, wear these shoes, or plaster that name across her clothing. She turned down two hundred thousand dollars worth of endorsements—didn't want them and didn't need them. She sent her regrets to the "Phil Donahue Show"—didn't have that much she wanted to say anyway.

And she vowed never to run another marathon.

With time, she changed her mind, though. Simply put, she loved running more than she hated the hoopla.

But before she could get back to the marathon, she had to deal with her first intimation of running mortality. In 1981 she underwent surgery on her Achilles tendons, an experience that forced her to confront the possibility that if she kept running she could do worse damage, damage that would leave her crippled. She thought about retiring then, but the call of the road was too strong. Convinced that her repaired tendons were not in further danger, she started training again.

Her training runs are legendary. She ran eight loops in the Maine countryside, ranging in distance up to twenty miles. She ran not once, but twice daily, often ending her day with a plunge into the Atlantic Ocean. Instead of dashing off to a local health club to strain against chrome-plated appliances, she split wood for her fireplace. She ran winter and summer, in subzero cold and blistering heat. Sometimes she would finish her runs with icicles literally hanging from her face. No matter how grueling it got, she never, ever broke off a training run. She always finished what she started. Other runners thought she was insane for training in such conditions. She thought it made all the sense in the world.

"I know I'll be in trouble the first time I give in," she said back in 1984, before her greatest triumphs. "I've been entertaining the thought more and more frequently. Then I realize that I've got plans."

Asked why she pushed herself so mercilessly, she told Jane Leavy of *The Washington Post:* "Every once in a while, there's a moment of joy, and that's what I do it for."

She also thrived on the competition. Her mother once said, "She grew up with boys," to explain her daughter's fierce will to win.

A long-time close friend, Ariane Sirop, said simply, "It's in her. She's the toughest woman I know."

She showed that toughness when she came back to the Boston Marathon on April 18, 1983. Like a runaway locomotive on a downgrade, she came back. At the starting line before the race, she handed her watch to her coach, Bob Sevene—an act that, for a runner, was either insane or the very soul of arrogance. Marathoners live by their watches, checking their pace at every mile against the schedule they set for themselves before the race.

Samuelson looked at it differently. "If you have a watch, you have barriers," Sevene explained at the time. And Samuelson wanted no barriers except those thrown up by the limits of her own strength, endurance, and will.

Running with a trailing breeze, she took the lead from the start and didn't look back. She ripped off a 2:22:43, which didn't just break the world record, it nuked it. In one bold stroke, she had carved nearly three minutes off the previous record. The time beat every men's Olympic marathon run before 1960. It beat the 1968 men's Boston Marathon and the 1972 men's New York City Marathon.

Almost as soon as she crossed the finish line, though, experts started questioning her achievement. They mentioned the favorable wind. But mostly they talked about Kevin Ryan, a male marathoner, who had run with her. Ryan was acting as a reporter for a local radio station, but runners charged that he had acted as a pacer for her. Pacers were then and are now common in any distance event from 1,500 meters on up. They set an early pace to help the elite runners run faster. Normally, they drop out before the race is finished.

But on the track, men and women do not race together, so a woman cannot have a man pacing her. This is what Samuelson did, the critics charged; it was illegal and Samuelson's record should not be recognized. She dismissed the charge as absurd, and The Athletics Congress (T.A.C.)—the national sanctioning body for track and field —agreed with her.

Samuelson had stunned the running world, but she had not yet conquered it. Although she held the record, the consensus was that Grete Waitz of Norway, who in the fall of that year would win her fifth New York City Marathon, remained the world's best. Another Norwegian, Ingrid Kristiansen, was also thought by many to be better. And finally there was Julie Brown of California, who in June of 1983—two months after Samuelson's record run—won the Los Angeles Marathon against a field of only women in 2:26:24. Considering the difficulty of the course and the absence of men to pace her, some observers went so far as to call Brown's race the greatest women's marathon performance ever.

The speculation was more than a friendly debate. There was a fervor to it brought on by the approach of the 1984 Los Angeles

Olympics, at which, for the first time in history, women would run a marathon for gold and glory. Until relatively recently, women hadn't been considered capable of running such a distance. They had been barred from competing in such prestigious events as the Boston Marathon. In the first New York City Marathon in 1970, only one woman entered the race; none finished. The following year, the first woman crossed the finish line in 2:55:22, more than half an hour and nearly six miles behind the first man. As recently as 1977, only one woman in the New York City Marathon could break 2:45.

Women literally had no idea how fast they could run a marathon. There was no history. Only when Waitz won her first New York City Marathon in 1978, with a then-world-record clocking of 2:32:30, did women begin to see the possibilities. And when Waitz returned to New York a year later to lop nearly five minutes off her previous record and break the 2:30 barrier, the idea that women could run long distances at a punishing pace without shattering their allegedly delicate bodies finally took firm root.

The Los Angeles Olympics became the watershed for women's distance running. Until 1984, women in the Olympics ran no distance longer than 1,500 meters—not quite a mile. The International Olympic Committee decided to add the 3,000 meters and the marathon to the women's Olympic competition in 1984. The 10,000 meters wasn't added until 1988.

The race that might sort things out before the Olympics was the World Championships, scheduled for August 1983 in Helsinki. Every woman who mattered was entered in the race—except Samuelson.

She deliberately passed up the world championships for several reasons. First, she didn't want to run too many marathons. She had run Boston in April. The Olympic marathon trials, slated for May of 1984, would choose the three-woman team solely on order of finish. The Olympics followed in August. She also didn't want to give anything away. While the world's other premier women marathoners would be testing each other in Helsinki, she would be running her training runs in Maine, keeping her strategies and her capabilities to herself. Although this was the first world championship women's marathon, the Olympic marathon was the one that really counted.

The World Championships turned out to be a tactical race in which none of the women could decide on tactics. Waitz, normally a frontrunner, had never before run a women-only marathon and was hesitant to react to early surges by four other women. Instead she stayed with the pack that ran behind the leaders, biding her time. The strategy paid off in the late stages of the race as she closed a 35-second gap and won with a somewhat pedestrian time of 2:28:09.

The victory reconfirmed Waitz's standing among women marathoners. She had run a tactical race, and she had won it, chasing down the frontrunning Regina Joyce of Ireland and outrunning everyone who tried to go with her. The second-place finisher, Marianne Dickerson of Illinois, was exactly three minutes behind—more than half a mile. A year before the Olympics, it was official: Waitz was the favorite to strike gold in L.A.

If Samuelson cared who the favorite was, she didn't say. She knew what she had to do, and she set about doing it, putting in her twice-daily workouts in Maine. Besides, she had other things to think about. She was to marry Scott Samuelson in September 1984, just after the Olympics. She had jams and jellies to put up. She had knitting to do. She had an old house to fix up.

When football players train, there are daily progress reports. Trainers talk about Moe Noodleman's hip pointer, BoBo Sternwheeler's back spasms, and Billy Joe Speed's strained medial-collatoral variable-interest incentive package. When runners train for a marathon, there are no daily reports and no troop of reporters waiting in the locker room after every workout. There is pain—daily pain. There are triumphs and setbacks, despair and joy, but few ever hear about them.

As the Olympic trials, which would be held in Olympia, Washington, drew near, the world heard nothing about the increasingly frequent pain in Samuelson's right knee. Sometimes the knee would just lock up and refuse to work. She'd try to run anyway, because that's the way she was.

"I went out on a training run in March and I felt something just like a spring releasing," she said years later. "I'll never forget the feeling, the sensation. I knew I had done something. I couldn't move my knee. I ran gingerly the following day, if that's possible. It felt okay. Then it came back to haunt me."

The T.A.C. rules were clear: To get into the Olympics, Samuelson had to finish in the top three at the trials. In other countries, the stuffed shirts would have told her she didn't have to run the trials, that she was the best they had, and she was in. But not in the United States. Rules were not made to be broken or even bent. There could be no exceptions.

"I took an injection of cortisone," Samuelson says. "That lasted about a week. Then the knee went again. I had another injection, but that didn't help at all. Then I started to really panic, thinking that the trials weren't that far away, and what was was I going to do?"

The first the public heard about her injury was in a wire-service report on April 24, 1984, just eighteen days before the trials. The report said:

"No woman ever has run a marathon faster than Joan Benoit, but it appears that the American won't be able to compete in the event in the Olympics.

"Benoit is scheduled to undergo arthroscopic surgery on her right knee tomorrow, and it is unlikely she will be in condition to compete in the marathon trial set for May 12.

" 'She can't run,' says her coach, Bob Sevene, in explaining why she's having the operation. 'It's so hard for all of us to swallow. Maybe we'll try to qualify her for the team in the 3,000 meters, but that would be a disgrace. She's the world's best in the marathon.' "

The doctors went in with an arthroscope through a small slit in the side of her knee. They fished around and hooked a chunk of cartilege that had been flopping around, causing the joint to lock. The problem was solved, but there were only seventeen days left before the trials. It didn't seem that anyone could recover quickly enough to endure the pounding on unyielding pavement it would take to make the Olympic team.

Samuelson says she realized much later that the surgery was a blessing in disguise. "I think I would have been overtrained," she says. "But I was forced to take time off because I couldn't run."

If others counted her out of the race, she didn't. As she convalesced, she thought about what she wanted and why she had worked so hard for so many years. "I just kept thinking of all the training that I put in during the summer when I could have been at the beach. I didn't go out on the roads in the middle of the summer—ninety degrees and ninety percent humidity—to just run around in circles. I had a mission to accomplish, and I just kept thinking back to those long runs. I knew at the time of my knee injury that if it was something that could be corrected, I would be on that starting line. That's when my mind took over. As long as I knew I was physically fit—and I was after arthroscopic surgery—then I'd be on the starting line."

As soon as she could, she was back on the roads training. But there were fewer than two weeks to go before the race, and she felt she had to make up the training she had lost before and just after the surgery. Trying to catch up and compensating for the weakened right knee, she pulled her left hamstring. The weekend before the trials, she went to a track meet as a spectator and could barely climb the bleachers.

She underwent another round of therapy as the days ticked by. By race day, she felt good enough to give it a go, and when they called the racers to the starting line, she was there. "If an athlete really wants something, he will persevere" she once said in an attempt to explain how she was able to compete against such odds. "The most important thing is you have to love what you're doing. A coach or a parent or somebody else can't tell you what it is you're going to do. If it doesn't come from within, obviously there's not going to be enough. If you don't love what you're doing, you won't persevere."

A lot of people who watched her line up that day felt sorry for her. They thought that Julie Brown would run away with the trials. They hoped that the small woman they called Joanie wouldn't get hurt too badly.

Their hopes were answered. The only hurt inflicted was by Samuelson on the other runners. She didn't try to coddle the leg along, and she didn't wait on the pace with the pack and hope to sprint it home with whatever she had left. She simply did what she had always done: she ran away from the pack and never looked back.

Her time was just over 2:31—not scorching, but faster than anyone else. Brown had been content to follow along, running just fast enough to make the team. No one else challenged.

"I won," Samuelson says. "Don't ask me how. If someone had passed me, I think I would have fallen apart."

But no one passed her. Because no one could.

Winning the trials would have been enough. She was a certified hero now. Few talked any more about Brown's performance in the 1983 Los Angeles Marathon as being the greatest in an all-women marathon. Samuelson's run from Olympia to the Olympics was now the performance of the ages.

Even so, she was not favored to win the marathon. In its preview of the Olympics, *The Runner* magazine polled seventeen experts in the sport and came up with ten first-place votes for Grete Waitz, five for Samuelson, and one each for Ingrid Kristiansen and Julie Brown. Accordingly, the magazine installed Waitz as the 2-1 favorite to win. Samuelson was the second choice at 4-1, and Kristiansen and Brown were listed at 6-1. No one else was supposed to have a chance.

It would be the first meeting between Waitz and Samuelson, and the self-absorbed gurus of running spent the months between the trials and the Olympics arguing the merits of the various candidates. Marc Bloom, an accomplished and astute writer on running, even composed an imaginary script for the race. Bloom spoke of Waitz as "a kind of running goddess, reticent and unemotional." Samuelson was "the spunky Benoit, twenty-seven, of hearty New England stock, as tough and as gutty as they come."

Bloom speculated that the favorites would run in a pack in a tactical race full of surges and countersurges. He saw Brown taking the pace out halfway through the race, and Samuelson and Waitz reeling her in together just three miles from the finish. He saw Waitz and Samuelson getting to the Los Angeles Coliseum together and racing for the gold on the final 600-meter lap of the stadium before the finish line.

It was a great duel, but only in the fantasies of the writers.

The women's marathon was set for Sunday, August 5, 1984. Just three days earlier, the Olympics had begun in an orgy of flag-waving and trumpet-tooting. The Soviets and East Germans (and other Eastern bloc countries), hadn't bothered to come to Los Angeles, ostensibly over security concerns—afraid, no doubt, that their athletes would wander out of the Olympic Village and up to Hollywood, never to be seen again. In reality, it was retaliation for the U.S. boycott of the Moscow Summer Games in 1980. The Eastern bloc runners weren't missed, however, at least not in the women's marathon, an event in which they did not excel. No one doubted that the fifty women from twenty-eight nations who gathered on the track in Santa Monica College Stadium to start the race were the very best in the world.

Johan Kaggestad, the coach of the Norwegian long-distance runners, proclaimed that Kristiansen and Waitz had prepared for every eventuality. Against the expected heat and humidity of Los Angeles, they trained wearing two warmup suits. They took medication that was supposed to ward off the effects of smog. They talked into tape recorders about how they would not fail and then listened to the recordings to reinforce the message.

Samuelson had simply run. In the weeks before the race, she moved to Los Angeles to run on the Olympic course, but she was so beset by running yahoos who wanted to test their speed against hers that she had gone to Eugene, Oregon, to run by herself and pick berries in the woods. She also made fourteen quarts of jam.

Eleven weeks earlier, Kristiansen had run a hard marathon in London in an unsuccessful attempt to set a world record, and there was concern about whether she had recovered sufficiently to win in the Olympics. But on the starting line there was no time for Samuelson or anyone else to think about those things. There was only the race, with a hundred thousand spectators waiting in the Los Angeles Coliseum to see them finish and hundreds of millions more watching around the world on television.

It began with a couple of laps around the Santa Monica College track, a start designed for maximum spectator participation. The runners lined up, the starter pulled the trigger on his pistol, and the race was on. Samuelson stood out as always, a tiny figure in a floppy white cap. Her official U.S. uniform, steel-gray with red piping, appeared several sizes too big for her. Her legs were still too short, and her feet still splayed out. Next to the tall, square-shouldered Kristiansen and Waitz and the sleek, powerful Brown, Samuelson looked like an orphan who needed to be rescued from a throng of killers.

For the first two miles and into the third, sportswriters took notes, checked split times, and debated the strategies they expected to see. They were having a grand old time, as were the television commentators.

And then it was over.

The race lasted fourteen minutes. Oh, the women would continue to run for more than two hours, but less than three miles into the race there was no more race. Not for first place anyway. That was settled.

On a slight upgrade, Samuelson had hit her accelerator and pulled away. And Waitz and Kristiansen and Brown and everyone else let her go.

"Because she wasn't in such good shape at the trial, Grete and I thought she would break down," Kristiansen said during the postmortem, when the writers and broadcasters went to work picking at the bodies, searching for causes of death.

"When she took off, I thought she would slow down later because of the heat," offered Waitz.

They didn't know Samuelson at all. They didn't know that the tiny woman from Maine didn't understand the words *slow down*. Maybe they should have taken note that Samuelson, unlike so many others —Kristiansen among them—hadn't bothered to wear a watch to check her progress. She didn't want limits. She just wanted to run.

The heat and the smog had been talked about so much that everyone except Samuelson was obsessed with maintaining a sensible pace. She was concerned only with how she felt. When her body told her she could run even a bit faster, she ran faster. To heck with the heat.

After ten kilometers—6.2 miles—Samuelson was cruising comfortably down San Vicente Boulevard with an eleven-second lead. It wasn't an insurmountable margin, but no one tried to cut into it. A mile later, she looked back and when she saw no one pushing her, she picked up the pace again.

The rest of the runners stayed in their comforting pack, watching each other and thinking that Samuelson would eventually die. Nearly ten miles into the race, there were still fourteen women in that pack, running safely along together. Almost a quarter mile ahead of them was Samuelson. By now, they couldn't even see her. Some wondered —and hoped—that she had dropped out, overcome by her own torrid pace.

"I thought I should go with Benoit," said Rosa Mota of Portugal, who would surprise everyone by winning the bronze medal. "But Ingrid and Grete are here. They should know what they are doing. Who am I to take the lead?"

By the halfway point, Samuelson was a minute and a half ahead of the pack. She was so far ahead that the television camera in the blimp overhead couldn't get her and her nearest competitors in the same shot. At about the same point, Brown dropped rapidly off the pace, eventually finishing thirty-sixth.

Yard after yard, mile after mile, Samuelson kept eating up the pavement. She ran through Marina Del Rey and onto the Marina Freeway, a stretch of concrete normally packed with commuters. That day it was occupied by one woman running alone as she did back home in Maine.

"I do most of my training by myself," Samuelson said after the race. "It felt fine."

"This was not going to be another Helsinki," said Sevene, Samuelson's coach, referring to the way the World Championship marathon had been run the previous year, with everyone holding back and letting Waitz outrun them to the finish. "It was not going to be sit around and wait for Grete to win."

The weather cooperated, with the temperature in the seventies and humidity around 80 percent. Although those are nearly tropical conditions for most marathons, it was nowhere near as severe as expected. And an overcast sky throughout the race kept the sun at bay. "I didn't feel a thing," Samuelson said.

When she exited the freeway at Mile 18, she again looked back, and again she needed binoculars to spot the competition. She was something like two minutes ahead of the world and feeling great.

Waitz, however, was not feeling so great. Around the 14-mile mark, her husband had told that she had to close the gap. In seven previous starts, she had never failed to win a marathon that she had finished. She tried, but she couldn't do it. No one could do it.

After the race, Waitz confessed that she had had back spasms the day before and that her legs were burning up during the race. But she refused to use that as an excuse. Samuelson "took a chance and succeeded," she said. "It was her day."

Knowing she could not be caught, Samuelson eased off the throttle in the last couple of miles. "I started to feel fatigued and let up a bit, but then I told myself, 'If you ease up too much and blow this race, you'll never forgive yourself.' So I picked up the pace again and that was that."

As she pulled closer to the stadium, the crowd—watching her incredible performance on a giant television screen—buzzed with anticipation. Finally, they saw her image disappear into the dark tunnel leading into the stadium. When she burst out into daylight, she was showered with the cheers of one hundred thousand spectators.

At first she did not respond to the cascade of noise. She kept running doggedly on, keeping her pace for the last lap around the stadium before she crossed the finish line. The race had been planned that way, so that if there was a duel to the wire, it would be for six hundred yards with one hundred thousand voices screaming encouragement. But the only duel that day would come almost half an hour later, when a woman named Gabriela Andersen-Schiess staggered into the Coliseum suffering from dehydration and heat prostration. Fighting only herself, she teetered and lurched painfully down the track. One side of her body had quit working, and she didn't seem to know where she was or where she was going. She only knew, somewhere in a part of her mind that was still working, that she wanted to get there. The crowd screamed encouragement at her for the five minutes it took her to make one lap of the track. Then she collapsed into the arms of waiting paramedics, who immediately started pumping fluids into her.

Samuelson didn't lurch or stagger or falter. The spectacle of Andersen-Schiess that would come later only cemented in the minds of the spectators the enormity of Samuelson's race. The conditions and the pace had taken their toll on everyone and all but felled Andersen-Schiess, but Samuelson was still fresh. If she had been pushed, she conceded later, she could have run several minutes faster.

After completing half of her final lap, Samuelson finally pulled her cap off, waved it to the crowd, and smiled. She finished the back stretch and came around the last turn, just a hundred meters from the finish line. As Samuelson made the turn, Waitz came out of the tunnel, her face a mask of pain and effort. Together they ran down the final straight, on either side of a row of orange traffic-control cones. They were side-by-side at last—except that Samuelson was a lap ahead.

Samuelson threw her arms up as marathoners do at the finish line. Her time was 2:24:52—not a record, but more than fast enough. She continued around on a victory lap, carrying a small American flag someone had thrust into her hand.

After the photographers had taken their pictures and the crowd had cheered itself out, she said that she had thought about the race Saturday night. "I said to myself, 'Are you prepared to deal with a victory?' I decided I was."

After the Olympics, she went through the hero thing all over again, but in the five years since her first Boston victory, she had learned how to deal with it. She signed a few endorsement deals, but nowhere near as many as were offered. One of them she signed not because it was the best offer, but because she used the product regularly and felt comfortable endorsing it.

She became a symbol for the women's rights movement, and was recruited for the cause. But she hadn't run all those miles for feminism or any other cause. She didn't aspire to be a chief executive. She liked her life and what she was. "If people want to make statements based on my running, that's okay," she once said, "as long as they don't take it too far. I run because I love to run. I'm not a strong women's rights advocate. I'm a quiet person. I'm not politically active. Women have shown they're capable of doing great things. If one of them is running, that's fine with me."

If life were a movie script, it would have ended there. She would have gone home to Maine to marry her Prince Charming, have babies, curl up in front of the big stone fireplace, and live happily ever after.

But she wasn't finished yet. She had had this goal for a long time of becoming the first woman to run a marathon under 2:20. She hadn't let go of that.

On October 20, 1985, she ran the Chicago Marathon in 2:21:21, another American record. Kristiansen, who by then held the world record with 2:21:06, ran in the same marathon. She managed to stay with Samuelson for nineteen miles before Samuelson's relentless pace wore her down.

In 1987, Samuelson became pregnant, and in October she gave birth to a daughter, Abigail. During labor, a nerve in her lower back was compressed, the nerve that controlled her right leg—the leg that had undergone arthroscopic surgery before the 1984 Olympic trials. Samuelson plugged gamely on, and in early November 1988 she entered her first New York City Marathon, where she would run against Waitz again.

She was not in peak form and could not keep up with Waitz. Several miles from the finish, a young volunteer who was taking water to another runner ran in front of her and both went down in a heap. She got back up and finished third in 2:32:40, more than four and one half minutes behind Waitz.

In 1989 she tried the Boston Marathon again, and she was running well when, halfway through the race, her right leg stopped working. Never one to drop out, she finished—in 2:37 and change, good, if that's the word, for ninth place—dragging the leg behind her. At the finish, she cried with hurt and disappointment. "I probably should have dropped out," she conceded, "but I've never dropped out of a race and I didn't want Boston to be the first."

In January 1990, she gave birth to a son, Anders. Waitz was chosen to be his godmother. Samuelson had run throughout her second pregnancy, and she thought that her back had improved. In November of that year, she entered the New York City Marathon, but pulled out at the last minute when her back again flared up.

What had been whispers were now practically shouts: Joan Benoit Samuelson—America's Joanie—was finished.

But then came Boston in 1991, and there was Samuelson on the starting line again. Again she took the early pace and forced the race, running as if every yard were the last. She couldn't hold the pace as she had before her injuries, but she finished fourth in 2:26:54. This time, when she cried at the finish line it was with joy instead of frustration.

She still wasn't finished. She probably never will be. She has given herself until the age of thirty-five (in 1992) to get her record. But she says she'll always run because running is her "sanity break." And if the record doesn't fall, she figures she'll be back when she turns forty and set some masters records. In the meantime, she might try to make the 10,000-meter team in the Olympics.

Al Oerter, who won an unprecedented four Olympic gold medals in the discus, wasn't speaking of Samuelson in 1984 when he talked about marathoners—not specifically, anyway. But she was surely what he had in mind when he said: "I guess I don't think of distance runners as good athletes. I don't think of myself as a good athlete either, for that matter. We're all too specialized. But when it comes to guts, when it comes to being able to apply your energies to a single goal despite the pain and exhaustion, then I'd have to say that the distance runner is head and shoulders above the rest of us."

Samuelson's way of saying all that is a simple and direct: "I like the challenge of it."

The Comeback Kid

Joe Montana's in the game, and you're in trouble.

The date: September 24, 1977. The place: the press box of Purdue's Ross-Ade Stadium. Notre Dame's sports information director Roger Valdiserri and Tom Shupe, his counterpart at Purdue, were watching the fourth quarter of a game that stood at 24 points for Purdue and 14 for Notre Dame.

Until then, Notre Dame coach Dan Devine had used first Rusty Lisch, then Gary Forystek, then Lisch again at quarterback. As the scoreboard testified, with 11 minutes to go, neither was getting the job done.

While Lisch and Forystek went in and out of the game, a third quarterback, a tall, skinny kid with the number 3 on his jersey, was standing by. Finally, his options evaporating, Devine sent Number 3 in.

When the Notre Dame team saw what was happening, they started waving their fists in the air. The leather-lunged contingent of Irish fans in the sold-out stadium joined in, celebrating as if George Gipp himself had been brought back to life and sent in to play.

Shupe didn't get it. This Number 3 was the third-string quarterback, the Irish were 10 down and going nowhere fast, and time was running short. "What's everybody yelling about?" he asked Valdiserri.

"Because Joe Montana's in the game," replied Valdiserri with a note of wicked relish. "And you're in trouble."

Before Shupe could say *Huh?* he understood better than he cared to. In the next 11 minutes, a near-certain Purdue win turned into a 31-24 Notre Dame victory, and it was all Montana's doing. He threw 14 passes, completed 9 of them for 154 yards, and put the 14 points on the board that sealed the game. Though he had played less than a quarter, United Press International named him its Midwest Back of the Week.

Joe Montana—the name had a nice ring to it. It sounded big and strong and unfettered. Shupe had seen him once before, two years earlier, in Montana's sophomore season. And if he had forgotten the name, it was understandable. Coming in late against Purdue in a game Notre Dame had wrapped up 17-0, he threw but one pass, his first ever as a Notre Dame quarterback. It was intercepted. Hardly the way to launch a legend.

The last pass Joe Montana would throw for Notre Dame came in the 1979 Cotton Bowl against Houston. That attempt worked out better than the first one Shupe had seen. It worked out so well, in fact, that it gets written about whenever a reporter somewhere is assigned to write a feature story about the Comeback Kid. That's when they haul out the Houston game and how Montana walked out of the training room and onto the field with a scant 7:37 left to play and the Irish facing a 34-12 deficit. By the time Montana was carried off the field, the Irish were the delirious owners of a 35-34 victory.

Only then do the writers move on to the National Football Conference Championship Game against Dallas in 1981, Montana's first year as an NFL starting quarterback for the San Francisco 49ers. Again with time just about out and no downs left on the scoreboard, Montana rolled right, pump faked, juked, and laid a perfect pass on the fingertips of receiver Dwight Clark—whom Montana couldn't actually see—to win the game and put the 49ers in their first Super Bowl.

Then there was the 1989 Super Bowl against Cincinnati, when the Bengals made the mistake of taking a three-point lead and then allowing Montana to have the ball with a whopping 3:10 on the clock and a mere 92 yards to go for the winning touchdown. Heck, he pulled that one out and still had 34 seconds left.

Those are just the big games. By the end of the 1990 season, Montana had won 32 games in college and the pros with fourth-quarter comebacks. He's done it so often that both the 49ers and Notre Dame have printed up lists of the comebacks to respond to all the requests they receive.

"Twelve years after he graduated, we still get as many requests about Joe Montana as we do about anyone," says John Heisler, who succeeded Valdiserri as Notre Dame publicist.

With football legends stacked in every corner of the Notre Dame campus—legends bearing names like Gipp, Lujack, Hornung, Rockne, Leahy, Parseghian, Bertelli, and Rocket Ismail—the one they want to know about is Montana, the skinny kid who once backed up Rusty Lisch, the kid whose arm wasn't supposed to be strong enough to play big time football, the one great Fighting Irishman who didn't win a Heisman Trophy.

Life's always been like that for Montana. Ever since his days at Ringgold High in Monongahela, Pennsylvania, he's had phenomenal fluidity, an extrasensory talent for getting out of trouble, an uncanny knowledge of defenses, and the ability to work magic, seemingly on demand. But he's also always had periods when his coaches overlooked him.

Joseph C. Montana Jr. was born June 11, 1956, in the coal-mining country of western Pennsylvania. His father, Joe Sr., had dreamed of being a quarterback himself, but work and life had cut those dreams short. So he put a ball in his only son's hand as soon as the tyke could hold it and taught him to be a quarterback.

Role models were as numerous as strip mines in the hills around Monongahela. The "cradle of quarterbacks" they call the region that spawned Johnny Lujack, Joe Namath, George Blanda, Dan Marino, Tom Clements, Chuck Fusina, Terry Hanratty, and John Unitas. Those were the people Montana had to look up to, people who one day would be compared to him. If baseball is more to your liking, Stan Musial and Ken Griffey grew up there, too.

Out of all of those strong-armed heroes, Montana's idol was Hanratty, who—as a sophomore in 1966 when Joe was ten—had taken Notre Dame to its first national championship in seventeen years. At that young age, Montana decided that he, like Hanratty, would go to Notre Dame.

By that time, Montana was already in his third year of PeeWee football. Kids weren't supposed to play until they were nine, but Montana's father had lied about his age and slipped him in a year early. Even as an eight-year-old, Joe could lead a receiver and put the ball in his hands.

Growing up, he was an all-sports star. He pitched three perfect games in Little League. He was good enough in basketball to get college scholarship offers, and good enough in baseball to get invited back to a pro tryout camp.

His life passed idyllically from season to season—indoors in winter, outdoors in spring, summer, and fall—with a ball always in his hand and great deeds at his fingertips. Then he got to high school and ran into a coach named Chuck Abramski.

As a sophomore, Montana was already six feet tall, just two inches shy of his full growth, but he weighed a spare 165 pounds. Abramski liked his skills but thought he needed more muscle to survive the pounding of high school football, coal-miner style. At the end of the season, which Montana had spent on the bench, Abramski told the young quarterback to show up for a summer weightlifting program the coach ran. It wasn't a request; it was an order.

Montana, however, had no intention of giving up his other sports just to lift weights for football. Although he wasn't the only player who didn't attend the program, he was the one Abramski remembered.

When Montana showed up for his junior year, he once again found himself on the bench as punishment for missing the weight program. Starting at quarterback in his place was a kid who was built like a tight end—which is the position he wanted to play.

Ringgold lost its first game that year (1972), and after two forfeit wins (a teacher's strike had halted football at some schools in the valley), the team faced Monessen, the conference's mightiest team. As would inevitably happen to many of Montana's coaches, Abramski was struck by an attack of good sense in the nick of time. He installed Montana at quarterback for the game, put the other quarterback at tight end where he belonged, and sent his team out to play. After scoring only six points in their first game without Montana, Ringgold scored 34 with him against powerful Monessen. Montana's numbers were 12 completions in 22 attempts for 223 yards and 4 touchdowns. A last-minute touchdown by Monessen forged a 34-34 tie, but even a tie was a major victory for Ringgold.

From then on, Montana was the quarterback. By the time he was a senior, he had grown to his adult height of six feet two, and he weighed 180 pounds. By the end of his senior season, he was a *Parade* magazine High School All-American, and the college recruiters were lining up at his door.

They were wasting their time, because Montana had long since decided that he would go to Notre Dame, where in that fall of 1973, Ara Parseghian was taking the Irish to his second national championship.

At Notre Dame, he found himself back at the bottom of the depth chart. His freshman year, he didn't get close to a varsity game and fared little better in his three junior varsity games. The other three freshman quarterbacks—Gary Forystek, Kerry Moriarty, and Mike Falash—each played more and threw more passes in the three JV games than did Montana. His entire freshman season boiled down to six passes, one completion, one interception, five rushes for seven yards, and ten punts for a 36.5-yard average. Hardly the foundation on which to build a legend.

He got his chance in the final game of the 1975 spring practice session, throwing 12 passes and completing 7 of them for 131 yards and 3 touchdowns.

Parseghian was no longer coach by then. Worried about his health and burned out by the enormous pressures of coaching Notre Dame, he had resigned as head coach after the 1974 season. Dan Devine was hired to replace him and got his first look at Montana in that spring intrasquad game.

"I asked my coaches about my quarterbacks when I first got there," Devine told *Sports Illustrated*'s Paul Zimmerman. "No one said much about Joe. He'd been something like the seventh or eighth quarterback. Then he had a fine spring practice, really outstanding. I came home and told my wife, 'I'm gonna start Joe Montana in the final spring game,' and she said, 'Who's Joe Montana?' I said, 'He's the guy who's going to feed our family for the next few years.' "

Devine apparently meant for Montana to do it from the bench, because that's where Montana found himself when Notre Dame began the 1975 season against Boston College. Rick Slager was Devine's starting quarterback.

Montana never got in the Boston College game. The next week, when the Irish faced Purdue, Montana got in at the end and threw his first pass—the interception. Against Northwestern the following week, Slager was hurt in the first quarter, and with Notre Dame on the short end of a 7-0 score, Devine called on Montana for the first time when it counted.

Montana did the job with a tidy 6-11 passing day, including a touchdown and 28 yards rushing as Notre Dame won 31-7. He started the next game against Michigan State, but after an early interception he was back on the bench, where he had a great view of a 10-3 loss.

Montana's teammates couldn't understand it. They could tell in the huddle that Montana was the man to lead them. "He was the guy who wouldn't overheat," said tight end Dave Waymer.

The comebacks everyone talks about are the ones Montana engineered on the football field, but his real achievement was bouncing back from each insult or benching, ready to perform if only he'd get the call.

In Game Five, he got the call. The Irish were playing North Carolina, and with 6:04 left in the game, Notre Dame was behind 14-6. Devine, facing what could become the second defeat of his rookie season at Notre Dame, turned to Montana.

That was Montana's first miracle finish. In the final six minutes, he threw four passes and completed three of them. One went for 39 yards and a touchdown. Another went for 80 yards—the third longest pass play in school history—and the winning touchdown. He also passed for a two-point conversion.

By now, Montana should not have been surprised to learn that his heroics had again earned him a seat on the bench. The next game, against Air Force, went worse for the Irish than the North Carolina game had. Slager's best efforts could put only 10 points on the scoreboard in the first 47 minutes. Air Force, meanwhile, was merrily rolling up 30 points and looking forward to a rare and delicious victory over the men from South Bend.

That time Devine surrendered to the inevitable with 13:00 on the clock. Montana went in, but this one wasn't as neat as North Carolina. He put the ball in the air 18 times, completing seven to his own team and three to Air Force. Still, he managed three touchdowns and won the game, 31-30.

That performance finally convinced Devine that Montana should start. But it was too late. There was no more magic left in Montana's arm. After a loss to third-ranked USC, Montana started the Navy game, broke a finger, and missed the season's last three games. Then, adding injury to insult, he separated a shoulder while practicing for the 1976 season and sat out the entire year, carrying his junior year of eligibility to 1977.

Montana came back healthy, but when the 1977 season began against Pittsburgh, he was buried more deeply than he had been two seasons before. As in his freshman year, Lisch and Forystek were ahead of him on the depth chart.

Notre Dame got by seventh-ranked Pitt without Montana, but they fell, 20-13, to Mississippi in the season's second game. Although it should have been a gold-plated "Montana moment," Joe never got in the game.

"We all knew he could do it, and he knew he could do it, but he wasn't playing," said Ken MacAfee, Notre Dame's All-American tight end. The team wasn't happy, and Montana wasn't happy, either. "I'm sick of the whole thing," he told MacAfee.

Devine insists he told Montana he hadn't played against Mississippi because he had not yet received medical clearance on his shoulder. Montana says Devine never said anything.

During practice the next week, Devine told Montana to get ready to play against Purdue. Montana got ready, and when game day arrived, there he was—back on the bench watching Lisch and Forystek taking turns getting hammered by the Purdue line. That was the game Shupe and Valdisseri were watching when Devine finally threw Montana into the fray in the fourth quarter with Notre Dame down by ten. The very fact that Valdiserri warned Shupe about Montana only underlined the fact that Devine was the last person in South Bend to figure out that Montana belonged in every game, start to finish.

After Purdue, Devine figured it out—and not a moment too soon. Montana started every game from then until he graduated the following season. And Notre Dame did not lose another game in 1977. Behind Montana's leadership, the Irish whipped fifth-ranked USC 49-19, then three weeks later slipped past fifteenth-ranked Clemson 21-17 when Montana ran for two fourth-period touchdowns.

At season's end, Notre Dame—which had climbed to fifth in the national rankings—accepted an invitation to take on number-one-ranked Texas, the only undefeated team in the nation, in the Cotton Bowl. That day, Montana needed no heroics as he led the Irish to a 38-10 win and the national championship.

Montana's senior season was a letdown for everyone. The Irish lost their first two games (to Missouri and Michigan) and were never in the national championship hunt. Montana did pull out the Purdue game with 17 fourth-quarter points, and he overcame an 18-point fourth-quarter deficit against USC, but only to see the Irish lose on a last-second USC field goal.

There the legend might very well have ended, but fate had one more test in store for Montana, a test of sleet and cold in a freak Texas storm at the Cotton Bowl on New Year's Day 1979.

Remarkable is not the right word for what Montana achieved that day. It's too pedestrian and doesn't nearly get at the full dramatics of the situation. Preposterous is a better word for the 1979 Notre Dame–Houston Cotton Bowl.

It started in Dallas with a storm—the coldest, nastiest beast of an ice storm that had ever tarried over a Cotton Bowl in the forty-three-year history of the game. The seats were coated with ice. The goal-posts were coated with ice. And the wind and cold cut through the bone to the marrow. With those conditions, there were 9 fumbles, 4 interceptions and 10 turnovers. It was an ugly, brutish, primal thing that turned beautiful in the end. And in between it had everything except spectators, who had taken one look outside that day and stayed home by the tens of thousands.

Not that any of those ticketholders would admit it today. Not after what happened, first to Joe Montana and then to Houston. Oh, no. If you had a ticket to that game, you ripped the stub off yourself, held it under the faucet, and crammed it in your pocket for an hour or two to make it look authentic. Then you showed it to your friends, whose eyes would grow wide as their lips formed the words: "*You* were at the Cotton Bowl?"

It started nicely for Notre Dame, with 12 first-quarter points on a Montana run and another rushing touchdown set up by Montana's passing. The second touchdown came with 4:40 left in the first quarter. The next Notre Dame touchdown wouldn't arrive for almost three quarters of an hour of playing time.

In the interim, to entertain those fans idiotic enough to go out in that weather, Houston capitalized on Irish mistakes (Montana threw 4 interceptions) to score 20 unanswered points for a 20-12 halftime lead.

The teams went to the locker rooms to thaw out. When they came out for the second half, Montana wasn't there. During the first half, the weather had sent him into a state of hypothermia. His temperature was ninety-six, and he was shivering uncontrollably.

The medics attacked Montana's chill with the best technology available to medical science: they piled blankets on top of him and fed him steaming cups of chicken soup. (Actually, it was boullion, but chicken soup has such a homey ring to it, that chicken soup it has become in official Irish lore.)

Back on the field, the Cougars were toying with Notre Dame, putting 14 more points on the board in the third quarter for a 34-12 lead.

Former quarterback Rick Slager was a law student at Notre Dame by then and a graduate assistant to the football team. Devine assigned him the task of running into the locker room every few minutes to see how Montana was doing. Every time he came back, Joe's temperature was a little higher, and Irish hopes dared to flicker yet a bit longer.

The third quarter slipped into the fourth, and although Notre Dame had managed to stop Houston, when the quarter was almost half over, Joe was still nowhere to be seen.

Finally, with 7:37 showing on the clock, Montana trotted out of the tunnel and onto the field. The flicker of hope became a tongue of flame. When Montana came out, Houston had the ball and was preparing to punt on fourth down. But Notre Dame blocked the kick and ran it back 33 yards for a touchdown. Technically, it was a defensive touchdown, but—what the heck—Joe Montana was on the sidelines, ready to go again, and the points, in history's sight, belong to him.

The score was now 34-18, and if the Irish hoped to win, they'd need a two-point conversion. Montana trotted onto the field and calmly dropped a pass in Vagas Ferguson's hands to make it 34-20.

The clock showed 7:25 to go, and the defense went to work. Less than two minutes later, with 5:40 left, Houston punted to the Notre Dame 39-yard line. Montana needed but five plays—three straight pass completions and two runs—and 1:22 to drive the team 61 yards for the score. He took it the last two yards himself and again passed for the two-point conversion that made it 34-28.

The defense ran out on the field and did its thing again, handing the ball back to Montana with more than two minutes left—an eternity for him—and only one more touchdown needed. Maybe he could have got it then. Certainly he should have got it then. But what's a great story without one last whipsawing of emotions, and what good is a Comeback Kid who can't take a bad bounce?

Notre Dame's bad bounce came with 2:05 to go. Montana had just run for a 16-yard gain when the ball popped out of his hands. The Cougars fell on it on their own 20-yard line.

Three plays later, Houston had advanced the ball to the 29, one yard short of the first down that would drive the stake through the heart of these pesky Northerners. But what to do? The clock, which couldn't run fast enough for their purposes, was stopped with 35 ticks between them and a serious party. They could kick it, but then that Montana fellow would have another shot at them. Or they could just get that lousy yard and the first down and that would be the end of it. Houston elected to go for it.

They came close to making it, too. But at least they had bled another seven seconds off the clock. There were 29 yards of turf between them and the goal line, and Notre Dame had to have a touchdown. A field goal wouldn't do. The Cougars would just have to stop this nonsense right here.

Fat chance. Montana took off on Notre Dame's first snap and

picked up 11 yards before going out of bounds. Eighteen yards to go. He took the snap again and hit Kris Haines for 10 more yards. Eight yards and enough time for one play—maybe two if Montana really got rid of it quickly.

Haines took off for the right corner of the end zone but slipped, and Montana threw the ball away just in time. Two seconds to go. Devine let Montana call his own play, and Montana told Haines to run the exact same pattern he had just slipped on. They snapped the ball, Montana went back, Haines ran the pattern perfectly, Montana threw the perfect pass, the gun went off, and all that was left to do was kick the extra point to give Notre Dame a 35-34 victory. Nothing to it.

That's how the legend was born. And you'd think that the National Football League scouts would have noticed. But they didn't. The drafting of quarterbacks is such a risky business that few scouts are willing to put their jobs on the line by flat-out declaring that a player is a can't-miss talent.

So they analyzed his arm and analyzed his style and decided he didn't look to his secondary receivers often enough and couldn't throw the ball through six inches of concrete. "Doesn't have great tools but could eventually start," one scout wrote (unwittingly echoing a report filed by a talent scout about Fred Astaire years earlier: "Can't act. Can't sing. Can dance a little").

When draft day rolled around in 1979, Joe Montana sat down and waited. And waited. And waited. Two rounds and most of the third went by before, with the eighty-first pick of the draft, the San Francisco 49ers decided to take a chance on Joe Montana of the University of Notre Dame.

It would be difficult to credit the 49ers with great daring or foresight. They did, after all, wait until the third round to draft Montana. But they were brighter than any other team. And, despite his college heroics, there were still those scouting reports.

In San Francisco, Montana was introduced to Bill Walsh's offense, which was built on what the coach called "quick, slashing strokes." It's been said many times that the offense was perfectly built for Montana, relying as it did not on a deep drop and balls flung sixty yards in the air, but on short, quick drops and perfect coordination between the quarterback and his receivers.

Montana's quick feet and ability to avoid trouble were key ingredients of Walsh's system. In fact, Walsh had Montana practice throwing off-balance and off the wrong foot so that when he got in a game and looked up to discover several large and angry bodies coming at him, he would be comfortable throwing while twisting and turning away from the rush.

You don't just toss a quarterback into a complex system like Walsh's. The 49ers were still building the team that would become the superpower of the eighties. For the time being, they had Steve DeBerg to run the team while Montana learned.

In his first NFL season, Montana played in sixteen games, but he started only once late in the season. He threw only 23 passes, but completed 13 of them for one touchdown and no interceptions.

The following year, he started seven games, including the last three of the season. Although the team finished at 6-10, Montana completed 64.5 percent of his passes—the best in the league—and in the season's 14th game, he performed his first NFL Houdini act, turning a fourth-quarter, 14-point deficit against New Orleans into a 3-point overtime win. He finished with 15 touchdown passes and only 9 interceptions.

By 1981, he was the full-time starting quarterback for Walsh, and he responded by leading his team into the playoffs, where the entire season came down to one fourth-down play against Dallas. The result was what is known in San Francisco simply as "The Catch."

It looked so makeshift when Montana and Dwight Clark pulled it off—Montana scrambling to his right, the Cowboys rushing him fiercely while their defensive backs stuck desperately to the 49er receivers, Montana pump-faking to get the rushers off their feet, spotting Clark and throwing it to where he thought Clark would be, then disappearing under more than a quarter-ton of flesh as Clark leaped. And caught. And went wild with joy.

It looked makeshift, but it really wasn't. Just as Montana practiced throwing off-balance, he and Clark also stayed long after practice was over to work on their patterns and options and timing. When the time came, Montana knew where Clark would be, and Clark knew where Montana would throw.

The next stop was Super Bowl XVI against the Bengals, where Montana, the kid, would be matched against Ken Anderson, the veteran. The experts looked at the matchup and decided the Bengals had the better quarterback. The experts were sort of right. Anderson passed for more yards and completed more passes than Montana, but Montana put more points on the board. A Bengals touchdown with 16 seconds left in the game made the 26-21 final score closer than it was. And Montana went home with his first Super Bowl MVP Award.

In 1984, Montana took the 49ers back to the Super Bowl, this time to face the Miami Dolphins. His list of fourth-quarter comebacks had reached eleven games in five years (and ten games in the last four). Even so, the Dolphins' rifle-armed quarterback, Dan Marino, was the experts' choice as the better quarterback. Again, the experts were wrong. After spotting the Dolphins a 10-7 first-quarter lead, Montana picked them apart, hitting on 24-of-35 passes for a Super Bowl record 331 yards and three touchdowns. He also rushed five times for 59 yards and went home with his second MVP trophy.

In 1985, the 49ers were knocked out of the playoffs by the Giants, who were becoming San Francisco's fiercest interdivisional rival. In the process of the 17-3 win, the Giants also beat Montana up pretty thoroughly. Lawrence Taylor, the Giants' all-Pro linebacker, dislocated Montana's shoulder on one hit, but Joe stayed in the game.

All of Montana's comebacks so far had involved scoring points in football games. In the first game of the 1986 season, however, that changed when Montana threw one of his twisting, off-balance passes and felt something go in his back.

They took him to a hospital, and the news that came back stunned San Francisco. Joe Montana had a ruptured disk, but of even more concern was the discovery that he had a congenital narrowing of the spine that restricted his main nerve trunk. Surgery could correct it, but he might never play football again.

Football is a game of heavy collisions. And the favorite target of every defender is the quarterback. If you're the quarterback, it's not as if you can hold up a hand to a 300-pound lineman or a 250-

pound linebacker and say, "I'm terribly sorry, but would it be too much of an inconvenience to ask you to hit me with a bit of delicacy? My back, you know. The doctors say it's not in good shape." If you're on the field with a ball in your hand, you're fair game. Anything less, and it wouldn't be football.

Montana knew that, but he also knew that he wasn't ready to quit. He listened to the doctors, filed it away, and nine weeks later—in the season's tenth game—he played again. He won five of the last seven games and again found himself facing the Giants in the playoffs.

The Giants were on a mighty roll that would take them to a huge Super Bowl win over Denver, and neither the 49ers nor Joe Montana was going to stop them. In the second quarter Jim Burt, the Giants' nose tackle, burst cleanly up the middle on a pass rush and ran his helmet into Montana's chin, knocking Montana out. But the back held up.

Montana wasn't invincible. The Giants proved that. Blanket his receivers, put pressure on him, and don't let him get outside—and you could shut him down. But that's easier to say than to do. After failing again to make the Super Bowl in 1987, Montana put it all together again for the 49ers in 1988.

The first indication that this would be a special season came in the second game, against the now-familiar Giants. As expected, the Giants played their usual bruising defense and coaxed just enough out of their conservative offense to get to the end of the game with a 13-10 lead. With less than a minute to play, the Giants had the 49ers pinned down on their own 22-yard line, 3rd-and-12. Montana took the snap and looked for his favorite receiver, Jerry Rice. He found Rice on the right sideline with two defenders converging on him. Montana delivered the ball, Rice turned upfield, the defenders collided, and seconds later the 49ers owned a 17-13 lead and the ballgame.

Few things would come easy to the 49ers that year. Montana was bothered by nagging injuries so that the Comeback Kid was suddenly becoming the Come Out Kid. Walsh started Montana's backup, Steve Young, in three games that year and relieved Montana with Young in eight others. With the changing quarterbacks, the team struggled through the season, and the benchings gnawed at Montana, who had bad memories of that particular seating arrangement.

"One bad pass, one bad series, and I'm out," he complained.

Walsh knew Montana was unhappy, but he didn't say anything. The coach was doing what he thought he had to. After losing the final game to the Rams, the club finished the regular season at 10-6, just good enough to win their division. Going into the 1988 playoffs, there were grumblings in San Francisco, not only because of what is euphemistically called "the quarterback problem," but also because it had been four years since the 49ers had last won a playoff game. What's more, Montana had not thrown a touchdown pass in any of three consecutive playoff losses.

The 49ers' first game in the playoffs was against the Vikings, who had done San Francisco a favor by eliminating the Rams (who gave the 49ers problems) in the wild-card round the week before. To show their appreciation, the 49ers abused the Vikings 34-9. Montana, reinstalled as the starter, threw three touchdown passes in the first half, thus ending the talk about his prior failings.

The following week Montana and the 49ers met the Bears, and Montana came through again, ignoring the blustery winds and passing for 288 yards, including two touchdowns to Rice. The final score was 28-3. The 49ers were going to the Super Bowl.

Waiting for them were the Bengals, who had romped through the playoffs and the regular season on the strong left arm of quarterback Boomer Esiason and the creative offenses of coach Sam Wyche, a former Walsh assistant who was said to know every move the 49ers would make. In the annual quarterback comparison, the experts again decided that Montana was outclassed by his opponent—who was younger, bigger, stronger, and blonder.

For far too many Roman numerals, the Super Bowl had been a boring affair consisting of two weeks spent convincing the world that it would be a good game followed by about ten minutes demonstrating that it was not. And lately it seemed the trend was toward bigger but not better blowouts.

All over the country, columnists whined, "When are we going to have a great Super Bowl?"

They should have known the answer, and the fact they didn't just showed that they hadn't been paying attention during Joe Montana's past fifteen seasons. It was really quite simple: we would have a great Super Bowl the day someone figured out how to get a lead on Joe Montana and then contrive to give him the ball with time left for one last drive.

That's exactly what the Bengals did. There was no help for it. The Bengals had staged a comeback of their own, and, with the score tied at 13-13, they found themselves in position to kick a field goal with just over three minutes on the clock. They hit the field goal for a 16-13 lead, kicked off, and when the kamikaze boys had finished their work, the ball was resting on the 49er 8-yard line, and the clock read 3:10.

As the 49er offense prepared to take the field, tackle Harris Barton remembers having an adrenaline fit in anticipation of the work that faced him. He was screaming and yelling at the kickoff team for committing a penalty when Montana walked up to him.

"Hey, check it out," Montana said.

"Check what out?" replied Barton.

"There, in the stands, by the exit ramp. It's John Candy."

Barton looked up in the stands and, sure enough, there was John Candy standing by the ramp. Suddenly, Barton grabbed tight end John Frank and said, "Hey, John. There's John Candy."

Just as suddenly, he thought, *What the hell am I doing?* He turned and ran out to the huddle, where Montana was waiting, clapping his hands, and saying, "Hey, you guys want it? Let's go!"

Montana may have been relaxed enough to point out celebrities, but while he was running on the field, he was thinking of Dallas and "The Catch." *Here we go again,* he thought. *We got another chance like we had against Dallas.*

"It was a tough position to be in," Montana later admitted. "But we had to be confident. We'd done it in the past."

He had done it in the past. He'd done it to Purdue, done it to Air Force, done it to Houston. He'd done it to Dallas, done it to the Giants, done it to New Orleans. Now he had to do it again. And with that realization, a crystal calm fell over him, and everything on the field slipped into place.

He passed 8 yards to Roger Craig out of the backfield, 7 yards to Frank, and 7 more yards to Rice, who finally went out of bounds. The clock stopped with 2:28 to go and the ball on the San Francisco 30-yard line.

Montana handed off twice to Craig for five more yards and a first down at the 35.

TIME!

After his huddle with the coaches, Montana went back to work. He took the snap, fell back, and hit Rice for 17 yards with 1:49 to go and the clock running.

Quickly up to the line. Hit Craig over the middle for 13 and a first down on the Bengal 35.

Montana had been shouting so many signals and instructions that suddenly (shades of hypothermia and chicken soup) he realized he was hyperventilating, and the precise green and white grid of the football field was swimming around him. He turned toward Walsh on the sidelines and motioned that he wanted another time out. Walsh didn't realize what was happening and motioned for him to keep running the offense.

Not wanting to throw an interception, Montana threw it over Rice's head and out of bounds. Clock stopped.

He drops back again, and now yellow flags litter the field. Illegal man downfield. Everybody move back 10 yards. It's 2nd-and-20, 1:15 to go. Bengals fans are apopleptic.

Montana changes his strategy. Now he just wants a field goal and a tie game to force overtime. He drops back and again hits Rice, who breaks away for 27 yards to the Bengal 18.

Run to the line, hit Craig for 10 to the 8; 39 seconds to go.

TIME!

Forget the field goal. The Comeback Kid can smell win now. On the next play he gets it. Montana to John Taylor in the end zone, the only pass Taylor has caught all day and the only one he had to catch.

The extra point goes through. It's 49ers 20, Bengals 16, and there are still 34 seconds on the clock—time enough for Joe Montana to drive his team to Venezuela, but not nearly enough time for the Bengals.

"This is probably the best," Montana says in the hurly burly of the locker room. And he's right.

It was the best because he had made it so. He had survived benchings. He had listened to the whispers that his career was finished. He had heard the home crowd chanting for Young, his replacement.

He had heard it all, and he had put it aside and done what he had to do. The following year, he would do it again, leading his team in the biggest rout in Super Bowl history over the hapless Denver Broncos. That gave him four Super Bowl rings, and only he and Steeler quarterback Terry Bradshaw could say that.

But 1989 against Cincinnati was the best. He had walked on the field, and every soul who watched him break that huddle with 92 yards to victory knew that Joe Montana, The Comeback Kid, was in command, and the opposition was in trouble.

Wonder Woman

My goal wasn't to be the best woman musher.
My goal was to be the best racer ever.

Susan Butcher isn't like you and me. She isn't like anybody. You can't say that about many people in a country where so many people spend so much time trying to be different that they all end up the same. And that's just the point: Butcher didn't set out to be a celebrity. Money to her doesn't mean fancy cars and yachts. It means dog food, an item more important to Butcher than indoor plumbing, electricity, or central heat. With anywhere from 100 to 160 dogs, she needs a lot of it—not pounds, but tons.

If your first thought about someone with that many dogs is that no matter how fine a person she is, you don't want to be her neighbor, don't worry. With her husband, David Monson, Butcher lives in Eureka, Alaska, 140 miles northwest of Fairbanks. If that's not the middle of nowhere, it's pretty darn close. The population of Eureka is pushing ten, and Butcher's nearest neighbor is seven miles away. The closest town to Eureka—Manley Hot Springs, a bustling metropolis of about a hundred—is twenty miles away.

Eureka isn't in your standard Rand-McNally atlas, but Butcher and her dogs have put it on the map just the same. That wasn't her intention, either. She'd just as soon that Eureka remained lost to cartographers. She likes where she is, and she likes what she does, which is race sled dogs better than anyone else in the world. It's a grueling sport, a contest that pits will, strength, endurance, and brains against the raw fury of the Arctic winter. The ultimate test of this sport is the Iditarod Sled Dog Race, which also goes by the name of the Last Great Race on Earth. It's more than a thousand miles long, and during the eleven or twelve days it takes to run it, the mushers get maybe fourteen hours of sleep. No one has ever done it faster than Susan Butcher.

Her accomplishments have made her more famous in Alaska than the governor and more controversial than the oil industry. And all because of her dogs.

Susan Butcher came to Alaska at the age of twenty. She wasn't so much looking for adventure as for peace, something she didn't get much of during her childhood in Massachusetts. When she was young, her parents got divorced, and her schoolmates made fun of her. As they so kindly put it, she was "dumb." She wasn't really, though. She actually had dyslexia, a disorder that causes the brain to scramble written words. Too bad no one knew that when Butcher was young and vulnerable. Because she was excellent in math, her teachers assumed her problems in reading and writing were due to laziness and a lack of concentration. Some of them lectured her in front of the class about her shortcomings.

On top of all that, she considered herself unattractive. The only things she did well were things girls weren't supposed to do—sports. She was an excellent athlete, shining at softball, basketball, and field hockey. She was also an avid swimmer and sailor, and she particularly liked sailing alone in dangerous weather. She dreamed about living in the wilderness.

Through sports, she found self-expression, and the friendship she didn't find in school she found in dogs. At first she didn't have a dog of her own, but there were a couple in her neighborhood that she made friends with. The dogs didn't object to her looks, and they didn't care how well she could read. She loved them, and they loved her back.

When she was fifteen, she was given her first Husky, and it was then that she decided what she wanted to do with her life: become a musher. That the idea—this was, after all Massachusetts—was preposterous didn't occur to her.

"I've always loved dogs and the wilderness," she says, as if that's all the explanation that is needed. For her it is.

She soon got a second dog, but her mother declared that the two Huskies were too big for their house. No problem, said Butcher, who was then sixteen. Just like that, she moved to Maine to live with relatives and finish high school.

When she graduated, she moved to Fort Collins, Colorado, to live with her father and attend Colorado State University, where she studied to be a veterinary technician. If she was going to race dogs for long days on the trail, she would have to know how to take care of them.

In 1973, the year she moved to Colorado, she heard about a race in Alaska that was being run for the first time that winter. It was called the Iditarod and ran from Anchorage to Nome.

"As soon as I heard about it, I said, 'I'm going to win that race,'" she says. She was eighteen years old.

When she got to Colorado, she talked about her ambitions. She got two more Huskies, and her stepmother bought her a used dog-sled from a woman who had fifty dogs of her own. When Butcher went to pick the sled up, she needed little more than ten minutes to talk herself into a live-in job helping to care for and train the woman's dogs.

She spent two years in Colorado, studying veterinary medicine, working with the dogs, and learning how to mush. But Colorado wasn't where she wanted to be. For one thing, there were too many people there. For another, she had lost both of her Huskies there—one killed by a car and the other stolen. Butcher wanted to get somewhere where there were no cars to run her dogs over and no people to steal them.

And so, at the age of twenty, she moved to Alaska with no intention of coming back. Of course, many people move to Alaska with the same intention, but most of them change their minds after a close encounter with the wilderness. Butcher was different.

The place she found was a log cabin in the Wrangell Range of the Rockies in eastern Alaska—not far from the Yukon Territory of Canada, and not close to anything.

"There were no roads, no civilization at all," she says. "There was no one within fifty miles of me." With three sled dogs she purchased shortly after arriving in Alaska, that's where she spent the winter. It was like heaven, she says. "Most people, if they actually got to experience it, would admire portions of it. But they might not want to do it for life."

She did. She spent two years there, earning money in the summer and training her dogs in the winter. One of her summer jobs was in the salmon fisheries. The other was on a musk-ox ranch. On the ranch, one of her duties was combing the big, strong-smelling beasts to collect the layer of fine fur that the animals grow for the winter and shed in the summer. The fur is called *qiviut,* and it makes terrific sweaters.

During those two years of living on her own on the last American frontier, she grew in strength and self-confidence. By 1977, she was ready to move even farther north. She found an old gold miner's cabin in Eureka and moved in.

A year later, she was ready to take on the Iditarod. She knew she wasn't going to win—she didn't have the dogs or the experience for that—but she wasn't going for a brisk stroll in the country either. "I definitely went in as a racer," she says.

It was the fifth running of the race. In previous years, three other women had entered, but they had no intention of even trying to win. As far as the men were concerned, that was the right attitude. After all, the Iditarod was a man's race in the last great man's state.

Butcher's first problem was dogs: she only had five, and she couldn't afford to buy any more. So she borrowed three dogs giving her a total of eight, which wasn't nearly enough. Not only didn't she have enough dogs, but the ones she had were mismatched. The smallest was thirty pounds and the biggest pushing ninety. The best Alaskan Husky sled dogs run around fifty pounds, far smaller than the Siberian Huskies or Malamutes that people buy for pets. The big dogs look good, and they're strong, but they don't have the endurance for a long race. You won't find the Alaskan dogs on any American Kennel Club pedigree lists. They aren't bred for show. They're bred to be athletes.

Butcher didn't finish in the money, but Joe Redington Sr.—the man who had started the Iditarod in 1973—kept an eye on her and was impressed with the way she handled her dogs and the way they responded to her.

In the following years, Redington helped Butcher learn. In 1979, he invited her along on a dog sled expedition up Mount Denali—the Indian name for Mount McKinley, the nation's tallest peak. The trek took forty-four days, and eleven years later Butcher and Redington remained the only two people ever to mush up the mountain. Another musher who befriended her was Rick Swenson, who lived in Manley Hot Springs and was on his way to becoming the first great champion of the Iditarod.

By her second Iditarod, Butcher had climbed into the top ten finishers. Whatever money she won she plowed back into her growing kennel of dogs.

To outsiders, she seemed to have extraordinary luck with her dogs. One male she bought for $600—not a large price—turned into the best stud in Alaska. Another dog she purchased for $250—one-quarter the cost of most good dogs—turned into Granite, her most famous lead dog.

More than luck was at work, though. Unlike other mushers, Butcher spent every day with her dogs. She didn't throw a joint of meat at them and get on with more important things. To her, there were no more important things. She worked them in teams of seven, spending fourteen to sixteen hours at it every day. In the summer, she hooked them up to an all-terrain vehicle, slipped the ATV into low gear, and let them pull that. In the winter, they pulled a sled.

She made the work playful for the dogs and showed her appreciation for their efforts. When she fed them, she greeted each dog by name and sang songs to them. She took them swimming with her in the ice-cold waters of a nearby creek. And every day, one dog would be freed from the chain that attached it to its individual plywood dog house and be allowed to be a housepet for the day.

The bonding between musher and dogs started at birth. As the puppies were born, she picked them up and stroked their wet fur and blew on their noses. Her intention was only to love them, but she was also implanting her scent on their very first memories.

Others thought her goofy for all the attention she paid her animals. She alone among racers personally raised every dog she strapped into a harness. And she didn't get rid of dogs that didn't immediately show talent. It wasn't crazy at all. What she was doing was forming a bond between human and canine that would create a championship team. And, as Granite proved, dogs responded to a show of confidence in them just as surely as people.

Granite had a great cardiovascular system and recovered quickly from exertion, but when she got him he didn't have the confidence necessary to be a lead dog. But Butcher stuck with him, and after about ten chances to lead the team, Granite gradually became a true leader.

In the early 1980s, Swenson was king of the mushers, and Butcher had become his strongest challenger. As she got better, she found herself at the center of a bitter debate that involved not her skills, but her sex.

"Women have no place in the Iditarod," Swenson declared. "Women belong in the kitchen."

"Right on, brother," echoed the men in the barrooms.

Alaskan males figured they were the most macho creatures on the face of the earth. Maybe down in the sissified cities of the rest of America women could do anything they pleased, but this was Alaska, where only the strongest, toughest, and most ornery survived.

There was comfort for their male egos in knowing that Alaska was the last refuge of real men—men so tough you could strike a highway flare on their cheeks. Why, not too long ago there was a bar either in Alaska (or next door in the Canadian Klondike, which is pretty much the same thing) that kept a toe in a jar of alcohol behind the bar. A human toe. Someone lost it one day a long time ago doing something real manly—trimming his toe nails with a chain saw or something like that. Anyway, he lost it and donated it to the bar, and there it stayed, getting kind of black and disgusting looking until the day one man bet another man that he wouldn't down a drink with the toe in it.

Real men don't back down on bar bets, so the toe was dropped in a drink and the challenged man downed it. The drink, not the toe. The toe went back into the jar of alcohol. Before long, everyone was proving his manhood by duplicating the feat, and the toe got quite a workout. That's a true story—mostly.

The point is that you had to be tough to live in Alaska, tough enough to drink a toe cocktail. Up there the saying "Some days you eat the bear and some days the bear eats you" wasn't just a saying; it was a fact of life. There are more ways to die in that country than in the New York subway. And the toughest test of all was the Iditarod. Just the cold alone was enough to chase most pantywaist interlopers back home to somewhere warm like Buffalo or International Falls. Jack Frost didn't just nip at your nose in Alaska, he nibbled on your toes, chewed on your cheeks, and foraged on your fingers. So if you were a woman, you had best busy yourself by cooking up a mess of mooseburgers and let the men attend to the dangerous stuff like the Iditarod.

Of course, most of the men doing the talking knew as little about running a team of sled dogs as they did about Petrarchan sonnets. By the time Redington started the race in 1973, even the Eskimos had given up on dog sleds and were driving snowmobiles. That was one of the reasons for starting the race, to get back to the adventures that had made Alaska great.

And the historical Iditarod on which the modern race was based was, indeed, a great adventure. That Iditarod had been a race, too, but not of man against man. It was a race against death. It happened in 1925, toward the end of the gold rush. A diphtheria epidemic had struck the gold miners up in Nome, a port city washed by Norton Sound on the south shore of the Seward Peninsula. Serum could save the miners, but there wasn't any on hand. There was serum, in Anchorage, but with Norton Sound frozen over for the winter, it couldn't be delivered by ship. With time a critical factor, a relay of dog sleds was organized to deliver the serum and save Nome. The name of the race came from the city of Iditarod, the halfway point of the old trail. Iditarod was a boom town on the banks of the Iditarod River that was born of the gold rush in 1908 and was dead by 1930. In its heyday, Iditarod was home to ten thousand. Today, it's home only to a few derelict buildings and the ghosts of the past, awakening once each year to witness the passage of the Last Great Race on Earth.

Butcher came to Alaska because of that race. She hadn't even considered that, as a female, she wasn't supposed to be there. "I never looked at it as some massive battle of the sexes," she says. "But it became an issue, and it was a real struggle for me, because I was the only competitive woman in the race."

She dealt with that by not thinking about it. "I blocked it out," she says. "I said the race should be musher against musher."

Since she was a musher, she didn't see why that shouldn't include her, especially since it was her life's work. "My goal wasn't to be the best woman musher. My goal starting from somewhere back in 1979 or 1980 was to be the best racer ever if it was within my capabilities," she says. "I hated being the best woman musher."

She nearly pulled it off in 1982 when Swenson, after some eleven hundred miles of neck-and-neck dueling, squeezed out a three-minute victory over her. Nearly every man in Alaska breathed a huge sigh of relief and ordered another round of beers, and maybe a shot of strong whiskey on the side.

Her superb effort made her an overnight celebrity, and for the first time, people in the lower forty-eight states heard about the incredible woman musher. *National Geographic* came up to talk to her, as did the television magazine show, "20-20."

She and Swenson were now bitter rivals, and most of the bitterness seemed to come from him. He took on the role of Bobby Riggs to Butcher's Billie Jean King, baiting her and all women while at the same time drumming up interest in the race.

It was a good thing, too. Before Butcher came along, the Iditarod was one of those goofy things that men do to break up the monotony of long winters which are otherwise distinguished only by twenty-one-hour nights and three-hour days. Butcher's presence turned it into an event worthy of the attentions of network television crews and *Sports Illustrated* reporters. Hard on their heels came sponsors who enabled the top racers to devote all their time to the sport. Before Butcher became a contender, the race was in danger of dying for lack of sponsorship. Her presence saved it.

Butcher finished second again in 1983 and 1984, so it was hard to question her fitness to compete—especially after 1984. That year the race was run on the longer of the two courses, 1,157 miles (versus 1,049). With 888 miles behind her, Butcher arrived at the checkpoint village of Unalakleet at the eastern end of Norton Sound. There she was told that the overland route to the next checkpoint, Shaktoolik, was closed because most of the snow had blown off it. The only alternative was to mush through the night over forty miles of frozen sea.

The first thirty miles of the crossing went smoothly. Then the ice started rolling and rumbling beneath her, and she knew it was about to break up. She yelled to Granite to turn for the nearby shore, but a great sheet of ice heaved upward above the swells running underneath it. When it came down it shattered, dumping Butcher, her dogs, and the 250-pound sled into thirty feet of frigid water. The dogs, with their thick, waterproof fur, could survive water that cold, but Butcher had only minutes before she would turn into a killer whale's Popsicle. As she hung on and kicked, Granite pulled the team through the break to solid ice, dug his claws in, and heaved himself out. As he pulled, the other dogs, harnessed in pairs, followed. Finally, they hauled the sled and Butcher to safety.

Even though there was little snow on the shore, Butcher had had enough of the Sound. She steered back to land where, instead of changing into dry clothes or building a fire, she kept right on going, dodging rocks and driftwood. To keep from freezing, she ran behind the sled in the minus-fifteen-degree cold. She remembers thinking, *This isn't too terrible. If it was minus thirty, I'd have to do something different.*

Having survived 1984, Butcher was overdue in 1985. Her lead dog, Granite, was by now the best in the business. Her breeding operation had produced a strong supporting cast. And she herself, at thirty years of age, was a well-seasoned veteran. And if it weren't for one crazy moose, she probably would have won.

She met the moose only 150 miles out of Anchorage. Though there were still 900 miles to go, she had set a speed record on the first leg of the race to Eagle River and felt confident that this was her year. Now on the second leg, she was running in the dark—it's almost always dark on the Iditarod—and navigating by the light of a headlamp when she saw a female moose blocking the trail. Now, the moose is the largest land animal in North America, and an angry moose is not something you want to encounter. Butcher had encountered moose before in her racing. Once, when she had gotten too close to a moose, it had panicked and run through her team to escape. This time she stopped well short of the beast so that it wouldn't feel cornered and could amble off at its leisure.

Only this moose didn't take the easy way out. It had been a rough winter for the local moose population, and this one showed signs of needing a good meal. Butcher figured later that, in its weakened condition, the moose—which viewed Butcher's Huskies as a pack of hungry wolves—didn't think it could outrun the dogs. That left only one alternative: attack.

Without so much as a trumpet call, the moose charged the team. Butcher's first thought was that it really was a shame she had decided not to pack a gun. As the moose reached the dogs and started kicking them with its hooves, Butcher thought to get the axe that she carried to chop firewood.

By the time she got to the axe, one dog was dead, another was fatally wounded, and the others weren't doing that well, either. Stuck in their traces, the dogs couldn't flee or effectively counterattack. Butcher's only thought was to save them, and she waded into the growling, bellowing storm and started hacking at the moose.

Her initial fury drove back the moose, but only for a moment. The moose attacked again, and so did Butcher. Most of her seventeen dogs, she says, "were trying to melt into the snow, but not Granite. He was trying to protect me and the team. Granite went for her hind legs. She got him in the head, and he was thrown against a tree."

For twenty minutes, the battle raged. Finally, Butcher saw a headlamp behind her. It was Duane Halverston, another racer, and he had a .44-caliber revolver. Four shots later, the moose was dead, and Butcher, who had taken a beating herself, was loading her incapacitated dogs on her sled. Thirteen of the seventeen dogs had been injured. Two were dead. Still, she was the first musher to get to the next checkpoint, thirty miles away.

There, she had to drop out of the race, not because of the injuries, but because by allowing Halverston to shoot the moose and pick up her dogs, she had broken a cardinal rule of the Iditarod by accepting outside help.

"You can get outside help in a life-threatening situation," she explained, "but if you do, you're out of the race."

When it was suggested that the rule seemed rather harsh, she replied, "But you're not dead."

Rick Swenson did not win the 1985 race, even with Butcher the victim of a technical knock out. That honor went to another woman, Libby Riddles, who had followed in Butcher's tracks to the upper levels of the sport.

Butcher thus did not become the first woman to win the Iditarod, but that was never her objective. A dozen women could win it before her. She just wanted to win it again and again until she was the best there ever was.

In 1986, she did it. With an enormous finishing kick over the last 250 miles from Unalakleet to Nome, she mushed across the finish line in Nome with television cameras in front of her and the aurora borealis dancing overhead. She not only won the race, she established a new record of 11 days, 15 hours, 6 minutes—knocking 17 hours off Swenson's record that had stood since 1981.

In 1987, she repeated the feat on the other Iditarod route and again set a record. In 1988, she racked up an unprecedented third straight win in the Last Great Race on Earth.

Times were great for Butcher, but tough on Alaskan men. "Welcome to Alaska," groused Swenson, "where men are men and women are men." No sooner had he said it than it was being printed on T-shirts. Other T-shirts proclaimed Alaska the place where men are men and women win the Iditarod. Still others called it the land of beautiful dogs and fast women. The male chauvinist crowd that had once crowed about how no woman could win the ultimate macho race now opined that women were actually better suited to dog sled racing because their extra body fat gave them greater energy reserves and endurance.

Butcher, five-feet-six and 140 trail-hardened pounds, figured that she did have greater endurance. But when you figured that men had greater strength—and you have to be strong to wrestle a 250-pound sled up hills and across broken ice—it was a wash. She had a simpler reason for her success: "A lot of it is dedication."

She won because she put more time into it, especially with her dogs. Her dogs viewed her not so much as a two-legged waiter, but as the leader of the pack. Because Butcher never mistreated them or pushed them past the point of exhaustion, they trusted her completely. Another amazing thing about her dogs was that they always seemed to finish a race stronger than they had started it. That, too, was planned. She made sure her dogs got ample food—three major meals and three snacks a day—and plenty of rest. Unlike other mushers, she didn't keep either herself or her dogs going with megadoses of caffeine and sugar. Caffeine can keep you awake, and sugar can give the dogs a jolt of energy, but after that jolt comes a crash. So Butcher runs on what she's got inside her.

With success, the awards and commercial offers started pouring in. She rounded up dog food and other sponsors, and she could have had more—enough to make her rich. But to the amazement of the celebrity brokers, she took only as much as she needed to run her operation and turned the rest down.

"I could do tons of talks," she says, "but then I wouldn't be any good. I have to train. I have to be there with my dogs because my success comes from spending more time on the sport than any other racer. I spend more time with my runners [the dogs that pull the sleds], more time with the puppies, and more time with the yearlings than anyone else. I personally know my dogs. More important, they know me."

Asked whether money is important to her, she answers, "Obviously not."

If you take the money, she explains, "you're basically compromising yourself."

When she told that to the agents, they told her she was crazy. The opportunity she had after three straight wins might never come again. "I'll gamble that it's not a once-in-a-lifetime chance," she replied.

She didn't plan to race the Iditarod forever. She was getting into her mid-thirties and wanted to take off at least a year to start a family with her husband, Dave Monson, a fellow musher and a lawyer. Before she did that, though, she wanted to become the first five-time

Iditarod winner, and she wanted to set the course records on a slew of other major sled dog races. Most of them she had already wrapped up by 1989, including the Kusko 300, the Kobuk 450, the Norton Sound 250, and the Cold Foot Classic 350. The John Beargrease 500 record fell in 1990.

The more she won, the more she grew into her role as a spokesperson for mushing. Her commercial endorsements required her to travel from Alaska to the lower forty-eight for four to six weeks each summer, a time when she had to leave her dogs in someone else's care.

At first, she had trouble dealing with all the attention. "I felt like people were trying to tear pieces of my skin off," she says.

Her trips to big cities were uncomfortable at first, too. "When you live in a city, you have no idea how much sensory input you're getting all day," she says. City dwellers can turn off the traffic noise, the smells, the continually changing visual panoply of the streets. Accustomed to the chirring of insects and the yapping of dogs, she absorbed every bit of that sensory input.

She was struck by how little control city people have over their lives. "And they don't even realize it," she observed.

A city person would argue with her. Of course they have control. If the faucet doesn't work, they just call down to the building superintendent. If they have a package that absolutely, positively has to get there overnight, they throw some money at a delivery service, and it gets done. If they want a romantic glow in the fireplace, they call some guy in Jersey who brings over a few sticks of wood.

It's an illusion, she said. In civilization, people think food comes from the grocery store. They don't see or think about the farm that grew it, the trucks that brought it there, all the people involved in processing it.

"We know where everything comes from," she said. "If we want to be warm, we have to chop more wood. If we want electricity, we have to generate it. We grow huge gardens. It's all very immediate. It's not very complicated, which is nice."

That was 1989. By 1991, things had gotten a bit more complicated as Monson, to run the family business, felt compelled to bring a cellular phone and fax machine to Eureka. But they still have to run a generator to make the gadgets work. And if anything breaks, they fix it themselves.

"There are times the lights will go out and I wish someone would fix the generator for me," she admits. But when she considers what that convenience implies, she gets over it. Sure, life in the wilds of Alaska isn't for the weak, but on the other hand, she doesn't have to go to aerobics classes to keep in shape. Just surviving keeps her and Monson in better shape than most of the human race.

To maintain her sanity, when Butcher comes to New York she requests a hotel room facing Central Park. As long as she can look out the window and see some green and trees, she's all right.

Although she managed to survive and even enjoy her trips to civilization, she told of a frightening moment in New York during one of her first visits. She and Monson were walking in the vicinity of Times Square, a section of the city as laden with sensory assault as any in the world. Without warning, her circuits overloaded, and she "had a major flip-out." She fairly screamed at Monson to get her out of there.

Sure, he said, let's take the subway.

The measure of their marriage is that she didn't strangle him on the spot. Instead, she suggested a cab might be more convenient. After telling her story, she said, "I can see why there are so many crazy people in New York."

She had hoped to win her fourth straight Iditarod in 1989, her fifth in 1990, and then retire. But in 1989, misfortune laid her low again. This time, she hauled into Iditarod in great shape, but during a layover there her dogs came down with dysentery. Not allowed outside help, she dosed the dogs with antibiotics herself and nursed them along the trail. For a time, they were better, and Butcher battled for the lead with four other mushers—Dee Dee Jonrowe, one of the half dozen competitive women now in the sport; veteran Joe Runyan; Swenson; and Martin Buser, a Swiss musher. With 77 miles—about 11 hours—to go, Runyan had a bare five-minute lead on Butcher. It was the kind of lead Butcher was used to overcoming. But the dogs fell sick again on that last leg, and Butcher knew they didn't have enough strength left to win. When Runyan pulled into Nome as the winner, the men in the crowd went wild.

Butcher had known that sooner or later she would lose an Iditarod. Too many things can go wrong to bank on victory, no matter how good your dogs and how stern your will. But she hadn't known how she would react.

As it turned out, she reacted very well. "I'm very proud of Joe Runyan," she said. "I heard it hurts to fall from the top, but when it happened, I thought, 'What are they talking about? Joe's put out a challenge I've got to beat.' "

It took her no longer than the next race. In 1990, she tied Swenson with her fourth Iditarod victory. She also shattered the last great excuse others (meaning Swenson) had used for her winning so often—that she won because she had a truly great lead dog, the redoubtable Granite. But in 1990 Butcher retired Granite, and she won anyway.

Now there was a new contest with higher stakes. Butcher had tied Swenson's victory total, but she hadn't broken it. In 1991, the race would be not only for the $50,000 first prize, but also for the distinction of being the first five-time winner.

When Swenson and Butcher lined up at the starting line in Anchorage on Saturday, March 2, 1991, for the nineteenth running of the Iditarod, they and a few other elite mushers were competing in a vastly different contest than the majority of the seventy-five mushers in the race. Most of the field, like the field in the Ironman Triathlon, had no chance of winning but was there for the adventure and the challenge. If their sleds broke, they had to repair them themselves. At the checkpoints, they had to melt snow to heat the water used to thaw and mix the dog food. If they wanted to catch an hour's sleep, they had to sleep on the floor of whatever building was offered or fight for a few available cots.

No outside help was allowed on the trail, but there were no rules against having someone waiting at each checkpoint with fresh supplies and water already heated and ready to mix with the food. And if a musher could arrange ahead of time for private lodgings for the fitful hour of sleep he or she might catch during the four-hour stops, that was okay, too. The top mushers had all of these advantages. They also had new sleds waiting at each stop in case they had damaged one on the trail. A few, including Butcher, had airplanes following overhead and sending information about the positions of the leaders to the next checkpoint.

There was grumbling about these advantages and talk of changing the rules to eliminate them. But dog racing, as with other sports, was not immune to the lure of technology and the quest for anything that would provide the winning edge.

As it turned out, the 1991 Iditarod was decided not by technology, but by old-fashioned derring-do.

The race was between Swenson, Runyon, and Butcher, and as they zeroed in on Nome, Butcher took over the lead. She was first to Unalakleet and the first out. She led going into Shaktoolik and was the first to Koyuk. The next leg ran to White Mountain on the south shore of Norton Sound, seventy-seven miles due east of Nome and glory. From there, it was a dash to the finish line, and everyone knew who was best at that.

But as the mushers left White Mountain, a blizzard closed over them. They tried to claw their way through the blinding snow and ice that—at thirty below zero and lord knows what wind-chill factor—literally scoured the skin off their faces. (Enter the Iditarod and get a free dermabrasion.)

Unable to see the wooden stakes tied with red ribbons that marked the trail, and fearing for the safety of her dogs, Butcher turned back. She had seen Swenson on the trail, and he wasn't having any better luck. From the way he talked, he wasn't going to risk it, either.

But Swenson would have risked anything at that point. Until 1982, he had been the greatest musher on the planet. Then Butcher had come along, and he hadn't won a race since. "If he doesn't win this year, he's going to kill himself," a musher told Detroit journalist Mitch Albom. Swenson himself had confided to another reporter that he thought so highly of Butcher, "If she weren't a woman, I'd punch her lights out."

For a full day, the people in Nome waited for somebody—anybody—to cross the finish line. While the blizzard raged, no one

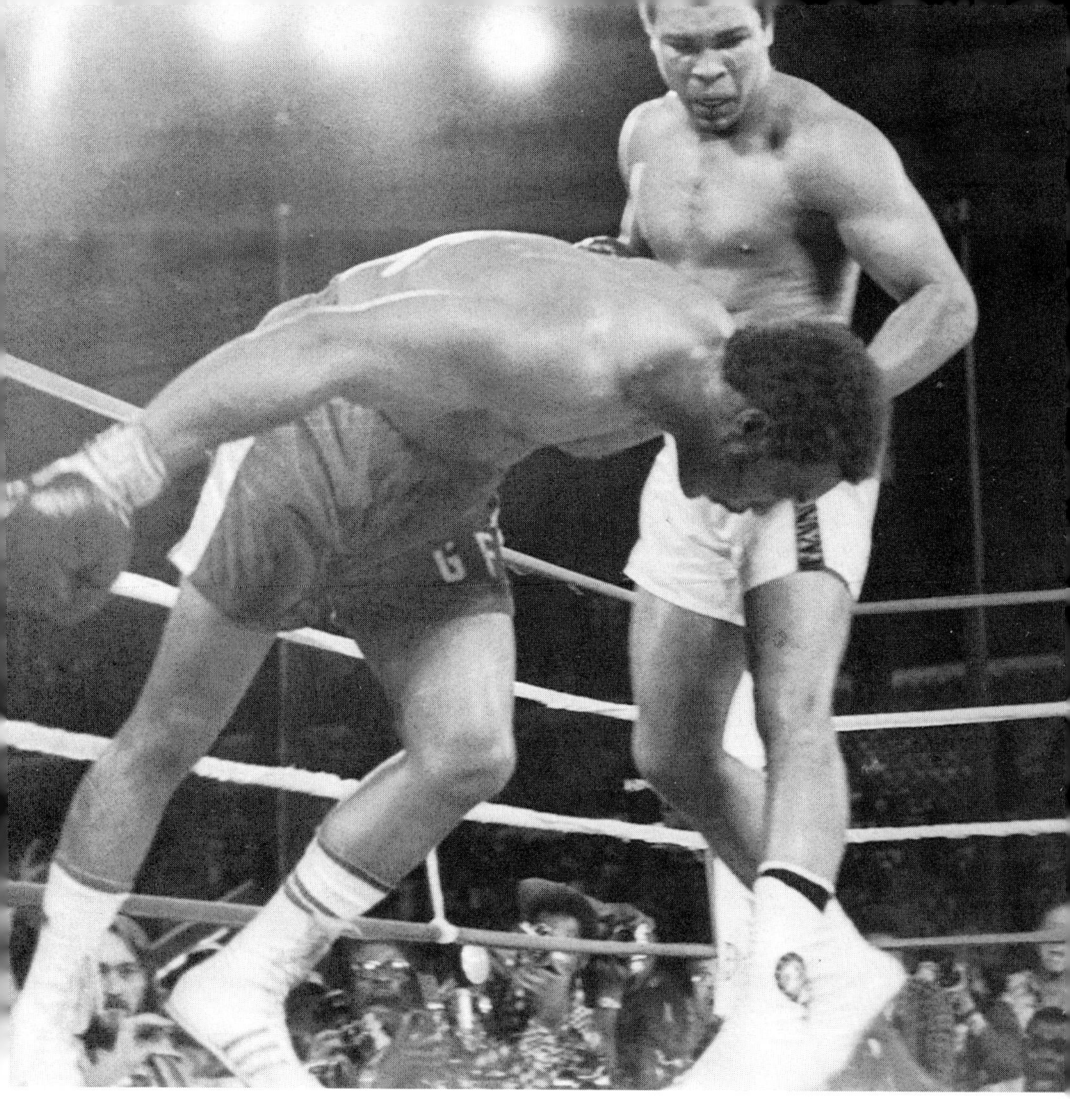

AP/Wide World Photos

The young George Foreman thought he was the toughest man on the planet. Then he met Muhammad Ali—and the canvas—on October 30, 1974, in Kishasa, Zaire.

AP/Wide World Photos

Seventeen years older and thirty pounds heavier, Foreman, tended by Angelo Dundee (left) and Archie Moore, fought for the title again against Evander Holyfield.

Courtesy of Zoe Koplowitz

With ten hours of the 1990 New York City Marathon completed and more than ten hours to go, Zoe Koplowitz (right) and her running companion, Hester Sutherland, take in New York City from the Queensboro Bridge.

Photo by Leszek Sibilski/Courtesy of Dick Traum

Dick Traum, founder of the Achilles Track Club and the first amputee to run a marathon.

AP/Wide World Photos

Jim Abbott at work for the California Angels.

AP/Wide World Photos

Joan Benoit Samuelson, winner of the first Olympic marathon for women, crossing the finish line in the Los Angeles Coliseum, August 6, 1984.

AP/Wide World Photos

Joe Montana at ease during a practice and at work, directing the game-winning drive against the Bengals in Super Bowl XXIII.

AP/Wide World Photos

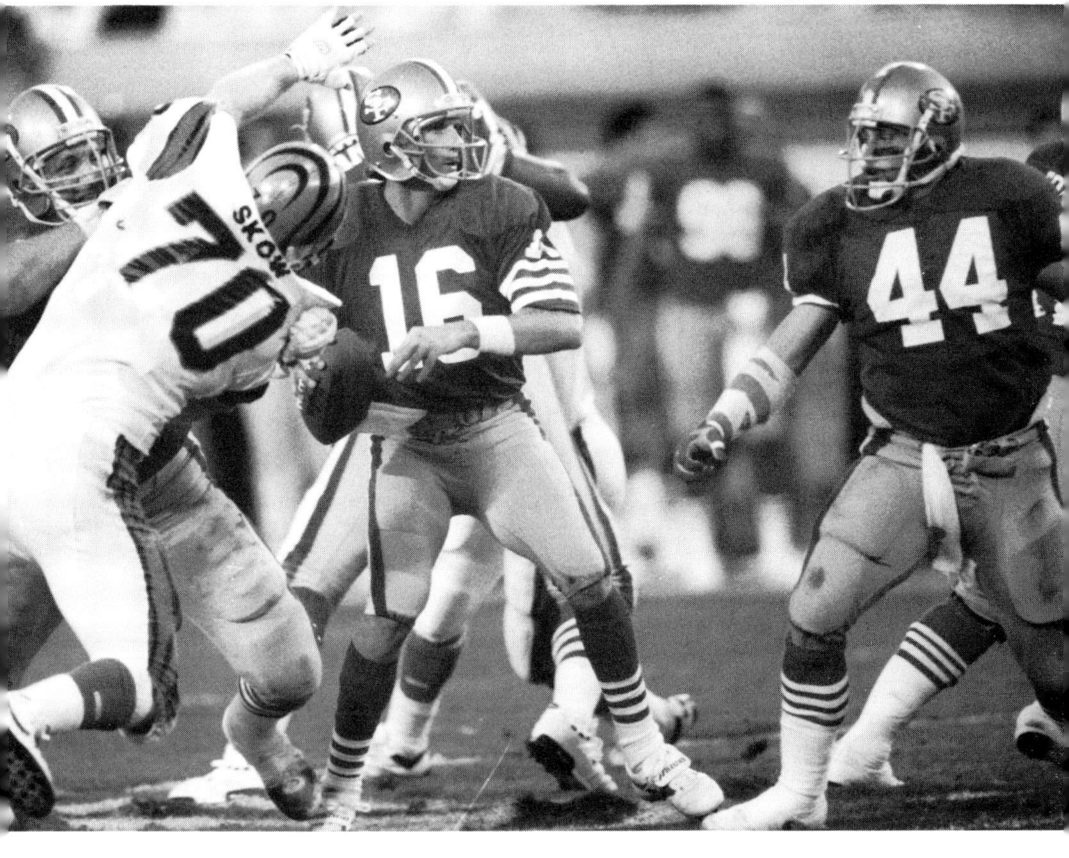

AP/Wide World Photos

Somewhere inside the ice-encrusted cocoon is Susan Butcher, four-time winner of the Iditarod, The Last Great Race on Earth.

Photo by Robert S. Townsend/*The Record*

Two days after being named to the 1991 NBA All Star Team, Bernard King (No. 30) took on three and four Knicks at a time in scoring 49 points in Madison Square Garden.

AP/Wide World Photos

Even heavyweight champion George Foreman had to smile when he presented Billie Jean King with her trophy for whipping Bobby Riggs in Houston's Astrodome.

AP/Wide World Photos

As King acknowledged the crowd on her way to the court, her mind was on the match with Riggs and a last-minute strategy change that would lead to her historic victory.

AP/Wide World Photos

Scott Hamilton got a hero's welcome when he brought his Olympic gold medal back to Denver, his adopted hometown.

Photo by Larry Brown/Courtesy of Tess Hyman

Howard and Tess—Dr. and Mrs. N. Howard Hyman.

Photo by John Decker/*The Record*

Teammates on the 1986 World Series champion Mets, Gary Carter and Darryl Strawberry were reunited on the 1991 Dodgers.

Photo by Steve Auchard/*The Record*

As a schoolgirl at Paramus Catholic in New Jersey, Anne Donovan stood head and shoulders above the competition.

AP/Wide World Photos

Bart Giamatti fields a question after declaring Pete Rose to be banned for life from baseball.

During the 1988 National League Championship Series between the Dodgers and the Mets, Giamatti, as league president, inspects the glove of Dodger pitcher Jay Howell. Howell was ejected from the game after an illegal substance was found on the glove.

AP/Wide World Photos

knew where Swenson was. They only knew that Butcher and the others had waited it out at White Mountain. Then, at 1:34 A.M. on Friday, March 15, Swenson crossed the finish line first.

But hadn't he been afraid of dying?

"What's my life worth anyway?" he asked as he sucked at a glass of whiskey (hold the toe). "If I had to go back and listen to three hundred sixty-five days of that crap—'How come women keep beating you?'—I'd just as soon be dead."

Butcher came in third and refused to second-guess herself. "At that point, my dogs could not endure another fifty-five miles in a storm," she said. "I made the decision not to continue."

If it had been only herself, she would have pressed on. But it wasn't just her. It was her dogs. As much as she wanted to win, their welfare came first.

"My whole strategy has always revolved around dog care," she said. "The better you take care of them, the better they perform. Maybe I could have got them to do it, but I didn't want to ruin their trust in the way I drive them."

During her career, the accusation that never went away was that she cared for her dogs more than she did for people. If it were true, it was understandable. When she was young and desperately needed a friend, dogs cared more for her than people did.

Asked how badly it hurt not to win, Butcher showed that she had changed. "I really wanted to win," she confessed. "It would have been a cute fairy tale. We could have hung up the harnesses and not raced Iditarod for a while. We want to start a family, and I think, even with this, we're going to do that."

Once she had tried to ignore being a woman in an alleged man's sport. She hadn't wanted the burden of a cause added to the weight of her sled. But she had come to understand even before her disappointment of 1991 that it was all right to be not just a champion, but a woman champion.

"Now that I've fought the fight somewhat unawares, I see that it is a good thing," she had said two years earlier. "I get hundreds of letters a week at home. I get them from women who have been inspired by what I do. This is wonderful, that something I do can help someone else's life."

Men might interpret every victory of a Rick Swenson or Joe Runyan as a reaffirmation of male superiority, but Butcher refused to turn that argument around. "Women aren't better," she said firmly. "It's a very equal sport."

And Swenson showed after he had won again that he recognized and appreciated Butcher's contribution to the sport. While he was making the rounds of the talk shows, David Letterman asked him about his animosity toward Butcher. Swenson dismissed it as just him talking to generate interest in the race. He mentioned how she had been considering retiring to have a child. "She's a great competitor," he said. "I had to beat her to get her back next year."

More than anyone else in Alaska, Rick Swenson knew that an Iditarod without Wonder Woman would be just another sled dog race.

Saint Bernard

I believe you can do anything in life if you are willing to put the time and work into it.

It should have happened in Phoenix, not Kansas City. Phoenix is a city named after the fabulous bird of mythology that was consumed by fire and then rose from its own ashes in undiminished glory. Kansas City is a stockyard, a place where cattle go to get butchered.

Butchered is what happened to Bernard King's right knee in Kansas City on March 23, 1985. When it happened, they said he would never be great again, just as they had once had said he would never be great to start with. But he had risen from the ashes before, and he would do it again. If no one believed that, fine. He believed, and he was the only one who counted.

King was an All-Star forward with the New York Knicks and on his way to becoming the first Knick ever to lead the National Basketball Association in scoring. The game that night meant absolutely nothing. The Knicks, riddled by injuries and hopelessly out of the playoffs, were playing the Kansas City Kings, a team bathed in a tradition of mediocrity that was looking only to the season's end when it could pull up stakes and move to Sacramento.

The sole bright spot for the Knicks that season had been King. Twenty-eight years old and playing for his fourth NBA team in his eight-season career, King was averaging 32.9 points per game. Earlier in the season, he had put together back-to-back 50-point games, and none other than Larry Bird had called him the greatest scorer he had ever seen.

It happened with 1:24 to go, with the Knicks, who would win but five road games all season, on the way to another loss. Kings guard Reggie Theus was going to the hoop and King, who had scored 37 points in the game, went up to try to block him. Before King left the ground, his right knee came apart. Given the sparse crowds the Kings attracted, it wasn't hard to hear the scream that tore from Bernard King's throat as he crumbled to the floor and writhed in pain.

The usual huddle of trainers rolled him on his back and asked him where it hurt. He said the knee, and they called for a couple of his teammates to haul him back to the locker room. There the Kings' team doctor, Howard Ellfedt, took a closer look at the injured joint and declared that it was probably a bad sprain.

Three days later in New York, Knicks' team physician Norman Scott cut a hole in the side of King's knee and poked an arthroscope inside to better assess the damage. What he saw wasn't good. The anterior cruciate ligament was shredded, leaving a nest of spaghetti in the middle of the joint. A hunk of cartilage had also ripped loose.

In other words, King told Paul Attner of *The Sporting News,* "My career was, for all intents and purposes, over. It was that simple."

It had been over for everyone else who had suffered such an injury. Oh, he still might play, as others had. He just wouldn't play with the explosive quickness and power on which his game was founded. "I didn't think it was fair for this to happen to me at the pinnacle of my career, not after all the work I had put into getting that far," King says. After Dr. Scott told him the extent of the damage, he allowed himself one day of depression. Then he decided that his career would not end. He decided he would be an All-Star again.

There were several options for dealing with the injury. One was to do nothing and hope that by building up the muscles supporting the knee, and by wearing a brace, King could restore enough stability to the joint to be able to play again—although not at the Himalayan level to which he—and the Knicks—had become accustomed. The other options involved surgery. None carried a guarantee.

King didn't want to make any decisions about a course of treatment until he knew everything there was to know about anterior cruciate ligaments and what happens when a person doesn't have one. He had medical books and journals brought to his room in New York's Lenox Hill Hospital. He called up other athletes who had suffered similar injuries and asked them what procedures they had undergone and how they had turned out. The news wasn't encouraging.

King didn't care. He told anyone who asked that he didn't want to just come back and play. "There was never any question I would play again, he says. "My will and my heart would make sure that happened. But the comeback wouldn't be complete until I was an All-Star."

He learned that the anterior cruciate is one of a pair of ligaments inside the knee. The ligaments are part of a system of four ligaments that connect the thigh bone—the femur—to the leg bone—the tibia. The other two, the collateral ligaments, are on the outside of the knee. The cruciate ligaments form an X in the knee, an arrangement that provides stability against twisting. Lose one of them, and the joint can still work, but it is unstable. King also learned that ligaments, unlike muscles and bones, don't regenerate. They can't be sewn back together, either.

Surgical procedures to repair knees had advanced considerably over the years. Some procedures involved transplanting tendons—the fibrous straps that anchor muscles to bones—to perform the function of the ligament. One procedure, pioneered by Knicks' physician Norman Scott, involved taking a thigh muscle that is normally connected to the leg, detaching it, and reattaching it inside the knee. His theory was that because he was using a muscle—the ilio-tibial band—instead of a tendon, the repaired knee could actually be made stronger through exercise. Other authorities questioned that theory, saying that the muscle Scott would use wasn't big enough. Scott had performed the surgery on other athletes, but none as accomplished as King.

After doing his homework, King brought in a half dozen surgeons. He didn't so much get their opinions as interview them about what they felt they could do. He told all of them the same thing: "I don't want to come back strong. I want to come back a superstar."

All but one gave him the same reply. Forget about superstar, they said. It simply wasn't realistic to think that the knee would function as it had before. The lone dissenter was Scott.

"I don't think I've ever seen any patient as well-informed as he was," says Scott. "I told him he had a chance to come back and be an All-Star, but you have to be a little bit tongue-in-cheek about anyone getting back to the level he was at." Scott promised King a chance, and that was all he wanted. He told Scott to go ahead.

The surgery was performed on April 1, 1985, and when it was over, King had an incision that ran from well above his knee to well below it. Forty surgical clamps held the incision together.

King's physical therapist was Dania Sweitzer. A former University of Miami swimmer, Sweitzer had begun her career working with stroke victims, amputees, and burn patients, then eventually switched over to athletes. Although she was full of enthusiasm and never said a discouraging word to a patient, going into the King rehabilitation, she said, "Up to now, nobody has been able to come back to professional basketball after such an injury." As for King's recovery, she said, "I think the odds are good. Bernard has a very good outlook about his future."

One of the first things Sweitzer said to King was, "Bernard, we're starting from scratch." And with that, King virtually disappeared from public view—not for a week or a month, but for two years.

No one but Sweitzer would know what King had to go through. No one would see the hours he poured into becoming not just good enough to play, but good enough to dominate again. At first there was optimism that King would be back with the Knicks and their prize rookie center, Patrick Ewing, in the fall of 1986. But then came outright anger and resentment at King for being so secretive. Finally, the Knicks let him go, figuring—wrongly—they were better off without him.

Call it a misunderstanding. King had spent a good deal of his professional life being misunderstood. Some of that was of his own doing, the result of his enormous pride and unwillingness to participate in the meaningless rituals that we often use to judge who is a good guy and who is not.

During most of his rehabilitation, King didn't talk to the media. He didn't show up at Knicks games or drop by at practices, and he didn't tell anyone why. He didn't tell anyone anything.

"I was going to do it my own way," he later explained. "I wanted to surround myself only with positive people. It seemed a waste of time to drive to games or practices when I couldn't play. The time was better spent rehabbing."

He set records for rehabbing. He spent five hours a day, six days a week with Dania Sweitzer. The seventh day he let her take off, but not himself. He never took a day off, never wanted one.

He says his work ethic comes from his parents, Thomas and Thelma King. Thomas King was a maintenance worker in a Brooklyn housing development. "I watched him work when there was snow, when there was rain, when he was sick. He gave everything he had, and he wanted to be the best at what he did." If his job was to sweep a floor, Thomas King didn't complain about the work or think it was beneath him. It was his job, and he took pride in doing it better than anyone else.

King's mother never missed putting a hot meal on the table for Bernard and his four brothers (including Albert, who also played in the NBA) and one sister. "We didn't eat frozen foods," King says. "She took care of the apartment and made sure our clothes were clean and sewn. That's hard work when you have six kids. So I emulated my parents. I work as hard at basketball as I saw them work."

Bernard King was born on December 4, 1956, and grew up learning what it meant to be tough. After starring in basketball at Fort Hamilton High in Brooklyn, he enrolled at the University of Tennessee, where he teamed with Ernie Grunfeld, who would also play for the Knicks in what was called the "Bernie and Ernie Show." From the very first, King was an All-American. As a freshman he was voted the Southeastern Conference's Player of the Year, a feat he repeated as a sophomore and junior. When he left after his junior year to enter the NBA draft, he was the second-leading scorer in University of Tennessee history, and his average of 25.8 points per game was the school record.

He was the first pick of the New Jersey Nets in the 1977 draft—the seventh player overall to be taken. He'd be going home to the New York area. Life, it seemed, was good.

Then Bernard King stumbled. In October 1976, he had been arrested in Knoxville for possession of marijuana and driving while intoxicated. He was suspended from the basketball team for the fall semester, but he came back strong in the winter, and when he entered the NBA draft, the Nets decided he was worth the risk. Then in

July, with training camp drawing close, King was arrested in Knoxville twice in one week. The first time he was charged with stealing a VCR from the university's athletic building, a charge of which he was exonerated. The second arrest was for possession of marijuana—a drug then at the peak of its popularity—and resisting arrest. He was nicked for a fifty dollar fine, but the damage to his reputation was more severe. Before he had played his first game, he was labeled a potential troublemaker. The arrests caused quite a bit of anxiety back in New Jersey, where the Nets were engaged in their perennial fight for respectability. But when King arrived in the Garden State, he proved to be an engaging and bright young man who said all the right things, including vowing to live not in New York, but in New Jersey.

The Nets were a sorry franchise in those days. They didn't even have a home arena but played in the Rutgers University field house in someplace called Piscataway. Considering that the team had been born in the now-defunct American Basketball Association and had played its first season in the Teaneck Armory, the college gym seemed appropriate.

King instantly improved the team. At six-feet-seven and a shade over two hundred pounds, he was a lean but tough scoring machine. He averaged 24.2 points per game that year and was a model citizen in every way. He even had a clause in his contract that gave him twenty-five free tickets to every game, tickets he distributed to disadvantaged kids who sat in a section that came to be called "King's Corner."

He was personable and never left an autograph unsigned. He didn't want to talk about the bad things that had happened to him, but he was willing to talk about life growing up in Brooklyn.

"I'm one of the toughest individuals I know," he once told journalist Mike Farber. "To grow up in New York, to face the challenge of New York, then college, then the media, you have to be tough. There were two approaches to city living: You can work for it, or you can take it. You can join a gang and have trouble with the law. I chose basketball, which didn't offer anything but a rim and some snow on the ground."

Even then, he had a highly developed sense of perspective about the world and about himself. "I don't use the word *ghetto,*" he said, when talking about his neighborhood. "If you tell a kid he's from the ghetto, he acts like a ghetto kid thinks he should act."

There were various theories about why he had gotten into trouble in Tennessee. His high school coach, Ken Kern, thought it stemmed from his rigid self-discipline growing up in the streets of Brooklyn. "He didn't want to get involved in anything wrong, so he went into seclusion," Kern said. "He never drank or fooled around with drugs. He wasn't out there living his experiences, so he denied himself a chance to learn from events. At Tennessee, he started to get out into society, and he wasn't equipped to handle it. He made younger mistakes at an older age."

If so, he wasn't the only one. On college campuses in 1976, marijuana was almost as common as textbooks. And if you could find a college kid who hadn't driven a car after drinking too much, all it proved was that the kid didn't have a car. But King was an African-American in a state south of the Mason-Dixon line, which made him more likely than a white kid to be noticed if he got out of line.

His only slips his first year as a pro were missing a practice and being late for a game—offenses for which he endured a one-game benching. Yet KING RETURNS TO COLLEGE FORM read the headline in one newspaper, a clear indication that his college mistakes weren't forgotten—or forgiven.

Every time something happened involving King, the press decided he was bad, and they hauled out his record to prove it. But he wasn't bad inside—until he had a drink.

King didn't know it then, but he was an alcoholic. "I'm not a very outgoing person," he would say when he had finally wrestled his devil to the ground. "I don't enjoy going out and partying." But as a marquee NBA player, he found himself being invited to a lot of parties, where he indulged in alcohol and whatever other drug was around. "To make myself comfortable," he said.

On December 18, 1978, during his second year with the Nets, he got a little too comfortable. Police in Brooklyn found him slumped over the wheel of his car at an intersection at 5:15 in the morning.

They found some cocaine in the car and determined that he was drunk. He also didn't have a license.

Anxiety levels were increasing with Nets management, but they stood by King, particularly as he was enjoying another outstanding year. Still, when the season was over, the team traded King and two other players to the Utah Jazz for center Rich Kelley. The Nets, who knew by then that King had an alcohol problem, insisted that they weren't unloading King. They said they needed a center, and Kelley was the man. Just the same, Kelley didn't even last an entire season with the Nets before he was sent to Phoenix.

If Tennessee had been culture shock, Salt Lake City, home of the Jazz, was culture shock squared. Under the best circumstances, life for an African-American in the lily-white city of the Mormons could be difficult. For King, it was a disaster.

His career with the Jazz lasted all of nineteen games, during which he played little and saw his scoring average drop to 9.3 points per game. King not scoring in double figures was like Babe Ruth going through a season with eighteen home runs. Something was obviously wrong.

He hit bottom on January 2, 1980. Again the headlines told of the arrest of a drunken King. And again cocaine was found in his apartment. Worse, he had been turned in to police by a woman who said that he had sexually abused her.

The Jazz suspended him immediately. He took a polygraph test that confirmed his story: he didn't remember anything that happened that night. Rather than face a trial, he pleaded guilty to reduced charges in the assault. He was ordered into an alcoholism rehab program in California (the same one former First Lady Betty Ford had graduated from) and put on probation.

He put the same energy into his alcoholism rehabilitation that he would later put into rehabilitating his knee. He joined a summer league in California, and when word got around about the apparent sincerity of his personal reformation, the Golden State Warriors, who desperately needed help, decided to take a chance. They traded with Utah, who wanted no part of King, to get him.

"I can't drink at all," King confessed when he joined the Warriors. "It's a disease. I've accepted it."

He came back better than ever. His average went back up to 21.9 on nearly 60 percent shooting accuracy, and his rebounding improved dramatically. The good citizen that had always been inside was allowed to come out and take center stage. He made the All-Star game for the first time, and to make that accomplishment even sweeter, the game was played in the Meadowlands Arena, the brand-new home of the same old Nets.

"People don't know me," he told the hometown New York press when he arrived for the All-Star Game. "My family and friends know me, but it's wrong for other people to draw conclusions. I'm not a tough person. I'm mentally tough when my back's against the wall whether it's in life or on the court. But I'm a relatively easygoing person. I think I'm a very feeling person."

Said Al Attles, the Warriors' general manager: "Bernard is a gentleman. He's one of the top people ever involved in the game of basketball."

At the end of the season, he was voted the NBA's Comeback Player of the Year. He followed that with another big season for lowly Golden State in 1981–82, bringing his scoring average up to 23.2 points per game. There was now no place to go but home.

King was a free agent at the end of his second year with Golden State, and after a nasty bidding war between the Warriors and the Knicks, he ended up in New York by way of a trade. The old stories were retold when he joined the team, but all was forgiven as long as he put the ball in the net.

King put the ball in the net.

They called him "Saint Bernard" in the Garden. In the 1982–83 season, he scored at a 21.9 clip and led the team to the second round of the playoffs. But in 1983–84 he dominated.

Unstoppable is a tough word to apply to an athlete, but if it fit anyone, it fit Bernard King. Opposing teams threw everything but the scorer's table at him. They didn't care if they fouled out three people guarding him, they just kept sending in the big, strong bodies with one order: Make that so-and-so work for his points. Work he did, absorbing elbows and forearms and knees while scoring at a 26.3 clip.

"Bernard is literally dominating games," said teammate Truck Robinson. "Defenses can't do anything about it."

At the end of December, he was voted team captain. At the end of January, he scored 50 points in a game against San Antonio. The next night—February 1—he scored 50 against Dallas. It was the first time in more than twenty years that anyone had scored 50 points on consecutive nights. (Wilt Chamberlain, the greatest scorer in the history of the game, was the last person to do it.)

"We couldn't stop him," said Dallas coach Dick Motta. "I guess no one can."

What made the performances all the more remarkable is that he wasn't trying for big numbers. He took only 30 shots in the first 50-pointer, hitting 20 of them. The next night, he again hit 20 field goals, this time on only 28 shots.

"What makes Bernard special is that he stays within the playing structure," said Knicks coach Hubie Brown. "He does not free-lance or razzle-dazzle or break up the offense. He just plays within the parameters we give him. He's the ultimate NBA player."

In the playoffs, he proved Brown right. The Knicks' first-round opponents that year were the Detroit Pistons. The series went the five-game limit, with King averaging 42 points. In addition, he twice led his team in rebounds. In the deciding game, played in Detroit, he out-dueled Isiah Thomas, the Piston's star point guard, 44 points to 35. He was the Knicks' leading rebounder as well, with 12, in a game that went to overtime before the Knicks won it.

Then it was off to Boston to take on the mighty Celtics. The Knicks dropped the first two games of the series in Boston, with King limited to a high of 26 points. After the first game, Cedric Maxwell, who had the task of guarding him, crowed that King would never score 40 points against him as he had against the Pistons.

For two more games—another Celtic win at home in which King was held to 13 points, and a Knick win in Game Three at Madison Square Garden, in which King hit for 24—Maxwell seemed a prophet. Then came Game Four and Bernard's revenge.

In the first half, King hit for 21 points. In the second half, he hit for 22 for a tidy total of 43 points. He hit with bodies draped all over him, hands in his face and elbows in his ribs. He shot fade-away jumpers, he slammed in alley-oop passes, he drove the lane. On defense, he held Larry Bird to 29 points. The Celtics tried Maxwell on him, then Kevin McHale—but to no avail. At the end of the game, the series was tied.

Back in Boston the magic carpet ride ended. The Celtics—with Bird, McHale, Maxwell, Dennis Johnson, and Robert Parrish—asserted their superiority. They smothered King (holding him to 24 points), won the seventh game, and then went on to win the NBA Championship for the fifteenth time. In addition, Bird beat out King for the league's Most Valuable Player Award, although it was difficult to conceive of a player more valuable to a team than King.

That summer, King did what he usually does—he worked. Every day he ran five miles and rode fourteen more on his bicycle. Then he worked on his game. The tendency with great scorers—or great hitters in baseball—is to think that the game comes easily to them. And it's true that there is a superior level of talent with the great ones. But the real difference is in the effort they put in. Larry Bird, Magic Johnson, Michael Jordan—all of them worked to perfect the shots that look so easy. So too did Bernard King.

The Knicks opened the 1984–85 season with high hopes that soon dissipated as player after player went on the disabled list. As his supporting cast melted away, King fell under even more intense pressure by opposing defenses, who treated him like a perennial opponent on boxing undercards. Early in the season, he dragged himself onto the court against the Spurs with a jammed right ring finger, a sore ankle, a hip pointer, a thigh bruise, and a strained knee. Then he scored 44 points, and the Spurs went home grateful he wasn't healthy.

Early in November, in a game against the Bullets, King dove for a loose ball and opened a major gash below his knee when he collided with the scorer's table. But he was soon back in the lineup, and on November 24, he ran off a streak of five games during which he averaged 39 points. In the fifth game, he scored 52 against the Pacers

—his third 50-point game of the season. "I stood behind Bernard in the first half and he hit his turnaround jumper," said poor Devin Durrant, the forward assigned to guard King for the Pacers. "In the second half, I tried to front him, and he beat me for layups. I tried, but nothing was going to work."

"If I was going to war, I would want Bernard King in the trenches next to me," testified Golden State coach John Bach after being burned in another game by King.

But even those performances paled compared to what King did on Christmas Day 1984 in a game against the Nets at the Garden. He hit 21 in the first quarter and 19 in the second for 40 by the half. In the second half, the Nets did everything but drop a safe on him and managed to hold him to 60 for the game—a Knicks record.

The season continued like that. King missed games here and there —seventeen in all—with a variety of injuries, but he played with pain that would have sidelined other players. It's safe to say he was never healthy the entire season.

"I worked on certain moves over the years that allow me to beat the double team and still take a high-percentage shot," he said when asked to explain how he could score when every defense he faced was stacked against him. He also explained why he worked so hard and what basketball meant to him.

"I had a need to find fulfillment when I was younger, and basketball was my emotional outlet," he said. "With any creative person, there is a great deal of emotion involved. To me, basketball is an art."

No one who watched him would argue that.

He turned twenty-eight in December 1984, and there was no sign that he was slowing down. Indeed, he believed he was getting better, and his league-leading scoring average supported him. "The way I look at it, I'm twenty-eight years old, still young, and the best years for Bernard King are still ahead of him," he said. "There are certain areas I can and will improve in. I will be much better in time than I am now. We all have certain fires within us, and we have to face the challenge of trying to be good at what we're doing. Fear is a big thing —the fear of failure. You have to be willing to face failure before you can succeed.

"I believe you can do anything in life," he concluded, "if you are willing to put the time and work into it."

He was willing. He was obsessed with the game, obsessed with being the best. He brought that same intensity to everything he did. He was a great admirer of Sidney Poitier, the actor, so he studied the way Poitier spoke and patterned his own speech after Poitier's. Unlike the speech of many athletes, King's was composed of complete sentences, devoid of cliches, and refreshingly free of slang and profanity.

He liked jazz music, but it wasn't enough for him to go to a record store and buy a few albums. He had to be an expert. He had to know what he was listening to, who performed it, how it was performed. He became a world traveler and a connoisseur of fine food. He collected art and got into acting, co-starring with Gabe Kaplan in *Fast Break,* a basketball film, and making appearances on soap operas and "Miami Vice."

He would talk about all these things freely. The only subject he wouldn't talk about was the past. It made no sense to talk about events that were over and couldn't be changed. He preferred to talk about the future and things he could yet do. And anyone who had ever thought there were limits on his future now believed that anything was possible.

Then came the night in Kansas City when everything he had worked so hard for was taken away by the betrayal of a body he had spent so much time conditioning. That he allowed himself only one day of depression over the injury was typical. That he would work harder than anyone else to return to active duty was also typical.

After Dr. Norman Scott put the knee back together, he declared, "Bernard will be fine. There's no reason to believe he won't be back and healthy next season."

Those were the words that Knicks fans had been waiting to hear. Further good news came when the season ended, and King's average of 32.9 points per game won the scoring title and earned him a place on the All-NBA Team.

But the weeks turned into months, King was nowhere to be seen. Fans and media anxious to hear about his progress were met by silence. Even his brother Albert, with whom he worked out, was sworn to secrecy.

One of the exercises prescribed for his rehabilitation was swimming. And here his will to get better met its sternest test. In the neighborhood where Bernard King grew up, there weren't a whole lot of backyard pools. "I wasn't a beach person," he said wryly. He was, in fact, terrified of water. But Dania Sweitzer, his therapist, insisted that workouts in water would speed the strengthening of his knee without putting stress on it.

King lived in Franklin Lakes, a well-to-do rural suburb in northern New Jersey popular with athletes. One of King's neighbors had a small backyard pool, a nonthreatening affair only four feet deep, and it was chosen as the site of King's first swimming session. Despite the shallowness of the pool, King showed up encased in life preservers.

He got in the water not because Scott and Sweitzer told him to, but because they explained to him the benefits of it. "He questioned everything," Scott says. "I've never dealt with an athlete who was so thorough or inquisitive. But once you explained to him why you thought he needed to do something, he said okay and never asked again. He was a perfect patient. His work ethic is the best."

Training camp opened in the fall of 1985 without King. The Knicks could only say his rehabilitation was progressing. The season began, and still no King.

There were sightings, however. It was discovered that he was working out at Ramapo College, a small Division III state school nestled in the hills of Mahwah, New Jersey. He'd go there by himself and work by himself, sometimes sharing the gym with the Ramapo College women's basketball team. Reporters, anxious for any scrap of information, quizzed the coach, Mike Ricciardi, about what he had seen.

"It seems like he's trying to gauge how long it will take until he can do everything automatically, without worrying about the injury recurring," Ricciardi volunteered. "He runs drills. Some days it looks like he can go full speed. Some days he can't. He's hot and cold."

What he was doing was teaching himself to play basketball again. He'd watch old game films of himself on videotape and then take to the court to re-create the movements he saw. It was slow work, even at the punishing schedule he set for himself.

Finally, in December, he gave a progress report.

Why didn't he come to Knicks' games to offer support to the team?

"I will attend some games if my schedule allows," he said, "but the biggest thing I can do for the Knicks is rehabilitate my knee."

He reported that he was working out without a knee brace, and that there was no pain or swelling in the joint. He said he was able to perform every offensive move in his arsenal.

So why aren't you playing?

"It's a matter of endurance, strength, and power," the ever-present Sweitzer replied. "He is not normal in those areas. By normal, I mean normal for Bernard King. He passed the point of normal for the everyday person months ago. But he needs to be explosive in his movements. He's not at that point yet."

So that's the way it would be. King would return when he could be King, and no sooner. It made sense to him, but the media and fans were beginning to lose patience. Even at fifty percent, they figured, he was better than most of the league. Why did it have to be all or nothing?

Because that's the way King wanted it.

The season ended, and soon the 1986–87 season was at hand. No one knew if King would show up at training camp.

On October 17, King gave his answer. He showed up at the team's training camp and joined in drills. Normally, training sessions are open to the press, but the doors to the gym were closed, and reporters had to press against the smoked-glass windows to try to get a glimpse of King.

He moved well to his left, they decided, but hopped off the right leg instead of driving off it. But he shot better moving to his right than to his left.

Such was the stuff of newspaper headlines. Not since Babe Ruth missed half a season with "the bellyache heard 'round the world" had an injury been the object of so much media attention.

Two days after King started working out with the team, disaster struck again. While running near his home, he stepped in a pothole and suffered a partial tear of the medial collateral ligament in the same right knee. He would be out, said Dr. Scott, at least a month. Maybe longer.

And there was another injury, a strain suffered while trying to do too much on a rehabilitation machine. Meanwhile, the Knicks were going nowhere.

With only six games remaining in the season, King finally declared himself ready to test the knee. His contract was ending with the season, and now the support he'd had when he was tearing up the league turned into criticism. The consensus was that King was only coming back to make a case for a new contract. If so, it was a decent case. In six games, he had scored at a 22.7 clip and averaged better than 35 minutes of playing time.

But it wasn't enough to impress Al Bianchi, the Knicks' new general manager. He was already saddled with Patrick Ewing's enormous contract, and he wasn't sure he wanted to risk additional millions on a player who had missed 185 straight games and would turn thirty-one years old that December. Besides, he thought that Kenny Walker, the team's top draft pick in 1986, would rediscover the scoring touch he had shown at the University of Kentucky but which he had lost in his first professional season. The debate raged in the newspapers and on the radio.

Sign him.

Let him go.

You can't live without him.

Who needs him?

The Knicks, Bianchi decided, didn't need him. He let King sign with the Washington Bullets. It was a bad decision, one of many that led to Bianchi losing his job four seasons later. Walker, a fine defensive player, never did develop as a scoring forward. In an effort to fill that role, the Knicks brought in Kiki Vandeweghe, a once-great forward plagued with chronic back problems. Although Vandeweghe had his moments, he couldn't fill the void left by King.

It took some time for the full weight of Bianchi's folly to sink in. In his first full year back, 1987–88, King averaged 17.2 points for the

Bullets—decent numbers, but nowhere near his former prowess and not enough to incite much anger back in New York.

The following year, he upped that to 20.7—good, but not great. And he was thirty-two years old, certainly close to the end of his career and unlikely to get better.

But he did get better. In 1989–90, he upped his average to 22.4 points and was on the verge of the complete comeback he had worked for.

That finally arrived in the 1990–91 season, when King astounded the NBA—astounded everyone but himself—by becoming a dominant player again. By January he was averaging 30 points a game and fighting Michael Jordan for the league scoring leadership. He piled up seven games of 40 or more points before the season was half over, including a 52-point number he dropped on the Denver Nuggets.

The 52-pointer got even King's attention.

"A lot of people, probably including myself, look at the period when I got back-to-back 50s as the height of my career," he said. "During my recovery from surgery, that was the magic level to work toward again. To come back after the entire knee was reconstructed, to come back from seeing forty metal staples running down the middle of my knee, to come back from being unable to lift my leg off the bed, to come back and get fifty points in a ball game again is one of the most special feelings in the world. It's something that I'm awfully proud of."

The truly amazing thing about King's performance was that he was a different player than he had been when he was scoring 50 points for the Knicks. Back then he had been a low-post performer who played with his back to the basket and scored from in close. Now he played facing the basket and scored from outside. Those who watched him said he had changed because of the knee. He pointed out that he had changed because the game had changed. All he was doing was what he had always done—finding the weak point in the defense and attacking it.

The only hurdle remaining was the goal he had set for Scott and himself in the week before his surgery: to be an All-Star.

On January 29, 1991, that goal was reached as well. With tears running down his face, he acknowledged his selection. "The doctors told me I'd never play again," he began. "For me, this is the culmination of my goal and my dream. My comeback wasn't completed until this moment occurred. It took six years to get here, but it was worth it."

As the luck of the schedule would have it, his first game after making the All-Star Team was against the Knicks in Madison Square Garden. As in his old Knicks days, he was playing for an injury-riddled team. As in those days, he was the focus of every defense, the target of every elbow. And as in those days, he could rise to an occasion and win games by the sheer force of his will.

February 1, 1991 was one of those games. With his parents and Dr. Norman Scott watching from courtside seats, King single-handedly took on the Knicks, and even the most rabid Knicks fans were delighted to see their team so abused by this remarkable man who had survived every blow fate and his own weaknesses could throw his way.

He hit his first shot, a sixteen-footer from the top of the key. Then it was a ten-footer from the right side. The Knicks put a tighter guard on him, and he popped out from a crowd in the lane, took a feed at the free-throw line, and in less time than it takes to say "swish," he turned, shot while falling away, and was hustling back on defense before the ball nestled neatly in the net.

He hit everything—left, right, and center. He drove, he pulled up, he hit the fade-aways. The game was his, invented for him. The moves he had practiced thousands of times, the endless hours he still put in conditioning himself, the passion he felt in his soul for this game of driveways and paved city lots—all of that washed over the game and possessed it. If he had lost any quickness, he more than made up for it by knowing at all times exactly where he was going—and where he had been.

At halftime, he had 20 points on 8-for-16 shooting, but the Bullets were losing by 9 to the Knicks. The points were nice, but he hadn't come to lose. Not on this night.

In the third quarter, he scored just 6 points but turned his attentions to defense and playmaking as he pulled down 5 rebounds and handed out 4 assists. The 9-point deficit had become a 2-point lead.

Then, in the fourth quarter, he took over. He hit his first shot of the period, a twelve-footer over a double team. Less than a minute later, he hit another twelve-footer. Then, on a fast break, he drove the length of the court, charged down the free-throw lane through a crowd of Knicks with the ball held overhead like a waiter carrying a tray, and calmly flipped the ball into the hoop while being hacked by Vandeweghe.

Anyone in the Garden who was still holding out for the Knicks gave up completely after that play. From then on, the whole building roared approval of King's every move. When he hit a thirteen-foot jump shot with 3:20 to go to give the Bullets a 9-point lead, the Knicks called time out, and now the place stood and cheered their Saint Bernard.

And King, who normally affects an all-world game face, left the court running almost daintily on his toes, cracked a smile, and thrust a fist into the air.

Back from the time out, the Knicks tried a new defense. As soon as King got the ball, four Knicks jumped on him like starving wolves on a pork chop. This time they stopped his shot, but at the expense of having the entire building erupt in laughter at their frantic efforts.

They couldn't stop him. No one could. When he sank two foul shots with 28 seconds to play, he brought his total to 49 points for the night, including 23 of his team's 32 fourth-quarter points. The Bullets' victory was assured.

His night ended there, a point shy of 50, the Garden crowd standing and cheering their old hero.

When the game ended, he ran across the court to embrace his parents and family. Then he sat down with the television crews to do the postgame shows. As King talked about what it meant to return to the Garden as an All-Star, Dr. Norman Scott, a tall and elegant figure, stood at center court and glowed with pride.

"As a surgeon, to get a guy back to this level, that's the ultimate, what you really want to do," said Scott. He chatted on about the surgery until King was done with his interviews and was walking back to the locker room. As King came across the court, Scott intercepted him. With a smile that could light a small city, King threw his sweaty arms around Scott, and the two hugged like high school sweethearts. They exchanged high fives, then King was off to do more interviews.

"Coming back to New York as an All-Star certainly is a big moment for me," he said. And, yes, he went on, it was satisfying to have such a splendid night "in front of the people who never thought I'd play, especially at this level."

There was no rancor in his voice, just the satisfaction of having achieved what he had set out to do. He passed up numerous opportunities to rip the Knicks for getting rid of him. "Playing with the Knicks was a dream come true," he explained. "I don't want to ruin the memory by saying anything negative."

It was unlike him to show the kind of raw joy that oozed from every pore that night. But, he said, "I worked awfully hard to get to this point. I deserve to relish it."

He was asked about the way he had responded to the crowd late in the game, when he had won it for the Bullets. That, too, was unlike him. "I've never milked anything in my career," he answered. "But, yeah, I took a few extra moments tonight. I thought I deserved it."

Few have ever deserved it more.

She Has Overcome

Trying the right thing at the right time, I think, is courage.

Dreams are easy. Everybody has dreams. But Billie Jean King was different. She had a vision.

She carried her vision for more than thirty years, from the time she was a young girl, and took it with her to Wimbledon, Paris, and New York—plus a thousand stops in between. And she never let it go. Now, at the age of forty-six, she is playing it out, and to tell the truth, as visions go it doesn't look like much.

It is early evening on July 21, 1990, in Florham Park, New Jersey. After a lusterless day, hot and punctuated by thunderstorms, the night is showing signs of drying up enough to get in some tennis.

A snug little stadium has been set up behind the Hamilton Park Conference Center, one of those modern hotel and meeting complexes that sprout up next to suburban office parks. There are a few thousand seats in the bleachers surrounding the single tennis court that is home to the New Jersey Stars, one of nine teams in a professional sports league called Domino's Pizza TeamTennis. Looming several stories above the court is the conference wing of the hotel, and on top of the building's roof are four loudspeakers of the type found in an average home. This is the public address system.

No TV cameras surround the court. Mary Carillo and Bud Collins aren't sitting in a tower commenting on the action. Only three or four reporters from suburban newspapers are on hand to chronicle the action between the Stars and the Sacramento Capitals.

There are four players on each team, two men and two women, and they are wearing ordinary tennis clothing, except that their outfits match and their names are stitched on their backs. The names are a good idea, because these players are mostly from professional tennis's vast underclass—that faceless mass of players who fill out the early rounds of tournaments and serve as sacrificial victims for the stars of the sport. The names on the Sacramento jerseys are Lindstrom, Schapers, Van't Hoff, and Whitlinger. For New Jersey, they are Barr, Sullivan, Harvey-Wild, and King.

King? Billie Jean King is one of the greatest tennis players in history. She has twenty Wimbledon titles to her name, but it has been the better part of a decade since she's played regularly on the pro tour. To compensate for lost youth, she is warming up with a tennis racquet so big it could have its own area code, and she's wearing long warmup pants when everyone else is wearing shorts. Surely she has somewhere better to be than Florham Park, New Jersey, and something better to do than sweat in public for the entertainment of maybe twelve hundred fans. It's not as if she needs the money, is it?

"I don't have to work. I could just do some customer tennis," she says, meaning play some hit-and-giggle doubles sets with corporate nabobs eager to match groundstrokes with a legend. "With my endorsements and stuff I'd be fine," she says.

But she has a reason to be playing TeamTennis for one night in New Jersey. She has a vision to sell, a vision in which men and women play tennis as equal members of a team, neither sex more important than the other, a vision in which tennis is not a sport of a few stars and a mass of faceless players drifting into town for a week and then evaporating until next year. In her vision, tennis is a team sport belonging to individual communities who can identify with players as something more than mere cannon fodder for the big names. Billie Jean King founded TeamTennis, and if by playing one or two nights a year she can wring a few more drops of ink for it out of stingy sports editors (who think that if it's not baseball, football, basketball, or hockey, it's not sport), then that's what she'll do.

"My primary focus and goal, the thing I care the most about, is TeamTennis," she says. "There's not any question. It's not even close. I don't think the public understands that about me at all. TeamTennis is my real dream. It's my greatest contribution to tennis."

She's right about the public. But the public doesn't understand much about Billie Jean King. Many people today don't remember or never learned what she did for women athletes at a time when no one took them seriously. And those who do remember think of King in a setting that dwarfs the little tennis stadium behind the Hamilton Park Conference Center.

How different Billie Jean King's night of transcendent fame was, and how far away from Florham Park. It was September 20, 1973. She was twenty-nine years old and the best woman tennis player on the planet. That night she played tennis before more than thirty thousand people who had paid up to a hundred dollars each for tickets. Fifty million more watched around the world on television. It was the largest crowd ever to watch a tennis match.

Her opponent that night was a snide and puckish little man named Bobby Riggs. It was a match between a woman champion at the height of her powers and a fifty-five-year-old former Wimbledon champion well past his prime in tennis—but at the very peak of his powers as one of history's great hustlers.

King had fought this match as long as a public eager for spectacle would let her. It was to be the best of five sets. There was money at stake—a lot for those days, but nowhere near what it would be today. "I made a hundred and fifty thousand for playing him," King says. She smiles at the thought. "What would that be today? Five million? Ten million?"

But no one except Riggs thought the money was important. What *was* important was an idea, but there was a substantial difference of opinion as to what that idea was. It was either that a woman was the equal of a man, or that any man—even an over-the-hill former champion like Riggs—was better than the best woman around. The name coined for the match was not terribly original, but it was to the point: the Battle of the Sexes.

The public bought it, and this one tennis match polarized the nation. People who didn't know foot faults from their elbows were suddenly tennis fans. Nothing like thirty thousand people had ever paid to see a tennis match before that day, and nothing like that number has paid to see one since. But this wasn't just a tennis match. It was a battle over the very structure of society. It was a war of philosophies and fundamental values.

Twenty years earlier such a match could not have taken place. Even if it had, it would have been a mere curiosity. It certainly wouldn't have turned into a crusade. In the fifties, sex roles were clearly defined: women tended the nest, men did the heavy work, and there was no question about who wore the pants in the family. But in the years between 1968 and 1973, everything changed. Women were being admitted to such male bastions as Notre Dame and Princeton. Yes, women had gotten feisty. From Angela Davis to Gloria Steinem, women were charting new agendas, breaking down old barriers, and demanding that they be treated as men's equals.

In 1972 Congress passed the so-called Title IX law, which required educational institutions receiving federal funds—virtually every college and university in the country—to provide women with the same opportunities as men. This meant that they had to support women's athletic teams, and give women scholarships. When the law was passed, there were no women's athletic scholarship opportunities in the United States, and thousands of high schools, colleges, and universities had no women's athletic teams at all.

Billie Jean King was at the center of the changes taking place in women's athletics, bucking established wisdom just as she would continue to buck it nearly twenty years later with her TeamTennis league. In 1970, she and tennis journalist Gladys Heldman led a group of nine women tennis players who broke away from the sport's governing body, the U.S. Lawn Tennis Association, and formed their own tennis tour. In 1973, they formalized their existence by creating the Women's Tennis Association.

Tennis had turned professional in 1968. Before that, there was a men's pro circuit, but the major championships such as Wimbledon and the U.S. Championships were officially open only to amateurs. Although athletes collected money under the table, so many great players were turning pro that the governing bodies of the sport finally agreed to put the money on top of the table. The open era had begun.

But tennis was more open for men than for women. The purses for women at the major championships were one-half to two-thirds the size of the purses for men. It was this inequity that prompted King and Heldman to strike off on their own, while still demanding—and ultimately getting—prize money equal to the men's in some major championships.

These were significant advances for women, the majority of whom were only starting to come to the startling conclusion that they were as good as men. Not all men shared that opinion, however. In fact, the concept of equality for women annoyed some men, angered others, and amused most. They made up names such as "libber," which had the same edge to it as the political epithet "pinko." The new brand of woman was denounced from fundamentalist pulpits and ridiculed in the media. These women, of whom King was a prime example, were getting uppity, and somebody had to put them down. Bobby Riggs was happy to oblige.

Women responded to the new epithets with one of their own—male chauvinist pig, or MCP. Although many men fit the description, few would admit it, particularly not young men whose chances of getting a date on Saturday night suddenly depended on being sensitive. But Riggs embraced the term. He bragged about being as piggy as they come. While King spent her time before the match getting into supreme condition and polishing her game, Riggs spent his thinking of new insults for feminists. The match became a great sociopolitical battleground. Did women want to be firefighters, police officers, and construction workers? Well, if the best of them couldn't beat a fifty-five-year-old bandy-legged man, what made them think they could keep up with men in any other profession? If they were so good, Riggs was saying, let them prove it. It fell to King to do the job.

King disliked the idea from the start. In her vision men and women played tennis on the same court as allies, not as enemies. The idea, she knew, was not to be against, but with.

At an early age, she had come to resent being on the outside looking in. Her younger brother, Randy Moffitt, was also quite an athlete, but Randy got to play Little League baseball, while Billie Jean Moffitt didn't. Why not? Because she was a girl, and girls didn't do those things. End of discussion.

She didn't think it was fair then, and she doesn't now. Preventing boys and girls from playing team sports together prevents them from working together when they grow up. "That's what's missing in our society—boys and girls working together," she says. "I can't believe that people separate the genders when they're growing up, and then when they get married and can't communicate, people wonder why."

King doesn't wonder. "There are no bonding experiences growing up. It's very bonding to play on a team together." And that was one thing that neither she nor any other girl could do growing up in the fifties—play on a team with boys.

To play against Riggs—a man—only echoed the boys against girls games of her youth and underscored the injustice. Again it was conflict instead of cooperation. But the role of warrior queen had been thrust upon her, and she couldn't ignore it.

Not that she didn't try. Riggs had been goading her for almost a year, and he was good at goading. In fact, he was famous in certain circles for his abilities to separate would-be heroes from their money. He had a hustler's knack for creating situations that his marks found irresistible and an uncanny ability to come through when the bets were placed. In 1939, he had gone to Wimbledon and bet a pile of money on himself at impressive odds to sweep the championships—singles, doubles, and mixed doubles. And then he had gone and done it. In the years since, he had concocted a series of money matches in which his opponents played by normal rules and he played with a broom, or with his foot in a bucket, or on a court littered with folding chairs. And he always seemed to win.

Like King, Riggs had vision. But his vision was one in which he always ended up taking a pile of cash to the bank. In 1973, he came up with the hustle of his life. He would goad these feminists who were so much in the news and use the hostility between the sexes to make a bundle. And what better way to do it than to challenge Billie Jean King.

In 1973, King was the greatest woman tennis player in the world. In 1972, she had won three-quarters of tennis's Grand Slam, winning singles titles in the French Open for the first time, the U.S. Open for the third time, and Wimbledon for the fourth time. She was an aggressive player, serving hard and charging the net. Nearly two decades later, *Tennis* magazine still ranked her forehand volley, backhand volley, and half volley as the best in the history of the women's game. In addition to her skill, she was well known as one committed to equal rights. No question about it: King was the perfect foil for Riggs's latest hustle.

But King wouldn't cooperate. Riggs challenged her and insulted her, but she ignored him. A match wouldn't prove anything, she said. If she lost, it would set the cause of women back to the days of her childhood. If she won, she would only have beaten an old man.

Riggs was undeterred. If King wouldn't play him, he would find someone else. That someone else was Margaret Smith Court, the great Australian star who in 1970 had joined Maureen Connolly as the only women to have won tennis's Grand Slam. Court was past her prime, but she agreed. A date was set—Mothers Day, 1973. Tennis insiders didn't take the match seriously. Many thought that Court, a considerably younger player, would win.

She didn't. In fact, she didn't even come close. Riggs, in perfect male chauvinist style, gave her a bouquet of flowers and then a thorough beating. The final score was 6-2, 6-1, and Riggs crowed that "a broken-down old guy like me can beat the best of them." He accused Court of choking, and he was not alone in that opinion. The luxury of choking was one of the fringe benefits of being a woman, he said.

Riggs and his fellow MCPs made so much out of the match that King was cornered. Somebody had to fight for women everywhere. "I went bananas when I saw those scores," King says of the trouncing that Court suffered. "I knew I had to play Bobby Riggs." Playing together could come later. Right now it was war.

Delighted, Riggs surrounded himself with as many curvy young women as he could find and did his best to drum up interest in the match. "I'll tell you why I'll win," he said at a press conference. "She's a woman, and they just don't have the emotional stability. She'll choke just like Margaret Court did."

As grown men guffawed, King smoldered. "That creep runs down women," she said. "That's why my feeling is like . . ."—she paused to find the right word—"hate." It was nothing personal, she said. "I like him for many things, but I hate him putting down women, not giving us credit as competitors."

And so it went, a war of words that was at once both merry and nasty. Riggs revealed that his training regimen included massive doses of vitamins, a self-therapy that was something of a fad at the time. King trained with the only thing she knew—old-fashioned hard work, and a lot of it. She also had an advantage that Court did not: she had been embroiled in controversy before. When the microphones and notepads came out, she knew what to say. When unflattering things were said about her, she knew how to react. "I had a very good understanding of what the process was going to be with the media," she says years later. "I knew what I'd have to go through. I thought I approached it psychologically, physically, mentally, and emotionally as well as anyone could have."

King knew what was at stake. She was twenty-six years younger than Riggs, but she was already being called "the old lady" on the tennis tour, which was then—as it is now—dominated by youngsters. Her knees were crosshatched with surgical scars. She was taking a chance and she knew it. "I think it took guts to go out on the court with Riggs," she says in retrospect. But she also knew that she had no choice.

When the day of the match arrived, the nation was wound up to a fever pitch. In Las Vegas, Riggs was a 2-1 betting favorite, which was probably a reflection of the fact that more men than women were betting.

The prematch setting was like that of a heavyweight title fight or a wrestling promotion, equal parts overblown pomp and circus. With brass bands, baton twirlers, bright lights, and props, it was more the atmosphere of a college football championship than of the ordinarily sedate sport of tennis.

Two hours before the match, King was in her dressing room fighting butterflies. "I was so nervous I was ready to vomit," she confesses. She was nervous, but she wasn't afraid. "I knew I had done everything I could to prepare. And I thought I had done a better job of preparing than he had."

Finally, it was time to trek out of the locker room and onto the court, which looked like a postage stamp in the middle of the vast Astrodome. Even the trip to the court was extraordinary. Riggs made his entrance in a rickshaw pulled by smiling and subservient young women. The crowd roared. Not to be outdone, King mounted a litter and was carried out by four husky and bare-chested young men, while other hunks shaded her with ostrich-plume parasols as if she were Cleopatra on her barge. The crowd howled.

The combatants dismounted and came to the net for the traditional prematch handshake. Both came bearing gifts. Riggs gave King a huge lollipop—a sucker. King gave Riggs a squealing suckling pig. Touché.

The fans were eating it up, but King wasn't concentrating on the looniness. She had more important things on her mind. The match was to be best-of-five sets, two more sets than women played in any championship. Riggs—figuring that the longer the match, the greater the chance that King would wear down, choke, or both—had requested the longer match. King had been delighted at the suggestion and readily accepted.

"That was really stupid," she says of Riggs's request. "I was a lot younger than he was. I mean, he should have prayed for two-out-of-three sets. He should have asked for best of one set."

Throughout her long training regimen, King had planned on playing her game against Riggs. She would serve, return hard, and attack the net as soon and as often as she could. That was how she had played from the first day she'd picked up a racquet. And that summer she had won her fifth Wimbledon title playing that way.

King was thinking about that strategy as she was being carried into the arena. As she visualized the match, she had a sudden realization. As she put it, "I went to Plan B."

One of the most difficult things for an athlete to do is to prepare to do one thing and then decide at the last moment to do something totally different. If there's the tiniest bit of doubt about the correctness of the decision, any early setback can start a chain reaction of second-guessing that won't stop until the game is lost. So the rule is: pick a course and stick to it until your opponent proves that your game plan won't work. That's how football teams do it. Set a game plan and adjust. But don't adjust before the game even starts.

But with the crowd going bonkers and the strobe lights popping in her eyes, King knew that her initial plan was wrong. "I realized that he liked the person he was playing against to generate the power and if I hit out against him like I planned, I would be playing into his hands. So I figured that I'd just soft-ball him to death. I'd hit junk. I figured I'd make him have to deal with that. And I figured I'd keep him in long rallies because I was in better condition. I just had an intuitive feeling that was the right course to take," she said.

And if it didn't work?

"I could always go back to Plan A."

This is what champions do. They have, in King's words, "a higher degree of self-awareness." They have the courage or the confidence or the skill—call it what you will—to do what they know is right, even if it goes against everything they've prepared to do.

Once she had made that decision, she says, she may have appeared to be smiling and joking with Riggs at the net, "But my mind was totally focused on my plan."

The Astrodome went silent as the match started. Then it went numb as King began to carve up Riggs like a Christmas goose. She won the first set, 6-4. The Riggs fans were nervous, but they figured he had a few tricks he hadn't played. Besides, it was best-of-five. He'd come back.

The second set went to King by the same score, 6-4. Now Riggs was the one awash in futile emotional energy. Clearly, he had bitten off more than he could chew: this woman had come not just to play, but to win.

Best-of-five became a whitewash and King took the last set and the match, 6-3. The crowd roared again as Riggs turned into a gentleman at last and congratulated his conqueror.

It was only a tennis match, a gimmick, but the effects of King's victory were enormous. The late Ted Tinling, who spent his life observing women's tennis—from Suzanne Lenglen in the twenties to Steffi Graf in 1990 (the year he died)—said that King's victory "was probably the most significant single event in tennis history."

King herself says, "Ours was then a macho society in which women's glamour was synonymous with helplessness."

She changed that. Girls who watched the match understood that they didn't have to be cheerleaders to gain entry to the playing field. Women athletes in all sports could thank King for generating support for their battle to have an equal right with men to sweat for pay in public. Tennis itself entered a decade of unprecedented expansion. Until King played Riggs, the game was still viewed as a pursuit for the idle rich. But King brought out the element of the prizefight at the heart of the sport. She brought it to a new audience. She made the women's game respectable.

The legacy did not die. King still cannot fly on a commercial airliner or walk through a hotel lobby without being stopped by people who remember September 20, 1973. She says, "The feedback I get is things like, 'You go way beyond tennis. You made me believe. You really helped me believe in myself.' It's amazing. On an airplane the other day, I had three different people come up to me and tell me that. One woman was crying. Then they'll talk to me about what's going on in their workplace."

If winning that one match were all King had done in her life, it would have been enough. For most people it would have been, but not for King. She had established the women's tennis tour. She had founded the Women's Tennis Association. She had established herself as the greatest woman player in the world. But that was just the groundwork. Her real work, her life's vision, had only begun.

By the time King conquered Riggs, she had been nurturing an idea for more than a decade, an idea she had first given shape in 1962 as a nineteen-year-old student at Cal State in Los Angeles. There she had talked about it with her friend, Larry King, a young law student with a flair for promotion and organization, and they had worked it out together.

The vision was team tennis, a concept foreign to a sport that was (and is) a genteel version of boxing, with two opponents striking at each other over a long match not with their fists but through the agency of racquet and ball. It was a sport that created stars similar to heavyweight champions. From Bill Tilden and Suzanne Lenglen, the stars of tennis had always been the show. And these stars and their sparring partners had roamed the world, playing their elimination tournaments first in one city and then in another. The stars prospered under this system; they still do. But they do so at the expense of tennis's ordinary players, who compete as well as they can and disappear from the tournaments when they lose.

King was a budding star in 1962. She had won the first of her record twenty Wimbledon titles in 1961 when she teamed with Karen Hantze to defeat Jan Lehane and Margaret Court, 6-3, 6-4, in the final of the women's doubles. But she had not yet blossomed. She was still two years away from her first singles final and four years away from her first singles championship.

Even then, she realized the first law of tennis. "You have to win to be recognized," she says. "If you're one of the top four baseball players in the world, you're something. But if you're the fourth-best tennis player in the world, you're barely recognized."

In 1990, for example, tennis was Andre Agassi, Steffi Graf, Jennifer Capriati, Martina Navratilova. "You never know more than a few men and a few women," King points out. "In baseball, basketball, or football, if you only know five or six players, you're not doing very well. You don't have an interest. But that's what happens in tennis. People do not feel connected to tennis like they do to a team. They attend because they want to see celebrities. I want tennis to belong to communities so that it becomes identified as a sport with people, instead of just celebrities."

And she wants boys and girls, men and women, to play together and contribute equally to the success of the team. That vision came to her much earlier than the formal idea of team tennis. It came when she was Billie Jean Moffitt, on the outside looking in at the team sports her brother could play but she couldn't.

Although King feels that she came by her pioneering spirit from her ancestors, she confesses that she doesn't know much about her family's roots. "Two of my grandparents were adopted," she says. "And one of my distant ancestors was an Englishman who came to America and married an Indian from Florida." Family history suggests that he left England one step ahead of the sheriff.

"It makes you appreciate the kind of guts it took to come to this country," she says. "That's one of our strengths as Americans. We're really spirited." And King is one of the most spirited. She sincerely believes that anything is possible, and if you talk to her long enough (say, five or ten minutes), she'll have you believing it, too.

She has needed every bit of her pioneering spirit and persuasive power, because ever since she wanted to play Little League baseball, people have been telling her that she couldn't do things. Naturally, they told her that this team tennis idea wouldn't work. And naturally, she didn't believe them. But there were other barriers.

The first presented itself when tennis entered the open era of professional competition in 1968. What was touted as a great advance for tennis turned out to be a slap in the face for women players. Consider that in 1970, Billie Jean King won the Italian Open and was handed a check for $600. Ilie Nastase, who won the men's side of the tournament, got $3,600. The United States Lawn Tennis Association (now the United States Tennis Association, or USTA) sponsored two tournaments for women, but the prize money wasn't much better.

So Billie Jean King, Gladys Heldman, and eight other women players decided to strike off on their own, ignore the USTA (which sanctioned tournaments), and create a new tour.

It was a bold decision, and the USTA immediately excommunicated the lot of them. What they were doing simply wasn't allowed. Most women professionals would not immediately join them, but they stuck to their guns. Backed by Virginia Slims cigarettes, they secured arenas and set up a tour. To publicize what they had done, the nine players each held up a dollar bill—their symbolic wages—and snapped a picture. The nine were King, Peaches Bartkowicz, Valerie Ziegenfuss, Nancey Richey, Kristy Pigeon, Judy Dalton, Kerry Melville, Rosie Casals, and Julie Heldman. Eight of them—Julie Heldman was injured and couldn't play—held their first tournament in Houston for a purse of $7,500—peanuts by today's standards, but a relative fortune to them.

They knew they wouldn't get rich. "But we had fun," King says, and fun is a concept that is increasingly foreign on today's tennis tour. "I knew my generation wouldn't get all the money," she goes on, "but I don't consider what I did a sacrifice. I think it was a building block. If you really want to do something, it's not a sacrifice. And I wanted to do it."

They played in high school gymnasiums, drove together from town to town, called up the local newspapers and begged to be interviewed. They handed out free tickets to their events and sometimes drew as few as two hundred people.

But at least they were masters of their own fate. They—not a roomful of men—were calling the shots, and they were having as much fun as they would ever have in their lives. As Peaches Bartkowicz once said, "We knew we were involved in something important."

The second year of their tour, 1971, King became the first woman athlete to earn $100,000 in a single year. Because of the tiny purses, she had to win nineteen tournaments to do it. But it was a milestone achievement, and it opened the door a bit wider.

By 1973, the tour that a handful of women had created around a kitchen table was established, and it was time to formalize it with an official governing body. King led the way in organizing the Women's Tennis Association, and she was elected its first president. The goal of the WTA was straightforward: to make a career in professional tennis economically realistic for women. For the first time, women tennis players controlled their own destinies.

Before tennis was opened to all players, amateur and professional alike, it had been a sport of white-flannel gentility. Players were expected to be polite both on and off the court, and dress codes were strictly enforced. The degree of conservatism in the administration of the sport was pointed out spectacularly in 1947 when Ted Tinling, who designed tennis dresses for the leading stars, created a pair of ruffled panties for Gussie Moran to wear under her tennis dress at Wimbledon. The lords of Wimbledon were so shocked at the scandalous lace trim that they not only banned the panties, they banned Tinling from Wimbledon for decades. Later efforts by other players to wear even a hint of color other than white met with similar resistance.

But the age of tennis professionals brought a new sort of creature to the court. This beast played for money, and for keeps. Young players such as Jimmy Connors and Ilie Nastase not only refused to make nice on the court, they came near to creating riots. They cursed linesmen and umpires. They threw racquets and made obscene gestures at anyone who annoyed them.

King and other members of the fledgling WTA recognized that image was all-important, so they authored a code of conduct for members and events, invoking a system of sanctions by which a miscreant player could forfeit a match if she persisted in violating the rules of tennis decorum. The code had the immediate effect of making the women's tour a much more civilized society than the men's. The WTA presented its women first as athletes and competitors, but also wanted them to exhibit the highest standards of sportsmanship. The system worked so well that the men's tour and the governing bodies of the Grand Slam tournaments eventually adopted the code as well.

Although King's match with Riggs was the single most memorable tennis event of 1973, the founding of the WTA was far more important. Knowing what she does now, King says she would have set the WTA up differently. "I would make us into a company and we would be receiving royalties from the tour," she says. "That's what we should have done. But we were very altruistic at the time." That is, they set the tour up knowing that its prime beneficiaries would come later on, when the tour expanded and prize money grew. In a company, all former players would have shared in the new wealth that they had helped create. As it is now, they don't, and that annoys King, who has always felt that the group—teamwork—was more important than the individual.

"There's no retirement for players of my generation, and I'm angry at the WTA, which I founded, for that. I think they should be taking care of the old players like Rosie Casals, Peaches Bartkowicz, Judy Dalton. All these players were suspended by their association so they could create the foundation and start building something. We're happy to pass it on to the next generation, but I think it's a crime that they haven't included the older players in their pension plan. I tried to get a pension plan started in the seventies, and they said we couldn't do it. They're doing it now, but they're not including the people who made it possible for the WTA to even happen."

The old fire rises as she talks about obligations. She searches for an analogy and finds it in baseball, another sport whose players take very good care of their own retirements but not of those who made the game what it is today. "Baseball should give Curt Flood a million dollars a year, *minimum,*" she says, speaking of the man who challenged the reserve system that bound a player for life to his team. Although Flood didn't win his case, he paved the way for the modern system of free agency. He made a lot of ballplayers rich, but lost his own career in the process. King understands that sort of courage.

"They could give him ten million dollars a year and still be ahead. His whole life was ruined so that the present generation of players could make all this money."

King turned thirty in November 1973. Her best tennis was behind her, although she continued to be competitive until she was thirty-nine. She won two more major singles titles, the U.S. Open in 1974 and hallowed old Wimbledon in 1975, and tacked on a string of doubles and mixed doubles titles at both Wimbledon and the U.S. Open. Her twenty total Wimbledon titles is an all-time record. The thirty-six-game set she played in the 1963 Wightman Cup competition against Christine Truman of England was the longest set ever played, and it's no surprise that King won, 6-4, 19-17. In 1983, twenty-two years after her first Wimbledon doubles title, she gave the tennis world one last thrill when, at the age of thirty-nine, she fought through to the semifinals of Wimbledon before losing. She finished the year by turning forty and being ranked thirteenth in the world—a phenomenal achievement. During her career, she was ranked first in singles five years and first in doubles twelve years.

But her major achievements were coming more often off the court. They seldom got the same publicity—or applause—as her tennis, but they were much longer lasting.

In 1975, she corrected another inequity by joining in founding the Women's Sports Foundation. She followed that by establishing the Women's Sports Hall of Fame. And she and her husband founded *Inside Women's Tennis* and *Women's Sports* magazines.

But the last quest remained—team tennis.

In 1974, the world was introduced to her idea. World Team Tennis began in a big way, with franchises in major cities and rosters populated with major stars. King herself signed on as the player-coach of the Philadelphia Freedoms. It was the first time a woman had ever coached a professional coed sports team.

The concept of the league was exactly what King had envisioned. Each team was made up of equal numbers of male and female players. To speed play, no-advantage scoring was used; that is, the first player or team to win four points won the game. Men's singles and doubles, women's singles and doubles, and mixed doubles all contributed equally to the team score. And raucous cheering—a no-no in tournament tennis—was encouraged.

What wasn't in line with King's vision was management. Although the teams played in major arenas and drew good crowds, the franchise owners quickly spent themselves into bankruptcy. By 1978, the league was history.

"Can you believe it?" King says, "The owners didn't get along. And they had a weak commissioner."

The league died, but not the idea. In 1981, she and Larry King (they later divorced) resurrected it. Calling the new league TeamTennis, they started small with four teams, all in California, and a short season. Instead of allowing franchise owners to bid for players and repeat the errors of World Team Tennis, the league signed the players to contracts, and players' earnings were based on individual and team performances.

In 1982, TeamTennis expanded to eight teams with franchises throughout the country. The following year, King made history again when she agreed to become commissioner of the fledgling league—the first woman commissioner of a professional sports league.

TeamTennis made a major breakthrough in 1985 when King convinced Domino's Pizza to sign on as title sponsor. Although the league was not exactly awash in publicity or public awareness, by 1990 it had nine teams playing for $450,000 in total prize money. The season lasted one month and consisted of seven home and seven away games for each team. King, who in 1989 had graduated to Chief Executive Officer, also landed a cable television contract and several local contracts for the league. In 1991, King scored a major coup by adding Jimmy Connors and Martina Navratilova—two veteran superstars—to its roster of primarily young and little-known players.

"Yeah, it's a struggle," she admits of the league's snail's-pace growth. "But most of the franchises are making money. That's a major step. Sacramento makes money. Los Angeles makes money. San Antonio makes money. Raleigh makes money.

"In Sacramento, they sell over two thousand seats for a match. In Charlotte, they get three to five thousand every night. When you consider our budget and the caliber of players we have, I think that's excellent. You can go to a major tournament on a Monday, Tuesday, or Wednesday night, and you won't have any more fans than what we have.

"Everybody gets so excited when four hundred and fifty thousand people watch the U.S. Open over the two weeks it's played. But that's not very many when you think that some baseball teams draw three million a year. I get cheesed off. I want millions of people watching tennis every year. Millions."

The way to draw those millions, King says, is to go beyond the current system in which two or three players are recognized as stars and instead establish hometown stars on local teams.

"I feel it's right for tennis," she says. "Tennis will never be a big sport with just tournament tennis. You can't get to enough people in enough time. In nine weeks, you can play only nine tournaments in nine cities—and you're always visiting. We are in nine marketplaces seven times each in one month. In tournament tennis, unless you win the tournament, you're not appreciated. That's the reason the game will never get any bigger. With TeamTennis, you start to appreciate doubles players because they contribute as much as the singles players. The city you play in may really take a shine to you.

"We don't want to replace anything. We want to be in addition to the professional tour. We want the same people on tour—if they're team players. If they're not team players, we don't want them."

It's a long speech, and she delivers it with the searing intensity of a tent-revival sermon. She repeats that she is not in a hurry. She is content to grow slowly—and sanely. Unlike all the other failed sports leagues—the World Hockey League, the World Football League, the

U.S. Football League—TeamTennis is not a get-rich-quick scheme. King is doing it because she believes in it, and she's willing to be patient. She's also willing to suffer the slings and arrows shot by the prophets of doom who look at her sensible little league and tell her it will never become a major league in the American marketplace. She's heard it all before.

" 'There's no way women's tennis will make it,' " she says, in a snide reenactment of the remarks she heard twenty years ago. "I had to hear that every day for two years, and now the women's circuit is playing for more than fourteen million dollars." She knows about the long haul. And she's willing to stick it out.

Billie Jean King is not in this for money, or even for glory. She has enough of both, and if she wanted more it would be easy enough for her to get. Her knowledge of tennis alone is worth a fortune. She proved that in 1990 when she took on the job of being Martina Navratilova's mental coach as Navratilova tried for the third time to get her record ninth Wimbledon singles title. The two previous years, Navratilova had failed. But at the age of thirty-three, with King's help, she succeeded.

King didn't teach Navratilova to hit the ball; Martina knew how to do that. What she taught her was how to win again after Navratilova's psychological edge had been worn away by too many losses to the tour's young tigers, Steffi Graf chief among them. "She asked me for help," King recalls. "She knew she needed it." And she knew King could provide it.

"I worked with her for fourteen months," King says. "Every day for those fourteen months, she had to keep a journal. Together with her coach, we taught her how to be honest with herself about her emotions. I knew that would be the hardest part for her. We gave her six pages of homework the night before the Wimbledon final. I told her to write down everything she had learned and what she was going to do to adjust."

After Navratilova's success, King was approached by another would-be pupil, Tim Mayotte, a serve-and-volley player who had reached the age of thirty and fallen from the top ten to forty-first in the world in the course of 1990. He knew he needed help and looked to King to get it. "It's groundbreaking in a way," Mayotte admitted. "Except for the Russian players, no men are being coached by women. But to me that was never a question. If someone knows the game, they know the game." King took him on, and Mayotte was astounded at her enthusiasm and knowledge.

"I feel her enthusiasm rubbing off on me. It's just fun to be on the court with her. But the thing that amazes me most is her knowledge of the game. It's almost humbling."

When King took on Mayotte, she set the rules, the first of which was that Mayotte would have to rebuild the serve that had made him one of the best players in the world. She had come to that conclusion after studying hours of tapes of his play.

Mayotte turned out to be her kind of player: he was willing to challenge himself. According to King, the willingness to take risks is a form of courage. "Not accepting limits, not playing it safe is courage," she says. "I think it permeates life. Being courageous—trying the right thing. If it's match point and at deuce, it's still doing what's right and not holding back. Pick your spot. Go through your rituals. Put yourself on the line.

"Each person is going to be different. If you're afraid to get up and give a speech, that may be the most courageous thing you can do. If someone finds out she has cancer, fighting it may be the most courageous thing she does in her life."

For Billie Jean King, going out on a court at the age of forty-six and playing TeamTennis doesn't take courage. She loves doing it. If the game doesn't go well (as it didn't on that July night in New Jersey), and people start shouting unkind things at her—she doesn't object. When she's bad, she's the first to admit it, no excuses offered or accepted.

"I hate playing poorly," she says after losing a doubles match with nineteen-year-old Linda Harvey-Wild. "But I love being on the bench yelling for my team."

Her enthusiasm is obvious. Playing for the New Jersey Stars for two nights, she is jumping up and down and throwing high fives around like a kid. Just seeing young tennis players playing in a league makes her feel as young as they are.

It's a feeling that is rare in tennis, the camaraderie that comes from being in something together. Because King wants everyone to be able to experience it, the professional league is only part of her scheme. Far bigger is the nationwide recreational TeamTennis program she has nurtured. As of 1990, she had established recreational leagues in 1,016 cities with tens of thousands of players of all ages and abilities.

It's just a start, she says. "I want TeamTennis to be the Little League of tennis." After all, kids play tennis on teams in high school and in college. Why not on the playground?

"Just imagine if we could get everybody together on this," she says, her eyes flashing. "But tennis people don't really network for each other very well. Everybody goes his or her own way, and that's it."

That way usually means looking out for number one, and King doesn't believe it has to be like that. "The tennis world is so small, and everybody's always protecting his own territory," she says. "I just laugh. Because we could really help each other a lot more."

It's late, and it's been a long day. The night's match is over, but she still has things to do. Somebody didn't put the drinks on ice in the reception room, so she does that. She wants to help Linda Harvey-Wild with her serve. There are interviews to do, cities to visit, programs to start—not to mention another tennis match tomorrow.

"I love it," King says, still as bursting with energy at midnight as she had been at noon, and thinking not about tonight's loss, but about what she can do tomorrow. It will be a new day, full of possibilities. "I don't want to keep talking," she says. "It's important that I do something."

So she'll play again tomorrow?

"I can't wait," she says.

Solo on Ice

The light is shining bright at the end of the tunnel. I'm just hoping it's not a train.

It wasn't exactly a scandal, but it raised more than a few carefully plucked eyebrows in Helsinki when Scott Hamilton competed for the World Figure Skating Championship in 1983 in a costume that didn't glitter. The very idea of going on the ice without sequins to sparkle in the spotlights and add something called "showmanship" to what was supposed to be an athletic contest was novel, maybe even downright risky. What, after all, would the judges think? Would they think a plain black costume devoid of twinkly things and embroidery too drab? Why, they might even deduct precious tenths of artistic presentation points.

On the other hand, what if the judges liked it? There was no telling what these people who glared with pinched faces at the skaters' efforts would or wouldn't like. As a rule, it appeared that they didn't like any music written by a living composer and any fabric not coated with sparkles. But once in a blue moon, a champion would arrive on the figure skating scene who dared to change the rules, and the judges would approve.

The best thing for the other skaters to do, then, was wait and watch, but not change anything—not for this competition, anyway. If Hamilton's gimmick didn't work, that was his problem. And if it did—well, there was plenty of time between the 1983 World Championships and the 1984 Winter Olympics to strip the sequins off their own costumes so they could all look like the champion.

So much ado about seeming nothing may sound silly, and it is. But we're talking about figure skating, a sport with nebulous objective standards judged as much on artistry and showmanship as on athletic prowess. It had been that way ever since Sonja Henie had dared many years ago to leave the ice and execute a leap and a turn in the air. That simple maneuver, and the panache with which she performed it, made her not only an Olympic champion, but also a movie star. And as the champion went, so went the sport. If Henie dared to become airborne and was rewarded for it, then everyone else would become airborne.

Once upon a time, men skated in costumes that looked like tuxedos. When they finally broke away from the going-to-the-prom look, they switched to glitter. And because figure skaters are more fervent followers than lemmings, once one man had sequined designs stitched on his clothing, all men did.

To be safe, skaters wear the same costumes, perform the same routines, and use the same music as whoever is the reigning champion. The tactic may be dull, but skaters can't worry about that. They're too busy worrying about how the judges will react if they dare to be different. They have all seen or heard of someone who tried something creative and was looked at by the judges as if he had bitten the head off a chicken.

Hamilton himself had gone the conventional route before 1983. Wearing sequins, he had finished fifth in the 1980 Olympics, and he'd won the U.S. and World Championships the previous two years the same way. So why was he trying to be different now? Had he gone mad? What would the judges think?

Hamilton didn't worry about what the judges thought. He pulled it off, too. He skated confidently on the ice for his free-skating program in Helsinki dressed in a simple black costume, and then he skated so well that they had to make him champion for the third straight year. Everyone went home to practice being like him.

They couldn't be like him, though, because what seemed risky to them wasn't to Scott Hamilton. Other skaters might think that nothing could be more alone and frightening than gliding out onto a sheet of ice in front of fifteen thousand people and a panel of judges who had probably graduated from the Spanish Inquisition School of Justice. There, without their coaches and psychologists and choreographers and costume consultants, they were pinned down by a spike of light and told to perform, knowing that the slightest slip, the merest stumble, meant precious points deducted from their score.

This wasn't like the first inning of a baseball game, where if you strike out you get up again—and there's always another game tomorrow. In figure skating, only the national and world championships—two competitions a year—really count. And even they are only preludes to the one shot every skater gets to fame and fortune, the Olympic Games, which come around but once every four years. The Olympics are the ticket to the big ice shows, where a skater can make a return on the years of amateur training. The champions become well-paid headliners. The also-rans skate in the chorus lines. Such brutal realities behind such a graceful, delicate sport.

But Hamilton could face the judges in a way that other skaters couldn't. He knew a different kind of loneliness, worse than anything a skater felt on the ice.

Scott Hamilton's life began on August 28, 1958 in Bowling Green, Ohio. Shortly after birth, he was adopted by Ernest and Dorothy Hamilton, two professors at Bowling Green University who had one other adoptive child, a daughter. Life in Bowling Green, a pleasant town surrounded by rich farmland and clean air, should have been idyllic for the young boy. And at first it was. Then, at the age of five, Scott got the disease with no name.

That's where this story really begins, in a doctor's office with a sickly boy being brought in by his anxious parents. Scott had symptoms of malnutrition, yet he did not lack for food. No matter how much or what he ate, his system showed little interest in digesting it.

The first doctor had no answers, so he sent Hamilton to the local hospital, where other doctors poked at him with instruments and invaded his body through every opening in an effort to discover what was wrong. When no one in Bowling Green could put a name on his disease, they sent him to Toledo, then to Ann Arbor, and finally Boston. At one point a doctor thought he knew what was wrong. Hamilton had cystic fibrosis, he announced. What's more, he had only six months to live. The tests went on, and it was determined that he didn't have cystic fibrosis, after all.

"They stuck so many needles in me, I was like a pincushion," Hamilton says. "They would put a device down my throat, then watch it on an X-ray screen as it worked through my digestive system. It was my first time on TV."

His laughter isn't forced. He is blessed with a native ability to find fun in the most desperate of situations. It wasn't the tests or the disease that was the hardest on him, though. "When you're young, it doesn't matter," he says of all the medical science he endured. What mattered was that he was a child away from his family, away from school, away from anything resembling a normal life. Oh, he'd get out of a hospital from time to time and spend a couple months in school, but then he'd have to go back in. He figures he spent a total of two and a half years in hospitals from the time he was five until he was nine.

"When you're that age, you should be with your family, and I couldn't be," Hamilton says. "My family did as much as they could to be with me, but they couldn't do everything." When he was in Boston, his mother's hometown, she would come and stay with her mother or her sister. "My mom used to sleep at the hospital as much as she could," he says. "And I had relatives there, and they would visit me a lot, so it was a little easier. It's not good for kids that age to be by themselves."

He made the best of his situation, though, and he even remembers his months in hospitals as fun. "There were a lot of other kids with me who were just as sick as I was or sicker. I was always around kids who were sick, so it didn't feel that my life was any different." With lots of time on their hands, the kids in the wards invented games to play. "It was like summer camp," Hamilton says. "The more time you spend in the hospital, the more time you have to figure it out, the more you can raise havoc."

In this camp, the nurses were the counselors, and the object was to drive them to distraction. "I was kind of mischievous. I was somewhat of a very minor vandal," he says, and you get the feeling that this man with the puckish grin and self-deprecating sense of humor is understating his accomplishments. One of his tricks was to hide when he knew that a nurse was coming to take him for more tests. Some of the tests were painful, and to a kid, a normal-sized hypodermic syringe looks like something you'd stick in a horse. Hiding was Hamilton's way of putting off the tests for a short time, during which he could sit in his hiding place and turn his fears into giggles as the nurses had conniptions trying to find him.

The kids would put medical equipment where it didn't belong and watch the nurses try to find it. And of course, there was always the food to play with. "The things we did with that were interesting," Hamilton says without elaborating.

He doesn't recommend the experience to anyone, but he does believe that all the time he spent alone waiting for someone to find out what he had and cure it helped him later in life when he became a skater. "I think it gave me a sense of independence," he says. "Later on, when I took up an individual sport when I really only had myself to rely on, I felt I could function on my own."

It is lonely on the ice, he says. Skaters warm up together, then leave the ice and pace under the stands as they go out one at a time to perform their routines. If the person ahead of you has skated well, the crowd will stand and cheer, sometimes for several minutes, as the skater circles the arena accepting armloads of flowers, kissing friends, and taking bows. When he finally leaves the ice, a door opens in the boards surrounding the rink. Then you skate out and the door closes behind you, leaving you all but naked in front of thousands of critical eyes.

"I was used to being by myself," Hamilton says. "And when they shut the door behind me, it wasn't as scary as it could have been." When he was alone as a child, though, he wasn't thinking about skating. He was too busy coping with his mutant version of a normal life.

From time to time, he got to go home and go to school. Because of his disease, he did very little growing, and he was too frail to do what the other kids did. When the class went outside at recess to play baseball, Hamilton was lucky to be well enough to simply go outside. Joining the game was out of the question.

None of this helped his social life. In the hospital, he had at least been like everyone else there—sick. In school, he was hopelessly different. The only thing that remained the same was the loneliness.

"When you're unusually small for your age, or fat, or whatever, you learn just how mean people can be," he says. "When I was going through it, I didn't really understand the adversity. I just realized I was a lot different from everybody else. And because of that, naturally, I was very lonely. I didn't have too many friends—or really any close friends. I couldn't do what everyone else was doing, and at that age kids don't understand. They call you lots of names."

Some people who go through similar experiences carry a grudge through life. Hamilton didn't. His years as an outsider only made him more self-reliant and more determined to make something of himself.

"I've always had something inside me," he says. "I've always felt that I had to achieve something, that I had to go way beyond what was expected. I think I was driven by always being the smallest in class.

"I'm not sure if the short-person's syndrome applies to me," he goes on, meaning that he doesn't feel as an adult that he has to prove himself constantly simply because he's so much shorter than normal. "But I know that occasionally, if somebody tells you you have a limitation, you want to prove them wrong. I don't think I had a big chip on my shoulder, but in many ways, I think all people have little chips on their shoulders."

He was nine years old when the doctors finally found a name for his problem: Schwachmann's syndrome. (*Schwachmann* is German for "weak person.") The syndrome was characterized by a partial paralysis of the digestive tract that prevented the absorption of nutrients from the food he ate. He was put on a high-protein diet that was injected into his stomach through a feeding tube threaded through his nose. And he was ordered to exercise moderately.

Home again, he remembers one Saturday morning going with his mother to watch his sister's figure skating club work out. Standing by the rink, the feeding tube still in his nose, he decided he wanted to take up skating. His mother signed him up.

"I wasn't a whiz, but I was small and coordinated," he says. Almost miraculously, the combination of brisk air and equally brisk exercise broke the back of the disease.

He was finally healthy, but he would never catch up on the four years of growing he had missed. Fully grown, he is barely jockey sized—five feet three and 110 pounds.

The kids were nicer to him when he went to school full time. "I was still the shortest kid in class, but I always had a bodyguard," he says. "It was usually the biggest kid in class. He'd look out for me."

Hamilton had no desire to play team sports, but he found that he could do well in individual sports. He took up gymnastics for a time and did well at that. And there was always the skating.

Skating did get him into one team sport when he was older. "I played hockey for a while," he says, "just so my friends wouldn't call me a sissy. I did pretty well, too. I played center and some defense. I led my team in assists because I was the only one who passed." Eventually, the other kids got too big, and Hamilton figured that if he continued to play hockey the day would come when he'd take a check, and they'd have to come and wash him off the boards with a fire hose. "I wanted to keep all my teeth," he laughs. "I wanted my nose to be straight. I didn't want any scars under my eyes. I decided to go with figure skating."

His small size was an asset as a figure skater, just as it is with a gymnast. With a lower center of gravity, it is easier to maintain balance, and a compact body is easier to control than one with a longer trunk and limbs. A small movement at the end of a short lever produces less force than the same movement at the end of a long one.

But if his size helped him technically, it initially hindered him artistically. He was, the experts decided, simply too small to be a champion. Why? Because all the previous champions had been larger. This is what passes for logic in Hamilton's sport.

And there were other stereotypes about champions to contend with. It seemed that most Olympic champions had been brunettes. "They had brown hair and brown eyes, and they were tall," Hamilton says. Being short and blond with blue eyes, he created another challenge for himself. *Enough of this,* he thought. *It's time to break the molds. John Curry, Robin Cousins, Jan Hoffman—they all look alike. Let's get somebody different in there and break it up a bit.*

Another thing that bothered Hamilton was the growing tendency to emphasize the artistic side of the sport. He had been taunted by other boys as a child because he was so small and weak, and going into figure skating had only confirmed that he was grossly lacking in the macho department.

"Not wanting to be called a sissy was a big motivation in the direction I took with my skating," he says. As role models, he chose dynamic, athletic skaters who projected power on the ice. "I related to the ones who were more athletic and not so *artistic,*" is how he puts it. "I related to the more masculine skaters."

Ron Shavers, a Canadian national champion who began his career in the mid-sixties, was one hero. Gordon McKellen, the U.S. national singles champion from 1973–75, was another. His third role model was Irina Rodnina, the Soviet pairs skater who had won three Olympic gold medals (in 1972, 1976, and 1980). "Those are the people I patterned myself after. They are the ones I looked up to when I was growing up."

Rodnina may sound like a strange role model, but she fit Hamilton's idea of what skating should be. She and her first partner, Aleksei Ulanov (she later teamed with Aleksandr Zaitsev, whom she married) used power and dazzling athletic moves in 1969 to dethrone the reigning world pairs champions, Lyudmilla Belousova and Oleg Protopopov, who had relied on grace and elegance.

Despite a bitter and painful personal split with Ulanov (who had taken up a romance with another woman skater), Rodnina skated with him to the gold medal in the 1972 Sapporo Olympics. Then, after acknowledging the cheers of the crowd, she skated off the ice in tears. That sort of will and ability to block out everything but the competition impressed Hamilton. "I liked the way she went after it every time," he said.

McKellen became his best friend among the skaters. "I liked Gordie's sense of humor and the fact that the guy had played halfback in high school," Hamilton says. "He was like my big brother. He taught me how to be a showoff on the ice. He taught me about girls. He taught me how to misbehave. And he had this great presence on the ice."

The same would soon be said about Hamilton, who projected more genuine humor and unbridled enthusiasm than any skater in memory. Much as he didn't fit the stereotype of the skating champion, he was too bright and energetic to ignore. In 1976, at the age of seventeen, he won the U.S. Junior National Championship. For the first time in his career, he dared to think about the Olympics, even though he knew he wasn't really pouring everything he had into the sport. "I was skating, but I was just going at it half-speed," he says.

Then, in 1977, his mother died.

Dorothy Hamilton had been sick with cancer for some time and knew she was dying. When she felt the end was near, she told her son that she wanted him never to miss a skating performance. Several days after her death, he skated.

Like catcher Gary Carter, who also lost his mother when he was young, Hamilton immersed himself in athletics to escape his pain and preserve her memory. "When she died, I decided I had been wasting my life," he says. "Anytime you lose a parent prematurely, you feel a great deal of guilt, and you wish it was you who had died instead. And then I thought, 'Well, what did she want more than anything?' I mean, she gave and gave and gave for me, and I was just screwing off. At that point, I said, 'Okay, I'm going to do this right.' "

Hamilton's mother had indeed given all she had to the point where, in 1976, the family could no longer afford to pay all his training expenses. At that point, his career had been saved by an anonymous benefactor who sponsored him. Now it was up to him to do the rest.

He worked harder than he ever had before, and by 1978 he knew that he could make the 1980 Olympic team. He was looking too far ahead, though. In 1979, when he should have been going to the World Championships to prepare for the Olympics, he found himself at home because he had failed to make the national team.

That was the turning point. He changed coaches—dropped Carlo Fassi and moved to Philadelphia to work under Donald Laws. He drove an old MG that didn't have a muffler, and he paid his living expenses by delivering pizzas at night. Every morning at 5:30, he'd fire up his roadster and roar off to the skating rink.

"I lived in a very quiet neighborhood," he says. "The neighbors were convinced that some lady in the neighborhood was having an affair with somebody who drove a car with no muffler and snuck off every morning before the sun came up."

He relished being on his own and looked forward to the solitary hours he put in working on his compulsory figures every morning. In skating competitions at that time, scores were divided into three segments. The first part was the compulsory figures, the origin of the sport. Few people ever watched the compulsories, even in the Olympics. A figure—two perfect circles describing a figure eight—was etched on the ice. Then, with judges standing on the ice and staring holes through him, a skater ever-so-slowly and carefully attempted to carve a perfect path on top of the etched circles, changing skates and moving forward or backward according to a predetermined pattern.

When the skater was finished, he stepped aside, and the judges literally got down on their hands and knees with their faces just inches from the ice, searching for errant scratches, sniffing at the slivers of ice that marked skate changes and turns.

Once the biggest part of the score, the compulsory figures gradually diminished in importance, but they were still the surest route to a championship. Since they required time—thousands of hours of repetition over many years—they were a measure of a skater's investment in his craft.

Often, the best skaters in the compulsories were not as good in the other two parts of the competition, the short program and the long program. In the short program, each skater had to perform the same prescribed jumps and spins and maneuvers in one choreographed sequence. The compulsories came first, followed by the short program, and then the long program. Most casual viewers of the sport think only of the long program, in which each skater gets four and a half minutes to knock the judges' socks off. But that is only part of the whole.

The great champions are great free skaters and great compulsory figure skaters as well. By winning the compulsories, a skater can build up a lead that acts as an insurance policy against accidents in the more glamorous short and long programs.

Casual fans and the media, however, didn't like the compulsories. They couldn't understand how someone who had run away with the long program could lose the competition just because they couldn't trace a stupid figure eight. Bowing to that pressure, the world governing body of figure skating eliminated the compulsory figures after the 1988 Olympics.

Had the compulsories not been around when Hamilton was competing, he might have done better at a younger age than he did. He was, after all, the one who wowed them in the long program. Yet he deplores their elimination for that very reason. "The compulsories have an excellence and a discipline that takes years of training to develop, and free-skating does not," he says. "You can be a fourteen-year-old little whipper and go out and do all kinds of tricks and stunts, but you may not have the maturity that other skaters do.

"Figures are the foundation of figure skating. You should use all three disciplines to find a champion and not base it on just one night. If you're hot or cold in the long program, that's the whole competition, but in the figures, work and time develop consistency. I really think that compulsory figures help find *the* champion."

Hamilton said this in 1990. He was thirty-one, and he had his gold medal and the successful and lucrative career that went along with it. So he wasn't talking in his own self-interest. It was the sport he cared about. Other changes in Olympic and international skating rules were opening the doors for professionals to compete in those showcase events. That hadn't been possible when he was competing. Back then, even though track and field athletes and skiers had long since been collecting sizeable payments for their work—either above or below the table—Olympic and international figure skating was strictly an amateur sport. It preferred that its athletes starved for their art.

Skaters talked about how it cost thirty thousand a year to skate—what with the cost of choreographers, sports psychologists, costume designers, coaches, and the healthy fees skating rinks charged for ice time.

Hamilton, whose family didn't have that kind of money, got by on eight thousand a year. Instead of renting ice time by the hour, he joined a skating club, which allowed him to skate as long as he liked, provided he didn't mind other people skating through his programs.

He could work on his compulsory figures on his own time. He picked his own music, helped choreograph it, and decided what to wear. The people who paid all those thousands didn't really need to, he says. "A lot of people pay huge fees to a coach to babysit their daughter for three hours a day—and teach her to skate. Those kids have no chance to work on their own, and it costs twice as much."

"I loved training," he says. "That's the thing I miss most about my amateur days—spending time on the ice every day, getting closer to your goals. Looking down at the compulsory figure and seeing the lines get closer together—that's just the greatest feeling in the world, and you have to do it by yourself."

Of his stay in Philadelphia, he says, "It was constant work, work, work. Every day I worked harder than I had ever worked before. Constant repetition, doing the same jump over and over and over again. I was like a machine. My ambition was at its peak. I found it easy to work so hard."

It's something that money can't buy, or even make easier.

Now it doesn't matter. Now promising kids can get sponsors or get paid to appear in ice shows and put the money in a trust fund to use for training expenses. "Pretty soon, it will be all professional," he says wistfully.

To many, it never made any sense to insist on amateurism in the Olympics. Even in the ancient Greek games, star athletes had sponsors and lived royally. But the modern Olympic movement, which began with the 1896 Games in Athens, was sponsored by aristocrats. The English nobility, especially, believed that the games should be for true sportsmen—namely themselves. If you made your living through the exertion of sinew and brawn, then you weren't a true sportsman doing it for the love of the game. One of the early Olympic rules prohibited manual laborers from competing: digging ditches and carrying hods of brick around for a living was considered the same as being paid to train.

But sport by sport the rules have crumbled, and soon there will be no prohibitions against professionals in any Olympic sport. Hamilton is not a crusty old conservative, but it does make him sad.

"I didn't have all the distractions from money," he says of his pizza-delivery days. "The best thing for me was to live in a basement and worry about the MasterCard bill. I could concentrate on my skating and not on all the distractions that money can buy. I don't know if I would have been as successful as an amateur if I would have had a lot of money around. Anytime a major distraction comes in, it really affects your performance. I'm grateful the money wasn't there."

This is not an opinion he has come to recently. Even back in his amateur days, when he was an international star and aiming toward the 1984 Olympics, he talked about the downside of celebrity. "The star trip is just the worst," he said then. "You just aren't as hungry to achieve as you once were. It's like working your whole life just to buy a Rolls-Royce, then you get it, and soon you've got McDonald's wrappers sitting in the back."

It's only "when you really want to achieve that you take risks," he says.

After the disappointment of 1979, Hamilton began his breakthrough. He made the 1980 Olympic team and headed up to Lake Placid, a village as peaceful as its name implied. Lake Placid had hosted the Olympics once before, in 1932, when Sonja Henie won her second gold medal.

Hamilton was by then becoming known outside the confines of his sport. His irrepressible personality won over not only fans but also his fellow athletes, who gave him the honor of carrying the American flag at the opening ceremonies.

"That was my fantasy Olympics," Hamilton says. He became friends with Eric Heiden, the twenty-one-year-old speed skater who would sweep every one of his events to become the first Olympian ever to win five individual gold medals in one Olympics. An avid hockey fan, Hamilton also got to watch the U.S. Olympic Hockey Team perform its "miracle on ice," beating the mighty Soviets and winning the gold medal. Whatever Hamilton did in his own event, in which he was not considered a threat for a medal, would be gravy.

"It was the hockey team's year. That's why I didn't win," he once said, tongue planted firmly in cheek. But he did finish fifth, a surprisingly good performance that marked him as someone to watch when the 1984 games in Sarajevo, Yugoslavia, rolled around.

But Hamilton didn't wait until 1984. In 1981, he seized center stage, beginning a winning streak that lasted through four straight seasons and Sarajevo. He won his first of four National Championships that February and followed it in March by winning the World Championships in Hartford, Connecticut. Between the two victories, his father, Ernest Hamilton, suffered a minor stroke, so he couldn't see his son crowned the new international king of skating.

Hamilton won the World Championships the hard way. Coming into the showcase long program, he was in third place in a competition led by David Santee, a veteran American skater who was a perennial runner-up. With everything riding on his performance, Hamilton stormed into his program with two big triple jumps that had the crowd gasping for breath. In the middle of the program, he hit another big jump, then turned a corner too fast, hit the ice with his boot, and crashed.

He was back on his feet in an instant, but to him that fall "seemed like it lasted thirty seconds." Many skaters simply lose it after a fall, stumbling through the rest of their program. But Hamilton finished his program perfectly, and when the judges—some of them almost smiling—held up a row of 5.9s and 5.8s (out of 6 possible points), the championship was his.

When he was done, he ran to a telephone to call his father, who was in a hospital in San Diego.

"How'd you do?" his father asked.

"I did okay."

"Come on," his father came back. "How'd you do?"

"Well," he began, and then he told him. Together, three thousand miles apart, they celebrated the victory they had worked so long for. At year's end, the U.S. Olympic Committee named Hamilton its athlete of the year.

In 1982, Hamilton repeated as national and world champion. Now he no longer had to fight the people ahead of him on the ice. He had to fight himself and that feeling of *What do I do now?* that eventually comes to haunt all champions in sports where the only possible finish is first. It's not like baseball, where a player doesn't have to win the World Series or a batting crown to be successful. In skating, once you've won, you must always win.

"You win, and you start to think, 'Gosh, I'm doing well.' Once you do it, you wonder how much more you can achieve." He slacked off, mentally more than physically, but he was brought back to reality in the summer of 1982 when he went to the U.S. Olympic Sports Festival and embarrassed himself on the ice. It was the jolt he needed.

"You get slapped in the face and everything comes into perspective," he said. He rethought his routines, scrapped the program he had been doing for several years, and constructed an entirely new long program that was full of technical subtleties his old program had lacked. It had power and grace. In the middle, it had comic relief. And it wasn't merely set to music; it *was* the music.

"Champions are those who survive best the risks they determine they must take," he said as he prepared for the 1983 campaign for his third straight national and world titles. "I have to put a lot of pressure on myself."

He was like Ted Williams, the great left-handed hitter for the Boston Red Sox and the last man to hit .400 in the major leagues—cursing himself, spurring himself on to the excellence he knew was inside, daring himself to be better.

"If you reach a certain level and say, 'Okay, I'm here, and I'm going to stay with the same program,' you're going to lose," he explained. "There's got to be improvement each year. I don't want to give up any ground."

With his new program, he came soaring back in the 1983 nationals in Pittsburgh. He won the competition wearing a dark costume with rivers of rhinestones on each shoulder and across his chest. But after the competition, he announced that he would go to the world championships, which closely followed, without glitter.

And that's how he came to so startle the establishment in Helsinki. If it seemed a rash act, it was carefully planned. He was firmly entrenched as world champion and thus whatever he did would be looked on more kindly by the judges than if some upstart had tried the same thing. And it was one year away from the Olympics, the perfect time to test the reaction to an idea that, in his mind, was long overdue.

"All the outfits had gotten beaded and everything," he explains. "I wanted to get into something that was more Olympic, something that I wasn't going to be embarrassed to see myself in a picture five years later."

He got the idea for a plain costume three years earlier, watching Eric Heiden in his form-fitting speed skating costume. "I thought that was real cool, so I developed it for figure skating," he says. "It's not heavy. Movement is effortless. You can do anything with it. It has a clean line, and that's all you want to show a judge."

By emphasizing the body, Hamilton focused attention back where it belonged—on the skill of the skater and not the deft fingers of a tailor. Hamilton didn't need sequins to draw attention. His skating was enough.

With his new fashion statement—or nonstatement—he declared the end to one of his quests. "I have been on a crusade to see the image of male figure skating changed," he said. "I hate crusades, but I also hate being stereotyped. It bothers me that some guys who came before me represented the sport in a certain way, and people assume I'm the same way just because we have a common skill. Just let it go at that. I'm tired of campaigning. From now on, I'm just going to skate."

With that speech, he tiptoed neatly around the center of the image problem that he was fighting, namely, that male figure skaters were a bit—shall we say—dainty.

And Hamilton was anything but. He still loved hockey, and he often found himself having to hide beer cans when official company came calling—bad for the image, you know. If prodded, he would admit the best thing about being famous was that, "Many of the girls I date find it impressive when people recognize me."

After winning his third straight national and world titles, Hamilton geared up for the home stretch to the Olympics and what everyone by now conceded was as certain a gold medal as there had ever been. "My Sure Thing Olympics," he called it, with a laugh that belied the pressure building inside. All the talk about his obvious superiority added to that pressure.

"He has overcome everything in his life," said former Olympic skater John Misha Petkevich, "as if none of it ever occurred. He's one of the most amazingly consistent skaters I've ever seen."

"I felt the pressure going for the championship for the third year running," Hamilton said himself. "But next year it will be worse—going for the Olympic gold medal and a fourth world title. I'm trying not to think about it."

He was living in Denver by then. He and his coach, Don Laws, had determined that he had done all the hard work in 1981–83. "Don knew that we had to just grind during those three years, and then in 1984 sit back and not let the emotion and the tension of the whole thing take over.

"A lot of coaches get in there and say, 'This is your one opportunity. This is the greatest competition of your life.' They put an extra something on it. But Don knew I should do all my work in those first three years, and in the fourth year just let it happen."

When the national championships rolled around at the end of January 1984, it did appear as if Hamilton was relaxed and ready. He talked easily about the routine he would use in the championships and repeat a month later in the Olympics. He talked about his "triple wow" theory of building the program. (The idea, he said, was to wring three "wows" out of the judges.)

"It starts out very technical to get the people's attention," he explained. "Then comes a slower section, quiet, with the people interested—well, sometimes. What the heck, it doesn't always work. Then, after a humor section, we have a big finish based on the illusion of strength."

Illusion, heck. There were no mirrors involved in what Hamilton did on the ice in Salt Lake City. In his long program, he wrung perfect scores of 6.0 from four of the judges, the first time so many perfect scores had been granted in a national competition in—no one knew how long. Afterward, Hamilton grinned slyly and said it hadn't been *that* good. "I've skated it better all week," he said.

There was purpose to what he said, just as there was purpose to the effort he put into the national championships. He knew the news of his scores would flash across the Atlantic to his Olympic rivals and put added pressure on everyone else in the competition to chase that new standard.

Three weeks later in Sarajevo, he was still the picture of confidence. "This is absolutely the best time of my life," he declared on arrival. He underlined that statement by taking first place in the compulsory figures. All those thousands of solitary hours had paid a dividend worth thirty percent of his score. Canadian champion Brian Orser, a brilliant free skater and Hamilton's chief competition, was seventh in the compulsories. Hamilton would literally have to skate his short and long programs on his backside to lose the gold medal. He was that far ahead.

Yet somehow that huge lead hurt him. Without the pressure of having to perform well, Hamilton was flat in the short program. Of course, flat is a matter of degree. What was flat for him was still better than everyone else in the world—except Orser, who beat him in the short program.

On gold medal night, the edge still wasn't there. He had wanted so badly to astound the world with his long program, but instead he found himself changing one triple jump into a single and another into a double. He didn't do anything horrible; he just didn't do anything spectacular. In practice, he had done the program perfectly twenty-three straight times. It just wasn't there the twenty-fourth time.

He won the gold medal anyway. To lose it, he would have had to finish fifth in the long program, which Orser won. And he was a hero in the eyes of the American public, which had seen enough of Scott Hamilton's skill and verve on their televisions back home to ensure sellout crowds for whatever ice show he chose to join after the Olympics.

But he hadn't gone out the way he'd planned. "Am I mad?" he asked rhetorically after the medal ceremony. "Yeah, I'm mad. I let outside things get to me, and I had never done that before. Things seeped into my concentration. I'm upset at my weakness. I wanted this to be the most memorable performance of my life." He paused.

Then the light went on again, and the mischief came back in his eyes. "I guess it's going to be."

Six years later, he was more analytical about what had happened in Sarajevo. He was in Minneapolis during the 1990 Olympic Festival to be inducted into the U.S. Olympic Hall of Fame, which would give him a clean sweep in the hall of fame department—U.S. Figure Skating, International Figure Skating, and Olympic. The 1984 gold medal had indeed opened doors for him, and he was now enjoying a career as a skater, choreographer, writer, and producer of ice shows. Still living in Denver, he was proud of the fact he had order in his personal life.

He saw his Olympic performance for what it was—a victory forged not in one day, or even three days, of skating, but over sixteen years that began when he was nine years old and asked his mother if he could take skating lessons.

"My whole strategy going into the Olympics was: Get a lead," he said. "Just watching all the people who came before me, you know you can't depend on anything. You can't depend on the best performance of your life no matter how hard you work."

And winning was the key, because for a figure skater, there's only the Olympics. Who, after all, remembers Hamilton's pal, Gordon McKellen? He won three national championships, but because he never placed in the Olympics, it was as if he didn't exist. You get one shot at it, and you had better be ready. It had been twenty-four years since the last American male skater had struck Olympic gold. Hamilton wasn't going to let it become twenty-eight.

When his time came, he was ready. He did what he had to do. And then he went from the Olympics to the World Championships —his last one—in Ottawa five weeks later. There, he nailed his program and won his fourth world championship. This time, he didn't think about winning it for America or anyone else. "I'm not thinking about beating anybody," he said. "I just would really like to do well for myself." He did that, and then he retired from a career built on delivering pizzas in a car with no muffler.

Six years later, he was skating more than he ever had as an amateur. "In many ways," he said, "I'm a better skater now. Athletically, I don't think I'm as strong as I was in '84, but I think as a performer I'm ten times the skater I was then. I've learned so much about audiences, about how to handle music and things like that."

He was working for himself, not for one of the big ice shows—which left him free to innovate. Instead of putting on a big splash of color and costumes, he developed shows with story lines. "I like to do characterizations," he said. "I like to do a little acting. It's more fun for the audience. You still get the athleticism, but it's done in a different way."

His ability to wow a crowd was greater than ever. When he took the ice, he could make every one of fifteen thousand people think he was skating only for them. He could make them laugh. He could make them cry.

And he did it in the strangest ways. Like the time he did a show in Moscow and realized the moment he started skating that he had completely forgotten everything he'd ever learned. "It was one of those things where I went up for that first jump, went upside down, tried to adjust in the air, and made it worse. I came down on my head. I lost all sorts of equilibrium, and every time I jumped again I fell harder. I fell on my head. I fell on my leg. I fell on my arm.

"I fell in love with the Russian people that night. After the third time I fell, they started clapping in unison. I wanted to hide under a rock, but the clapping gave me all sorts of strength to hang on. So I went into the last jump—a triple. I'm thinking, 'I can hardly stand on my left leg and I've got to do a triple jump. This is going to be a lot of fun, ladies and gentlemen.' I hung on somehow and I landed it. It wasn't pretty. But the place just erupted. They went nuts."

The experience was so humiliating that he actually thought about retiring. But on the way home, he ran into Lynn Swann, former Steeler great, at an airport rental car counter. He told Swann what had happened. Swann just listened and said calmly, "If you're in anything long enough, everything will happen to you."

"I thought that was wisdom," Hamilton says.

He didn't quit.

Hamilton doesn't take any of his successes for granted. A couple years after the Olympics, he was spotted practicing for a show in a

T-shirt that read (before the sentiment became popular): LIFE'S TOUGH. THEN YOU DIE.

It was a joke, and it was also the truth he had learned as a young boy who was supposed to die but didn't. Hamilton never forgot about the other kids in the hospitals where he spent a good part of his childhood. Few people do more charity work than he does. "I'm available," he says, "for anything my involvement will help."

There is a Friends of Scott Hamilton Foundation, set up by "two ladies who like skating." He raises money for the Make a Wish Foundation, the charity that gives kids with terminal diseases a chance to realize their one great dream, be it going to DisneyWorld or to a ballgame. He does a lot of work for the Pediatric AIDS Foundation and the American Cancer Society. He dispenses funds to promising young skaters to defray training expenses. He has his own foundation through which he develops programs for kids to help other kids. "If we can get children working for other children, it can affect them for the rest of their lives," he says.

What's next for Scott Hamilton?

"Golf," he says. "I've got nineteen years to get good enough to play the Senior Tour."

Life's turned out to be very good, and he knows it. Yes, he admits, "The light is shining bright at the end of the tunnel." And then there's that twinkle again as he adds: "I'm just hoping it's not a train."

One of a Kind

You can rise above anything, even if you don't know what you're rising above.

You won't see Tess Hyman on "NFL Today" or ESPN. Television cameras don't prowl the corners of Giants Stadium where she hangs out. Not that she's hard to find. Just go out in the windswept parking lot an hour or two before the game. Walk over to the northeast side of the stadium—the side that looks out past the big, white hatbox that is the Meadowlands Arena, over the hulking stone spine of the Palisades, and across to the Oz-like skyline of Manhattan. You'll find her there, at the gate for the handicapped.

You can't miss her. She's the tiny woman with the big smile who greets each handicapped fan with a warm hello and a bit of small talk. Nearly all of them are men, and she calls them "my boys." They call her Tess.

"It's just Tess," she says. "No one knows I have a last name."

Most of the men come in wheelchairs, although there have been some who have arrived on litters. Some drive their own specially equipped cars and vans. Others are brought by friends and relatives. Still others are brought by veterans' hospitals and disabled veterans' organizations.

They come from four states, two hundred of them every day there's a Jets or Giants football game at the big stadium in the New Jersey meadowlands. Cerebral palsy sufferers, paraplegics, quadriplegics—the victims of wars and accidents and the cruel chances of birth.

It doesn't matter how they came to their situations, not to Tess. It only matters that they need a friend and that seeing a football game is sometimes the best therapy in the world. Tess Hyman is that friend. For fifty years she's been there for them—first with her husband, Dr. N. Howard Hyman, a Manhattan dentist, and now by herself. She loves these men, each and every one of them.

They come to the games because of her. The special wheelchair section that wraps around the east end zone of Giants Stadium at the back of the lower deck is also there because of her. Not that Giants Stadium is the only one in the country with facilities for the handicapped. What's unusual is that at Giants Stadium the handicapped do not have to pay for a ticket. Not for regular season games, and not for playoff games, either. The spaces, therefore, aren't held on a season-ticket basis like the rest of the seats in the big stadium. They are rotated from a list that Tess keeps. Some ten thousand fans have been on her list over the years. Each week, two hundred go to a professional football game. Tess figures it's the least she can do for people for whom so little else is done. She knows as few people do what a difference a football game can make in a shattered life. It started long ago with a simple act of kindness.

Dr. N. Howard Hyman was an outstanding dentist. His services were sought out by the likes of Walter Winchell and Arthur Hammerstein. But he also took in patients not nearly so wealthy. One day, a young man came in for dental work. He had been a soldier, and he was blinded in the line of duty. As he waited to be treated, he whistled a song from *The Red Mill,* a popular musical on Broadway at the time.

Making conversation, Hyman asked the young man if he had been to the play.

"How can I afford to on what they give me?" the man replied bitterly.

"He had so much belligerence," Tess says. He was still angry at the world for the harsh turn his life had taken. Most people would have changed the subject, but not Howard Hyman. He knew people in the theater, and an idea popped into his head.

"Suppose I could get you a ticket to the play?" Hyman asked the man. "Would you like that?"

"Who wouldn't," the man said, as if only an utter dolt would ask such a question.

Hyman called his friend, Richard Rodgers, explained what had happened, and soon had a ticket for the man to *The Red Mill.*

Not long afterward, the man came back for more work on his teeth. The song that earlier had been on his lips was now in his heart as well. "He was a changed person," Tess recalls. The simple act of going to a play, of getting out into the world again, pulled him out of his swamp of self-pity and anger.

That's how it started. Having seen the results of such simple therapy, Howard Hyman started calling other Broadway producers. Theaters weren't sold out every night, and when tickets were available, Hyman got them for other disabled veterans. "From that time on, he got tickets for everything," Tess says. There was no problem finding takers for the tickets. The veterans' hospitals were full of soldiers who needed a lift.

It wasn't planned. It just happened. From plays, Hyman proceeded to baseball and football games. In those days, the football Giants played in the Polo Grounds. Howard Hyman and Tess would drive men to the stadium and wheel them out onto the sidelines—there were no wheelchair ramps or sections—to see the games.

They organized parties in fancy hotel ballrooms, and Tess invited every young, single woman she ran across—hairdressers, manicurists, secretaries and receptionists—to come and help. One year, after they had been at it for a couple of decades, they organized a trip for thirty handicapped veterans to the Orange Bowl in Miami. "We took them down there for a week," Tess says. "We chartered a plane to take them down. It took a year to get it all together." As with everything else they did for their "boys," the trip was first class.

They did it by themselves, dipping into their own funds when there was no other way. It was something they believed in, but it wasn't always easy convincing others. The doctors and the staffs in the veterans' hospitals weren't always thrilled about the outings that the Hymans kept planning. Tess said they'd sometimes propose an outing and one official or another would object. "What good can one time out do?" they'd ask.

A lot of good, the Hymans insisted.

"But they don't have anything to wear," the argument would go.

"Let them wear what they have on," the Hymans replied.

They got their way, too. They weren't people who were easily discouraged.

Tess Hyman, you see, hadn't had life handed to her on a silver platter. She knew that few things come easy. But she also knew that a handicap isn't the end of life. That she learned from her mother, a feisty woman who lost her hand when she was three years old, lost her husband when she had four young children, and never missed a beat.

"*There* was a courageous person," Tess says. "She was born Rosa Burke in Midway, South Carolina. She lost her mother when she was just sixteen months old. When she was three, one day she saw some smoke coming out of a little building about a half mile away from the house, and she went to see what it was."

The nanny who was caring for her didn't see her walk away, and no one else saw her as she toddled to the building. It was harvest time, eleven years after the end of the Civil War, and the cotton was being brought in. The building that Tess's mother went to housed the cotton gin, a steam-driven contraption that separated the seeds from the raw cotton. The little girl put her hand out to catch the seeds as they fell out. The machine grabbed her hand and chewed it off.

"I don't know how long she was there bleeding before they found her," Tess says. "But she rose above it so magnificently."

That she did. She married Julian Sternberger from South Carolina. He was the salesman for a family shoe business and he traveled the country around Sumter, finding outlets for the company's shoes. He was good at what he did and eventually went as far as Cuba opening new accounts.

But Tess's father had a congenital heart condition, and as he grew older he became less able to get around. He was told that a move to the mountains might be beneficial, so he looked for a town where he could breathe more easily. He found it in Saluda, North Carolina—population around three hundred fifty.

"He was a little over forty when we moved," she says. "He had to give up his business. We were able to subsist on what money he had saved. We had no running water, there was a privy outside, and twice a week my mother would bring in a tin tub to give us kids a bath. My mother, with her one arm and four kids, pulled that tub in and took care of everyone. It was pretty pioneering."

Tess was three years old when the family moved to Saluda. The twentieth century was not yet ten years old. She remembers herself as a funny-looking girl who lived by her quick wit and ability to invent a story. "I wanted to be in the circus," she says. "It was the only way I got attention. I made up stories. That's the way I got away with a few things."

School wasn't easy for Tess. Although she was a good speller, she wasn't a good reader and she didn't know why. She suspected that she was stupid. To anyone who knows her, the idea is preposterous, but it always took Tess much longer than the other kids to read and write.

She and a sister took up the violin, but reading music was no different from reading words: she couldn't do it. A retired musician —Mr. Bushnel—lived in Saluda. He had played in the orchestra of the great John Philip Sousa and had moved to the mountains, just as Tess's father had, for the clean, fresh air.

Mr. Bushnel taught the girls to read music, except that Tess couldn't do it. Unwilling to admit her failing, she learned to memorize pieces and play them back by ear. The trick was to get her instructor to play it first, a talent that Tess perfected over the years. "I was always tricking my music professors to play the piece first. They'd tell me they wanted me to play, but I'd think of everything to make them do it. I tried to keep people from knowing I couldn't read very well."

This was more than seventy-five years ago, and the word *dyslexic* hadn't been invented. In those days, the usual word for Tess's problem was *dumb*. And for most of her life, Tess believed she was.

Even today, her eyes swim when she remembers the humiliation she endured for seventy years before she was able to put a label on her affliction. It's one thing to lose a limb. Then at least you know what your problem is. It's something else entirely to have something wrong with the way you see words and numbers, something that for most of your life doctors and psychologists don't even know exists.

"They discovered when I was in the first grade and learning to print that I would print my name with the *T* crossed on the bottom and all the *S*s backward. The teacher told my mother the problem. She was terribly upset and took me to an eye doctor, but he said it wasn't my eyes. I went to a better doctor, and he said there was no problem. Finally, my little sister, who was sixteen months younger, caught up with me in school. That upset me very much."

"I never felt sorry for myself," Tess explains. "I just felt inadequate. I felt that everything I did was so much harder for me than for the others. I can't carry seven numbers in my head at the same time, so I'd invariably dial the wrong number on the telephone. When I worked in an office, it would take me all day to do what the girl next to me took three hours to do."

Tess's father died when he was forty-eight. All the fresh air on God's green earth couldn't save him from a heart that just wouldn't work. There was no future in Saluda, so Tess's mother packed up her four children and moved to New York City. Tess was eleven years old.

The first order of business was to find work. Western Union was hiring telegraph operators, and Tess's mother applied. She had learned Morse code as a teenager twenty years earlier despite this problem with her right hand, which wasn't there. But she had never sent code professionally. Telegraphers had to send and receive code at the same time, and the people at Western Union told her she wasn't equipped for the job. But the plucky woman went to school and learned to do it.

She got the job. With time, she became an office manager. "She just overcame all of her obstacles," Tess says. "When she didn't know what to do, she asked for divine guidance, and she always got it."

"She was forty-four when we moved to New York, and she had never worked a day in her life, but she learned," Tess says with pride. "She worked for Western Union more than twenty years."

At seventy-six, she was struck by a car that threw her nearly twenty feet in the air. When she landed, her body broke in too many places, and the tiny woman went into a coma. For over a week Tess and her two sisters sat at her bedside. Tess says she never doubted her mother would pull through.

The right arm that had lost its hand when she was three had been badly broken, and the doctors wanted to amputate. She didn't have a hand to start with, they said, and the arm was so badly damaged, she wouldn't be able to use it. But Tess refused to allow it, so they put in a plate to hold it together. The arm ended up two inches shorter than it had been, but Tess's mother learned to use it again when she recovered.

For she did recover. Confined at first to a wheelchair, she locked herself in her bedroom and taught herself to walk again. She lived until she was ninety-eight, a testament to will and determination that is mirrored in her daughter.

Tess was enrolled in New York City schools, but because of her dyslexia she was put back three classes. "I was a big girl and fat," she remembers. "I hated to be the biggest girl. I stayed in school through the eighth grade and graduated, but I got the diploma by feigning a nervous breakdown. I was sixteen."

Her quick wit had carried her through, and although she remembers with fondness playing the violin in the school orchestra, her most vivid memories of school can be summed up in three words: "It was torture."

In those days, at the dawn of the roaring twenties, a sixteen-year-old girl with an elementary school diploma was considered ready for the job market. So Tess, despite feeling "like somebody who'd been defeated from birth," went to work. Her first job was with a tobacco importer, where most of her day was spent hand rolling cigarettes. Then she caught on with Paramount Studios as a stenographer.

Through the job with Paramount, she had an opportunity to go to Europe with a young singer from Montgomery, Alabama. The girl's name was Florence Star. She was not quite eighteen years old, but she had a voice that was pure honey. Tess was twenty-four.

Going to Europe was an enormous adventure in 1930. It took a week to get there, and people didn't stay for a couple weeks and return home. Tess and Flo—as Star was called—planned a two-year tour. Although they were quite young to be traveling alone, Tess's official job was to be a chaperone for the young singer. She ended up being her business agent as well.

Those were glorious days on the Continent, magic days. Josephine Baker was the toast of France, and Ernest Hemingway and the Lost Generation had made Paris a center for American writers and artists.

But London was Tess and Flo's planned destination. Tess still has publicity photos of the beautiful young Florence Star. "Beauty and Dance at the London Coliseum" reads the caption on one early photo.

"She was beautiful," Tess says of her charge. "She had a gorgeous voice. We went over to sing in the nightclubs in London."

Star was supposed to have bookings in advance, but when they arrived in London the bookings evaporated. So there they were, stranded, with no confirmed work.

Tess doesn't use the word despair, and she doesn't understand the concept of quitting. She took Star to the Royal Academy where she had her take dance lessons for six weeks, thinking that another skill might increase her chances of finding work. Then the two went to Paris.

Tess set about looking for a theatrical agent to represent Star. "I couldn't get any agent to represent her because she wasn't quite eighteen," Tess says. "They said, 'She's jail bait,' 'Go home and grow up,' and, 'The French don't like them so young.' "

Finally, Tess talked to someone in the theatrical business who advised her to represent Star herself. "But I don't speak any French," Tess protested. "I wouldn't know if she were being offered a job if I took her to an audition."

"Find a little bit of courage and take her," Tess was told.

And that's what she did. There was a casting call for a new show, and Tess took her young charge. They had purchased a dress for the audition, a lovely, demure dress with a full skirt puffed out with crinoline. When they got to the audition, however, all the other aspiring actresses were wearing practically nothing.

"When I saw all those naked women parading around showing everything they had, I said, 'What chance does she have with this costume? She sings so beautifully, but no one will notice.' "

Nobody was taken the first day. The next day Tess brought a pair of scissors with her. Just before Star was to go on, Tess brought out the scissors and told the singer, "Flossie, you can't wear that outfit, and we have nothing else. I'm going to cut off the skirt so you can show your legs.' "

To this day, Tess doesn't know how she thought of such a thing. "I was only twenty-four," she says. "I don't know where I got the knowledge to think of these things. It used to amaze me."

The trick—and Florence Star's voice—worked. She was hired the next morning for the new show at the Casino de Paris. She was to be the second lead singer. The lead singer was Josephine Baker.

Overnight, Tess and Star went from joblessness to the center of Paris's café society. Tess particularly remembers a party during the Christmas holidays that Josephine Baker threw at her estate in the country outside Paris. After the last show of the evening, Baker engaged limousines to take the cast and other guests to the estate. More than two hundred people came, including such literary lions as Erich Maria Remarque and John Dos Passos.

"It was a wonderful evening. We got there after the last show and left after breakfast," Tess remembers. "Josephine Baker was an amazing person. She was gorgeous. Her skin was like glistening Karo syrup that they put some spangles in. She could turn to Erich Remarque on one side and speak perfect German, and then turn to someone else and speak perfect Spanish."

So it went for two unforgettable years. Then they went home to the Great Depression. Tess did all right, though. She always had a knack for landing on her feet. She got her old job back and got married. When the marriage didn't work out, she defied the conventions of the day and ended it.

And then she met N. Howard Hyman, D.D.S.

She met him thanks to an oyster. Tess was eating the oyster, and she chipped a tooth on a piece of shell. A friend suggested that she go to Dr. Hyman. In time, they fell in love and got married. It was the second marriage for both, and it was made in heaven.

"I think we had the greatest love that any two people could have," she says of the man whose company she cherished for thirty-four years. "In all my life, I've never known a couple that had the happiness and love that we had for each other. One of us could almost feel what the other was thinking. My vision has never been great, but I have excellent hearing. He never wore eyeglasses, and he practiced dentistry until he was seventy, but his hearing was slightly impaired.

We had a pact. I was to be his ears for life and he was to be my eyes. Sometimes he'd say to me, 'You know, I can't even have a bad thought because you hear what I'm thinking.' "That's how close we were."

But for all their closeness, Tess could never tell her husband of her difficulty reading. It was too private, too painful. She didn't want him, of all people, to think—to know, in her mind—that she was dumb.

Then when she was seventy-five years old, she saw a story on television about something called dyslexia. It sounded like what she had. In secret, she made an appointment with a psychologist. She told her husband and the housekeeper—a woman named Tessie—that she was going to the dressmaker.

The psychologist's tests went on for hours. When Tess got home several hours late, she says, "Howard was pacing the floor in one direction and Tessie was pacing in the other. I couldn't talk. I was afraid that if I said anything, Tessie would hear and I didn't want her to know I was a moron."

When Tessie finally went home, Tess told her husband that she had something called dyslexia. "What are you crying about?" he asked her. "Isn't it wonderful to know something like that?"

"It is," she replied, "But it's such a shock to me because maybe if I had known sooner, I could have done something about it."

She had done much *despite* it. And she would continue to do more. The special bond between Tess and her husband was their work with handicapped veterans, their willingness to share the fruits of their success with others who weren't as fortunate. Along with that was a determination not to fail.

It would have been easy to give up on any or all of the hundreds and thousands of men they helped. These were men who had gone to war and glory only to wake up in hospitals without their sight or without limbs or without the ability to walk. The bitterness and despair were heavy in those wards. The doctors and staff were primarily concerned with maintaining life and not as interested in repairing destroyed psyches. That's where Tess and Howard did their work.

The walls of Tess's New York apartment are covered with plaques, photos, and proclamations testifying to their work. She has boxes of even more photographs and mementos. As she goes through them, every story comes to life again.

"Here's a man from Turkey," she says, picking up a picture. "He was a double amputee. He hadn't been in the country three years when they put him in the Army.

"And this was a blind general, Melvin Maas," she says, looking at a testimonial given to her and Dr. Hyman at a dinner in 1962. The inscription reads: "Congratulations to my very dear and wonderful friends on your night of nights. I know firsthand of your contributions to uncounted thousands. Too bad every community doesn't have a Tess and Howard Hyman, but that would be the millennium, and we're not ready for that."

There's a plaque from 1961 inscribed to: "Broadway's only real angels for opening the doors of the living theater to many of us who might not otherwise know its magic."

There's an exquisite piece of calligraphy given to them by the Institute for the Crippled and Disabled. A paraplegic inscribed it holding the calligraphy brush in his teeth. It is signed with names like Graziano, Kowalski, McQuade, Romano, Russell—an ecumenical and international community of people touched by the kindness of Tess and Howard Hyman. The text itself is a poem: *There are men who live in castles/and men who live on a throne,/or graceful ivory towers/secure in their dreams and alone./But our hearts are grateful and humble/to have founded a bridge that would span/the road to the house by the road/where dwells a friend to man.*

It wasn't easy being friends with many of these men. They didn't want friends. They didn't want life, not on the terms that had been handed to them by bombs and land mines and bullets.

A newspaper clipping begins: "As near as he can remember, the first words N. Howard Hyman, D.D.S, ever heard from a hospitalized amputee were, 'Mind your own goddam business.' The wounded soldier in the next bed was more polite. He said, 'Don't be a nudnik.' "

Tess listens to the paragraph being read and immediately remembers the man. "His name was Morris McGee," she says. "He was very belligerent and arrogant, and every time we went up to the veterans' hospital, he would say to Howard, 'Oh, I guess you're here to pester me again to get out of bed. Well, I'm not walking today, so get out.' He was very insulting to Howard.

"This went on for maybe three or four months. Finally, we heard that this man had been an actor who played bit parts. He had been in a movie with Mae West. And we learned that he had also been a football player. He was so bitter about being a paraplegic, so angry with life that if he could have held a knife, I think he would have ended it all. We couldn't get him out of the bed. He didn't want to go anywhere. He didn't want to do anything."

Howard Hyman took the insults and the rebuffs. He did a little more research and learned which football team the man followed. He waited until that team was coming to New York to play the Giants at the Polo Grounds. Then he went back to the recalcitrant Morris McGee.

"If you send me away this time, I'll never come back," Howard said. "I have one ticket left for the game this Sunday. I'll save it for you if you want to go. Otherwise, I'll give it away."

"Morris said, 'Doc, if it's only to get you out of my goddamn hair, I'll go.'

"That was the first time he ever went out with us," Tess recalls. "From then on he became a new man."

McGee committed himself to his rehabilitation and got out of the hospital. The Hymans lost touch with him. Then, some twenty years later, Tess was visiting friends in New Jersey. She was looking up a number in the phone book when she came across the name Morris McGee. Curious, she called the number, and her old friend answered. "Tess," he said, "you wouldn't believe what's happened to me."

It was all good. He had gone back to college and become a college professor. He had married. "He had mellowed and rejoined the human race," she says.

Tess doesn't know how many stories like that there are. "There are thousands," she says. "I never stopped to count them."

They started with one blinded veteran from World War II. That one became a flood. Then came Korea and more broken bodies and spirits. Then Vietnam. There was never a lack of customers for the special service Tess and Howard Hyman provided. And on their part, there was never a lack of willingness to continue helping.

Not all of the stories have happy endings. One picture brings back a particularly poignant memory. "He was a typical boy who came up paralyzed," she says, looking at the picture. "They wanted to amputate his leg. He didn't have the use of it, and it was ulcerated. He said it looked good seeing two shoes at the end of his legs. They said they had to amputate or the infection would spread. He said, 'Over my dead body.' He died."

Tess and Howard never tired of their work and never let themselves be deterred by the failures. The walls covered with plaques and the boxes of pictures attest to the fact that there was much more joy than sorrow.

They took their clients to operas, ballets, concerts, Broadway shows, dinners, baseball games, and football games. The football games played by the New York Giants became the most popular attraction, and the Giants, owned by Wellington and Jack Mara, were generous. They provided the free tickets, and they allowed wheelchairs and litters to be rolled out onto the grass surrounding the football field, first at the Polo Grounds, and then at Yankee Stadium.

When the Giants accepted an offer from the New Jersey Sports and Exposition Authority to move to a new stadium being built in the East Rutherford meadowlands, they called on Tess and Howard to help design a wheelchair section and to eliminate barriers for the handicapped. When Giants Stadium opened in 1976, Tess and Howard were there to greet the first two hundred handicapped patrons and escort them to their stations in the east end zone.

Howard Hyman died in December 1981 at the age of eighty-five, but Tess wouldn't allow his program to die with him. Instead she expanded it, taking on the added responsibility of distributing passes to New York Jets games as well.

She's still at it. Her health doesn't allow her to come to every game, but she's there more game days than not, standing at the gate before the game and standing next to a pillar in wheelchair section 121 during the game.

"I still don't understand football," she confesses. "I'm too busy taking care of everyone to watch. I just turn around and look when the crowd starts making a lot of noise."

Nearby is a plaque announcing that the section over which she presides is officially the Dr. and Mrs. Howard Hyman Memorial Wheelchair Section. Tess is as proud of that as anything.

Many of the men she first served have no doubt died. And she doesn't know every person who comes through the gate as she once did. But she still collects stories. Like the one about the man she had to deny admission to. He was in a wheelchair, but his shoes were worn on the bottom. He was faking, trying to take advantage of her charity.

Or the one about the wheelchair-bound friend who asked her to feel his leg one cold and windy afternoon. "I beg your pardon," said Tess, her old-fashioned sense of propriety offended.

"I have a new battery-powered heater," the man said with a sly grin. "I can't feel if it's too hot, and if it is, it could burn my legs."

"Why didn't you tell me?" she asked.

"Because it's more fun this way," he replied.

She loves those little stories, stories that show how getting out into the world can restore a zest for life. There are big stories, as well.

A few years ago, she got a call from a woman who was a volunteer worker in a hospital in New Jersey. The woman was helping care for a man, a former athlete and football coach, who had an undiagnosed disease that left him paralyzed. He was unable to move or speak, locked in despair in a body that would do nothing for him, not even communicate. She wondered if perhaps going to a Giants game would help.

Tess arranged for tickets, and the man was wheeled in and rolled up to the railing, where he could look out across the perfect green of the football field.

"His eyes danced," Tess says. "That's the only part of his body he could move. And his lips tried to mouth words."

The following week, the woman called Tess again. Seeing a football game had stirred something in the man. He had turned the corner from despair to determination. The following year, as football season was starting, the woman called asking for tickets again. The man had improved significantly, had regained some muscular control, and was learning to use a computer. "And," the woman told Tess, "We're going to be married. It's all because of these football games." At the wedding the following year, he got out of his wheelchair and stood with the aid of braces. He mouthed the words, "I do."

That's what makes it worth it to Tess. If there's one thing she can't understand, it's why there are so few others willing to do what she does, especially retired people who don't know what to do with their time.

"The most important part is that you can rise above anything, even if you don't know what you're rising above—if you do the best you know how, if you're not a selfish person, living for yourself alone," says Tess.

She knows. It's what she does. It's what her mother did. It's what her husband did.

One summer, she says, her secretary at the foundation went away, and she was snowed under by paperwork. But she had an idea, and she took it to a club to which she belongs, most of whose members are retired women.

"I knew many of them at the club," she says. "So many are unhappy. A lot of them had been secretaries and office managers. We had a meeting, and there were four or five hundred of them there. I asked them if any of them wanted to help, I could use a volunteer for a couple hours one or two days a week to take dictation.

"You know, I couldn't get one person to help. They were always wailing about the fact that their children didn't come to visit them or didn't care about them. Everything they said was a complaint. Yet they wouldn't do anything to help someone else."

It's a mystery to her, as is the idea of giving up just because life hasn't been as kind to you as it has been to the next guy. She didn't give up, although many times she could have. Why should anyone else?

When it is suggested to her that maybe she's simply more courageous than most people, she blushes.

"I don't have courage," she protests. "I've persevered."

The Gamer

If I had sat out and waited until I was one hundred percent before I played, I would have missed half my career.

Sometimes courage begins at home. It did for Gary Carter. He learned it by watching his mother die. It happened a long time ago, when the man they still call Kid really was just a kid and the world seemed as perfect as a storybook.

Life began as an American fairy tale for Gary Edmund Carter. The second son of Jim and Inge Carter, he was born on April 8, 1954, in Culver City, California. The life he was born into was straight out of "Leave it to Beaver." The postwar boom was in full swing. The nuclear family was real then, with Mom keeping a spotless house in a neatly trimmed suburb, Dad bringing home the bacon, and polite but high-spirited boys saying "yes, sir" and "thank you, ma'am," paying attention in school, and winning the big game with last-minute heroics.

Today, Gary Carter's biography sounds too goofy to be real. He actually went to a high school called Sunny Hills, where he was an honors student and the quarterback of the football team. In his junior and senior years, he captained the football, basketball, and baseball teams. A whole slew of colleges wanted him to play football, including his hometown university, UCLA, but he chose instead to pursue a baseball career with the Montreal Expos.

His first year in the minor leagues, Carter was named Most Valuable Player of the Eastern League All-Star Game. Then, playing winter ball in Puerto Rico, he was named MVP of the Caribbean World Series. In his second year he was an all-star in Class AAA, the highest minor league. By his third year of professional ball, he was in the big leagues, representing the Expos in the All-Star Game and being named National League Rookie of the Year by *The Sporting News*.

Carter would go on to play in ten straight All-Star Games—eleven overall—and be named MVP in two of them. He would set a National League record for games caught and would share a record with Yogi

Berra for being the only players in Major League history to hit home runs on four consecutive Opening Days. He would be one of the leaders of the 1986 World Champion Mets. And through it all, he remained as polite as a choirboy, rarely using an expletive stronger than *gosh.* He signed autographs, gave interviews, raised more than a million dollars for charity, and navigated the shoals of life by the glow of his trademark hundred-acre smile.

It's the sort of life you run into only in books and television shows —and bad ones at that. Real life just doesn't happen that way, so people always figured Carter must be hiding something behind all the teeth and good cheer. Because no one could be that—well, that *nice.* But although Carter really is the perfect kid from the perfect family, people don't realize that behind his smile he carries permanent sorrow. When he was twelve years old, his storybook life had a head-on collision with reality.

Inge Koller had been an athletic girl, a swimmer and a lifeguard. When she grew up she married Jim Carter and became a homemaker in the new American Eden, Southern California. Culver City, where Gary Carter was born, is just west of Los Angeles. Fullerton, where he grew up, is southwest of the City of Angels and just north of Anaheim, a sleepy land of orange groves that Walt Disney was changing forever.

As a boy, Gary Carter adored his mother, and it's clear that the feeling was mutual. "I feel very much that I've gotten a lot of my athletic abilities through her," he says. "My father was my coach and manager in Little League, but Mom encouraged me to go out and play. She never told me to quit playing ball. She loved to see me play. She knew that I was all boy."

Carter smiles when he talks about his mother, and his eyes show that he can see her still. And through him you can almost see her, too: a woman of infallible good cheer, helping her neighbors and her community, doing the right thing in a world that hadn't yet learned to question the fundamental values of decency and family. She wasn't always delighted when young Gary would trudge in dirt-stained, tired, and happy from playing ball until it was too dark to see. But, says Carter, "She always held dinner for me. She realized and accepted that I was always out doing something—playing ball out in the street, shooting baskets back in the alley."

Life sped by like that for eleven idyllic years, and then it fell apart like a cheap suit. Late in 1965, just before Christmas, Inge Carter was told that she had an acute form of leukemia. She was one month shy of her thirty-seventh birthday, Gary was going on twelve, and his brother Gordon (also a fine athlete who would play minor league ball for two seasons) was almost sixteen.

Inge Carter didn't want her family to suffer. "She didn't let us kids know anything," Carter says. "My father didn't let us know, either. We didn't know she was dying. She kept running the house, kept trying to clean and cook, kept trying to be Mom."

The two boys could sense that something was wrong, though. Mom tired easily and couldn't do the things she had always done. But Gary didn't know what leukemia was, and he didn't know what his mother knew—that the disease was eating her alive.

By May 1966, the boys finally realized how desperate things had gotten. "There was one week when we finally knew she was in a lot of pain and hurting," Carter says. His voice grows thick. "She went in the hospital, and I remember saying 'I love you, Mom' and 'Hurry back.' "

He figured she would be back. After all, hadn't she always been there? "As a twelve-year-old, you just don't comprehend those things," Carter says. "I talked to her every day on the telephone when I came home from school."

But on May 21, 1966, there was no phone call. Inge Carter had been released from her pain. "The day she died, everybody went to the hospital but me," Carter says. "I never did see her alive again. The next time I saw her, she was lying in the coffin. It looked like she was asleep."

Although the twelve-year-old boy wished she were sleeping, he knew she wasn't. "And that was devastating," Carter says. "I'll never forget that. It's very difficult for me today to go to a funeral because I visualize her and what she meant to me—the way she raised me. She was a loving, caring, very congenial person, and everybody admired and loved her. The funeral procession was the biggest the little town of Fullerton had ever seen. There must have been a hundred and fifty or two hundred cars." He says this with pride but no joy.

Losing his mother did something inside Gary Carter. For one thing, he threw himself into sports—lost himself in them. It was his way of blocking out the emotional pain. As long as he was on a diamond or a field or a court, he didn't have to face the pain inside. For another, it gave him a reason to succeed: he would do it for her.

"I threw myself into sports to try to forget a little bit," he says. "That was my motivation—to play sports and forget about the death of my Mom, or try to. You can't forget about it totally, but sports was my outlet. I did it every day all year round. That's all I did." And he had a talent for sports. Both of the Carter boys did, but it was Gary who stood out.

"It really became a testament to her," Carter says of his achievements on the playing field. "I felt this was what I wanted to do with my life. I worked at it. I've always tried to go out and play the game as hard as possible every day. I've never taken it for granted. That's why I appreciate it so much, because it's not always going to be there."

Life's not always going to be there. Gary Carter knows that all too well. Late in the 1990 baseball season he reflected on that. He was thirty-six years old, nearly the age his mother was when she died. "To think I would be gone in less than a year, that would be devastating," he says, thinking of what that time must have been like for his mother. "I feel like my life is just beginning. Then to all of a sudden just see it vanish. . . ."

The man who is seldom at a loss for words lets the sentence die in midair. Then he picks it up again in a way that gives insight into his incurable optimism. "It gives me a lot of hope," he says. He's a religious man, and he believes his mother died for a reason, just as he believes he plays baseball for a reason. "My Mom was the one who always taught me the right things and how to handle situations," he says. "I feel like she's always been a part of my life even though she hasn't been here." She didn't live past thirty-seven, but in his mind she is still alive through him. And he is making that life as full as possible. He plays for her.

The joy Carter projects on the playing field—the fierce smile, the high fives, the intensity—belies the fact that it has not been easy for him to play as long and as well as he has. It has, in fact, been for most of his career physically painful. The pain began when he was a senior in high school and he tore ligaments in his right knee while playing football. Before the injury, he says, "I ran a four-six forty." Twenty years and four operations later, he ran just as hard, but not nearly as fast.

It's frightening to think what Carter might have done with two healthy knees. In 1986 he enjoyed a glorious season, tying what was then the Mets record for RBIs with 105, clubbing 24 home runs, scoring 81 runs, and playing 132 games. And then he started to decline, principally because he couldn't push off on his right knee when he was batting. By 1989, the knee was so bad it looked like he was smuggling a softball inside it. He lost all his power at the plate and found it increasingly difficult to throw out base runners. The press said he was simply too old to play, and the fans picked up on it, booing him in Shea Stadium, where once they had stood and chanted *"Ga-ry! Ga-ry! Ga-ry!"* whenever he had won another game for the Mets.

He might have helped himself by admitting that he was badly hurt, but he didn't. It isn't in him to complain about an injury. He learned that from his mother.

"What I learned about courage is that she went through a lot of pain that was a lot more severe than anything I've suffered in my career," he says. "When I play with some of these aches and pains, people say, 'Gee, you're crazy for doing that.' I don't think so, because I know what my mother had to go through. Compared to her, anything that's happened to me is nothing." She didn't complain, and Carter won't either.

The damage to his right knee has been his most debilitating injury, but there've been plenty others. An examination of Gary Carter's body is like a tour through a medical text on sports trauma. On his left foot, his small toe is a misshapen stub of flesh that looks more like a wart with a nail than a toe. "That's Flipper," he says, flicking it with his other foot. "I broke it so many times they finally just took the bone out." He's had two broken thumbs, cracked ribs, torn ligaments and muscles, and taken at least five hundred stitches.

One of Carter's biggest scars is also one of the most telling. It starts at the bridge of his nose, runs an inch or two due north through the furrows of his expressive brow, then does a duck-hook over the right eye, where it dies in the eyebrow. It's significant both because it happened on a ballfield and because he ran into a brick wall to get it.

In 1976 Carter, who had played his first full season for Montreal the previous year, was playing left field in an exhibition game against the Red Sox when Dwight Evans "hit a BB over my head." Carter turned to chase it (remember, this is an exhibition game), and didn't stop until he'd run into one of the few things tougher than he was.

"The ball tipped off the top of my glove," he recalls, "and boom! I went into the brick wall. When I came off the wall, I wiped my forehead, saw the blood, and knew I was hurt."

Hurt isn't the half of it. Carter's forehead was laid open like a side of beef. Some players—maybe most players—would have given up right there. But Carter still had a job to do. "All I could think about was picking up the ball," he says. "I threw it in to our shortstop, Tim Foli, and held Evans to a triple."

He says this last with considerable pride. And he is practically apologetic when he admits that he left the game to get sewn back together. "But I was back on the bench before the end of the game," he adds.

"Yeah," Carter admits years later, "it was just a spring training game." Then he laughs, as if leaving bloodstains on an outfield wall somehow falls under the heading of fun things to do in the pursuit of a game.

But that's the whole point for Gary Carter. It is a game. It is fun. And to get the most fun out of it, you have to play just as hard as you can. For Carter, every day is like a new season. He loves getting dirty and collecting bruises like a schnauzer loves gnawing on mailmen. It's what made him happy when he was trying to forget his loss, and it still brings him the approval he first got from a mother proud of her ballplayer son.

Carter was playing the outfield in 1976 because the Expos—the team that took him fresh from high school in the third round of the 1972 draft—were trying to develop Barry Foote as their catcher. But within a year, Foote was gone and Carter was firmly entrenched in the position he would define for the next dozen years—behind the plate. It is probably one of the few times in baseball history when a man had to be put behind the plate, where he could only be run over and assailed by foul balls, to protect him from himself. "I've always played with reckless abandon," Carter admits.

Reckless abandon? It's more like the joyous abandon of an eight-year-old who, like Peter Pan, has decided never to grow up. "If your leg fell off, you'd probably swear it was only a flesh wound and insist on playing," someone once suggested to him. "You're darn right," Carter replied. "I thoroughly enjoy this game."

A lot of people, he's been told, look at the abuse he's endured in the pursuit of pleasure and figure that he's got more guts than a slaughterhouse floor. "It's more like stupidity," Carter laughs.

It's more like a refusal to quit, no matter what his body and other people tell him. He flat-out enjoys the game, and he won't give it up until it gives him up. The measure of his enjoyment is in his nickname—Kid. They called him that when he came up. It stuck through baseball middle age. And when he was hanging on at the end of his career, the name still fit.

"That's Gary," testifies Bob Sikes, assistant trainer of the New York Mets and for five years an up-close observer of Gary Edmund Carter. "He's a Hall of Famer, and Hall of Famers have something special."

Sikes feels Carter showed that something special during the 1989 season, his last as a Met. Carter had gone into the season needing a fourth surgical procedure on his right knee. Things were floating around inside the joint, making every step painful, and squatting down behind the plate 120 or more times a game didn't make things any better. He refused to sit down, though. Every day he'd come to the park early and climb into the whirlpool bath to get the blood flowing. Then he'd have his knee taped and mount an exercise bike for ten or fifteen minutes. "That was just to loosen the knee up so he could play," Sikes said.

But playing was a mistake. "I should have had the surgery before the season started," Carter admits, "but I thought I could help the team." As for enduring pain without complaint, he says, "I thought that's what you did."

Throughout his career, Carter's critics charged that he was more interested in himself than he was in the team, but those charges never stood up to the evidence he provided. No one interested in his own statistics would have played with injuries that hurt those numbers. And no one interested only in himself would have put himself in harm's way as often as Carter did.

He won games even when he didn't hit. One game in his first season with the Mets stands out. Playing the Pirates at Shea Stadium, the Mets got off to a 4-0 lead in the first inning, but then hardly got a hit for the next three or four hours. The Pirates eventually tied the game and sent it into extra innings. The game ended up going eighteen innings before the Mets won it on an error. But it wouldn't have gotten that far without Carter, who caught every inning. Twice in extra innings, Pittsburgh sent runners home with a chance to go ahead and twice Carter took tremendous hits at the plate but held on to the ball and got the critical outs. Once he dove three rows deep into the stands behind home plate to snare a foul pop and stifle another rally. He didn't have a hit, but he won the game just the same.

Carter also won a lot of games with his hitting. In his very first game as a Met, he had a passed ball, got hit by a pitch, got called out on strikes, allowed a horribly slow runner (a pitcher yet) to steal second, then won the game with a tenth-inning home run. In 1986, his 105 RBIs tied the team record and helped take the Mets to their first postseason appearance since 1973.

In 1980 Frank Cashen, a ruddy little man given to bow ties and putting together winning baseball teams, was hired to resurrect the Mets. The team had been born as a cosmic joke in 1962, became the "Amazing Mets" when they won their first World Championship in 1969, and repeated as league champions in 1973. Then things fell apart. By the time Cashen arrived, the team was nearly as miserable —but nowhere near as much fun—as it had been in 1962.

At first the rebuilding went slowly as Cashen assembled a professional organization and used the team's high draft choices to stock the farm system with outstanding young talent. By 1983 Cashen felt he had enough of a foundation to look for one or two veteran leaders who could take the team back to the top. The first player he obtained, in a 1983 midseason trade with St. Louis, was first baseman Keith Hernandez.

Hernandez immediately turned the Mets into contenders, and in 1984 they finished a strong second to Chicago. Only one more piece was needed to put the team over the top. Cashen found that piece in Montreal, where Carter, once the golden-haired idol of the city, was being blamed for a series of frustrating seasons. Two years earlier, Carter had signed a seven-year contract with the Expos and built a home in Montreal so he could live there year-round—something virtually unheard of for an American ballplayer. During the winter months he toured the province of Quebec, drumming up fans and business for the Expos. He even learned French.

But all his efforts only made him disliked by some of his teammates, who began to whine that Carter was a publicity hound. Their evidence was that when someone asked him for an interview, he granted it; if a camera was pointed his way, he smiled for it; and if someone asked for an autograph, he signed it. In short, he was doing what his mother had taught him—being cheerful and polite.

Fans and the press picked up on the complaints about Carter, and he became a scapegoat in Montreal. Later it was revealed that at least one of the complaining teammates had been using drugs. No wonder the player disliked Carter. The Expos had shown great promise but had not been able to cash in on it, and management decided that an example had to be made. After the 1984 season, they traded Carter to the Mets for four players. Montreal thought it had made a good deal, but the Mets ended up in the World Series.

"Many have said that Gary Carter put us over the top," Frank Cashen said some years later. "And that I would not dispute. He gave us class and dignity." Not to mention home runs and RBIs.

The same qualities that had come to grate on the Expos charmed New York. On the first day of spring training, Carter, a certified superstar, was seen picking up trash off the locker room floor and lugging bags of baseballs out to the practice fields—chores normally assigned to rookies. Before going to camp, Carter studied a Mets press guide so he would know something about his new teammates and be able to greet them by name.

"He just knows the right things to say and do," said Davey Johnson, Mets manager at the time. "He's going to be a good guy to have around. He's so enthusiastic about everything."

After his first practice, Carter signed autographs and talked about how wonderful the Mets were going to be and how happy he was to be with them. "He just never stops," said Mets public relations director Jay Horwitz. "He's just so enthusiastic about anything we do."

"It's the way I am," Carter explained.

The love affair between New York and Carter was mutual. Carter got the big hits, directed a young pitching staff that would become one of the best in the majors, and guarded home plate like a pit bull. It didn't matter what else was happening to his game—if he got the ball with a runner charging in from third, the runner was out. They could hit him with cleats or shoulders or come in a M1-A1 tank—it didn't matter. Once the ball was in his glove, Carter never dropped it.

Despite Carter's presence, in 1985 the Mets fell agonizingly short of a championship. They had gone into St. Louis three games behind the Cardinals with six to play. If they could sweep, they would be tied for first with three games left. They won the first two games, but in the third game—which they had to win—they fell short a run, and it was Carter who made the last out on a fly ball to right. The Carter critics were delighted.

The following spring was payback time both for the Mets and Carter. The team vowed it would not fail again. That year, 1986, they marched through the National League like Sherman through Georgia. By June Whitey Herzog, then the manager of the defending National League champion St. Louis Cardinals, had conceded the divisional title to the Mets. Herzog was more than prescient. The Mets won 108 games and took their division by 21½ games.

The playoffs were a different story. Facing New York was a Houston Astros team led by pitchers Mike Scott and Nolan Ryan. The first game of the series set the tone, as Scott beat Dwight Gooden and the Mets 1-0 on five hits. Throwing a split-fingered fastball that the Mets insisted was aided by illegal scuffing, Scott struck out fourteen. Carter contributed three of those whiffs and added a groundout for an 0-for-4 day.

The Mets won Game Two in Houston, with a fourth-inning double off the wall by Carter driving in the first of five runs Ryan would surrender. But the rest of the day Carter struck out again, flew twice to center, and bounced into a double play.

Going into Game Three, which the Mets would win 6-4 on a Lenny Dykstra home run in the bottom of the ninth, Carter was 1-for-9. After the game, he was 1-for-13, although he reached on an error and scored in the sixth. In Game Four, his miseries continued. Scott was back on the mound and Carter popped out, struck out with a man on second to end the fourth, bounced out to the pitcher, and flew out to center to end the game with a man on second in the bottom of the ninth. The Mets lost 1-0, the series was tied, and Carter's old tormentors in Montreal were pointing to the proof that Carter could not come through in the clutch. Sure, in 1981—the only year the Expos made the playoffs—Carter had hit .429 in the postseason. But in the end the Expos lost horribly. Although Carter had six RBIs and three runs in the first playoff series (the majors had split-season champions that year because of a midseason players' strike), he had no RBIs in the championship series against the Dodgers that the Expos lost after leading two games to one—despite seven hits and four walks in five games. Left unmentioned was the fact that while Carter hit .438 in that series, the rest of the team hit just .169.

After Game Four, Carter could have run and hidden. A lot of players would have. But he gritted his teeth and stood up to an interrogation about his slump. He listened to stories about Mike Schmidt going 0-for-20 once in the postseason, of Gil Hodges hanging up an 0-for-15, of Tony Perez rendered hitless. He talked about bearing down and keeping his confidence.

It rained the next day, giving Carter more time to think about his sins. The following day, October 14, 1986, the series resumed under leaden skies with Ryan taking on Gooden at Shea Stadium. Things were no better for Carter. He bounced out to Ryan in the first and flew out to right in the fifth. The Astros had scored in the top of the fifth, and in the bottom of the inning Darryl Strawberry had tied it with a home run, the first Met hit off Ryan. They got another hit in the seventh but could do nothing with it. Carter popped up to short in that inning. When the game went into overtime, Carter got up again to lead off the tenth and grounded to third. He was now 1-for-21.

But the Astros couldn't push a run across against Gooden, either, despite nine hits in ten innings. And so the game ground on through ten innings, then eleven, and finally twelve.

After reliever Jesse Orosco put the Astros down in the top of the twelfth, the Mets brought the top of the order out against Charlie Kerfeld, who had taken over from Ryan in the tenth. Kerfeld was a rookie, but he was football big—six-foot-six and a reported 235 pounds (although he looked more like 250, give or take a cupcake). He was a righthander who acted like a lefty, and his hometown was someplace called Knob Noster, Missouri. He threw hard. Very hard.

Kerfeld had breezed through the tenth and eleventh innings on three strikeouts and three ground balls. No one had come close to a hit. He started the twelfth the same way, getting Lenny Dykstra on a grounder to first. Finally Wally Backman, hitting second, nicked him for a single to left. Kerfeld compounded his problem by throwing wildly to first on a pickoff and allowing Backman to go to second.

With first base open and the dangerous Keith Hernandez up, the Astros elected to intentionally walk Hernandez to get to Carter, who was standing in the on-deck circle with a bat in his hand and a 1-for-21 monkey on his back.

As Carter stepped in, the crowd began chanting—pleading, really—*Ga-ry! Ga-ry! Ga-ry!*, Carter dug in and stared at Kerfeld, forcing himself to forget his failures and concentrate on the job at hand. All season long he had risen to the big moment, leading the league in game-winning RBIs. But could he do it now in the most pressure-packed situation he had ever faced?

Despite their barroom bravado, most fans haven't the foggiest idea what it takes to walk to the plate in the bottom of the twelfth inning with a divisional title at stake, tens of thousands of fans imploring you to be a hero, and some mountainous Baby Huey character from Knob Noster, Missouri, throwing balls at you that hiss like bullets and look like aspirin tablets. Factor in a horrific slump, and most mortals would be looking imploringly back at the dugout, hoping that a pinch hitter will be sent out.

Not the Kid. Carter wanted to be at the plate. He wanted redemption the way a shark wants bleeding meat. "I'm not an oh-for-forty hitter," he would explain afterward. Maybe not, but there was no evidence to suggest he wasn't about to become a 1-for-22 hitter, either.

Kerfeld's first three pitches whistled past outside the strike zone. Then he poured in a strike that Carter took. He threw another fastball strike on 3-1—a hitter's pitch—but Carter could only foul it off for strike two. Another foul ball. And then yet another, and still another foul ball.

By now the fans were apoplectic. Once again Carter dug in. Backman danced off second. Kerfeld glared down from his height for the sign. He poured another BB through the strike zone.

Carter swung hard and level, and this time he hit the ball square. It shot up the middle, past Kerfeld, and into center field. As Backman scampered around third and headed for home with the winning run, Carter ran for first with both arms thrust straight up. When he got there, he was buried by his happy teammates, as the Astros retreated to their clubhouse.

Billy Doran, the Astros second baseman, had felt a premonition about what would happen. While Kerfeld was walking Hernandez to get to Carter, Doran was chatting with Backman on second base. "I hate to see Gary up with a man on second," Doran had said. "He never quits."

Carter himself said much the same thing. "The most important thing," he explained to the same crowd who two days earlier had grilled him about his slump, "is to keep your head up and maintain your confidence."

The series went to Houston, and the Mets closed it out in Game Six in what was perhaps the best playoff game ever played. Behind

3-0 to Bob Knepper, the Mets tied the game with three runs in the ninth. They went ahead 4-3 in the fourteenth, but the Astros tied it in the bottom of the inning. The Mets finally won it in the sixteenth after scoring three runs and giving up two. Carter wasn't the hitting hero in that game, although he walked to extend the ninth-inning rally and singled twice. But he helped stifle the Astros' three-run first-inning rally by throwing out a would-be base stealer and threw out another in the twelfth. And he caught every inning.

As the Mets celebrated their return to the World Series after a thirteen-year absence by dousing one another in cheap champagne, Carter roamed the locker room, seeking out the other team leaders. He found Keith Hernandez, wrapped him in a bear hug, and kissed him. He did the same to Darryl Strawberry.

"We did it," he kept saying. "We did it."

There was no doubt then that winning was what mattered most to Carter. He felt an obligation to his team that took precedence over his own health. This was something else he had learned in the wake of his mother's death, and this lesson came from his father.

"For four and a half years after my mother died, my father was there for us," Carter says. "He didn't date. He didn't go out. He came home promptly after work to cook dinner. He got up early to make breakfast. He devoted his life to being both Mom and Dad for my brother and me. He could have gone out and dated. He had no reason to always be home other than for us kids. But he wanted me to get into baseball."

So he did what he could to help make that goal come true. Jim Carter waited until Gary was in his last year of high school before he took up his own life and remarried. Gary Carter never forgot that sense of priorities—first the team, then himself.

If the Houston–New York playoffs had been spectacular, the World Series between the Mets and the Red Sox was nothing less than Homeric. Giddy from their heroics against Houston, the Mets sleepwalked through the first two games of the Series in New York and went to Boston trailing two games to none.

Earlier in the season, the Mets had played an exhibition game in Boston. Carter, a dead-pull hitter whose power was to left field, took his first look at Fenway Park's legendary Green Monster left-field wall and drooled. During batting practice, the first fly ball he hit—a routine fly—plopped comfortably in the netting atop the wall, and Carter turned around and grinned like a toddler who has just discovered candy. He had won a home-run hitting contest earlier that day with five dingers in ten tries. During the exhibition game, he doubled off the wall.

But this was the World Series, and one thing on which hitters agree is that trying to go for that wall will mess you up. In the first inning of Game Three, Carter came up with two men on and one run in, and he promptly doubled off the wall to drive them both in. He singled in another run in the ninth, and the Mets won easily.

The next night Carter hit two balls over the wall, drove in three more runs, and—as if to prove that he wasn't thinking about the Green Monster—added a double to right field. The Mets won again, and the Series was tied two games apiece.

In Game Five the Red Sox struck back, hammering Dwight Gooden for nine hits and four runs in four-plus innings. The stage was set for Game Six back at Shea Stadium.

There's not much that hasn't been said about Game Six of the 1986 Series. The Red Sox sent six men to the plate in the first and six more in the second and came away with a single run each time. The Mets tied it in the fifth, and the Red Sox went ahead again by a single run in the seventh. They would have had more runs, but a spectacular throw from left field by Mookie Wilson and Carter's refusal to yield at home plate nailed Jim Rice with what would have been the Sox' fourth run of the game. In the eighth inning, the Mets, trailing by a run, got pinch hitter Lee Mazzilli around to third on his single, a sacrifice bunt which turned into a fielder's choice, and another sacrifice bunt. With runners on second and third, one out, and Keith Hernandez coming up, the Red Sox elected to do what the Astros had done. They walked Hernandez intentionally to have right-handed reliever Calvin Schiraldi pitch to right-handed Carter.

Carter came through again. Ignoring the temptation to go for the fence, he lifted a sacrifice fly to tie the game.

The tie held until the tenth inning, when Dave Henderson's home run, Wade Boggs's double, and Marty Barrett's two-out single put the Red Sox up by two, 5-3. The Sox were only three outs away from winning their first World Series since 1918, the year before Harry Frazee had cursed the team by selling Babe Ruth to the Yankees. Schiraldi got the first two outs quickly—fly balls to right by Backman and Hernandez. Only Gary Carter, the man who wasn't good enough for Montreal, stood between the Red Sox and victory.

Carter lined a single to left center. Kevin Mitchell followed with another single to center. Ray Knight came up next and hit yet another single to center, scoring Carter and sending Mitchell to third.

Shea Stadium was rattling with noise when the Red Sox called Bob Stanley out of the bullpen to face Mookie Wilson. Stanley worked the count to 2-2 on Wilson. He threw two more pitches, and Wilson barely fouled both off to stay alive. Then, trying to come inside, Stanley uncorked a wild pitch that allowed Mitchell to come in with the tying run and sent Knight to second. The crowd was in a frenzy.

Wilson fouled off two more pitches from Stanley before finally connecting. He didn't connect very well, though, hitting a ground ball that hugged the dirt down the first baseline straight at Bill Buckner, who stooped on gimpy legs and waited for the ball to settle in his glove. As everyone knows, the ball scooted under his glove. Knight came around third and stomped on home, the Mets won the game, and the Red Sox rolled over and died two days later in Game Seven.

It was chaos on the field and in the Mets' clubhouse after the miracle of Game Six. Keith Hernandez slumped in front of his locker with a goofy smile on his face, a six-pack at his feet, and a cigarette in his hand, telling how he had come back to the clubhouse after making the second out in the ninth inning and popped open a beer while watching what he thought would be the Mets' requiem on TV. Mitchell was telling how when he played with Schiraldi in the Mets' farm system, Schiraldi had bragged how, if they ever faced each other in a game, Schiraldi would get him out with a slider. So Mitchell looked for a slider, got it, and stroked his clutch single. Knight was talking about his hit and Wilson was recounting how he got out of the way of the wild pitch that scored the tying run.

And Carter?

Carter and several of his teammates had been hired by local newspapers (in Carter's case, the *Record,* of Bergen County, New Jersey) to write a daily World Series diary. One player, writing for the *Daily News,* had kissed off his column one day in Boston, leaving the paper in the lurch. Others gave perfunctory attention to their journalistic duties, which consisted of telling reporters what they wanted to have put into story form. But Carter, who was being paid relative peanuts for his work, took it seriously. It was, after all, a commitment. So immediately after Game Six, he alone delayed joining the celebration so that he could meet with the reporter assigned to him and do his job. Only a ballplayer dedicated enough to learn French would show that much responsibility. The difference between Montreal and New York, though, was that no one in New York criticized Carter for being a good guy.

His attitude and his play made him a hero of the highest order for the Mets. His nine RBIs in the World Series tied him with Yogi Berra for the most by a catcher in the Fall Classic. In the thirteen combined games of the playoffs and the Series, he had ninety-nine putouts and six assists and did not commit a single error. After the season, *The Sporting News* named him its National League catcher of the year for the sixth time. He held the National League records for most years leading the league in games caught, putouts, and chances accepted.

But all the games he had caught were taking their toll. In 1987, he slipped to 20 home runs and 83 RBIs. In 1988, when the Mets won their division again, he had only 11 home runs and 46 RBIs, and his days as a clean-up hitter were long gone. In the playoffs against the Dodgers, he managed only six hits as the Mets lost in seven games. Yet he still came up with 4 RBIs, including the game-winner in Game One.

His right knee was hurting, but he wouldn't give in. In 1989 he came to training camp bursting with confidence. "Last year was a very disappointing year," he admitted. "Nobody has higher standards for myself than I do, but all I can do is keep working hard. I can still play the game. I'm not going to fret or worry about things. I'm going out to have fun."

The 1989 season turned out to be anything but fun. By late May it was clear that Carter wasn't his former self. He was not only not hitting his weight, he was barely hitting Mary Lou Retton's weight. As he floundered, the boos grew louder, and what were once whispers about his faded abilities were now amplified speeches on New York's sports talk shows. Why? Because he was trying to play and win on a knee that most people would have trouble walking on.

Although Carter understood that people will always boo, it hurt just the same. "People have the right to cheer, boo, or whatever," he says. "But instead of giving me credit for trying, people were saying I was washed up and didn't belong out there. I was disappointed and kind of upset with the way that was handled. I felt I was trying to be part of the club, trying to help them win. In a pennant race, I was out there to prove that you can try to play through pain."

That much he proved. You could try. And you could suffer. And you could refuse to give in.

Just as they had in Montreal, his teammates were saying that Carter was no longer a leader in the clubhouse. Such treatment by teammates and fans have made other players sullen, but Carter kept on hustling, kept on being a good guy, kept on smiling. It was increasingly clear that the only thing he couldn't do was play.

On May 29, Carter finally had his knee operated on. After cleaning out all the garbage that had accumulated since his last surgery 3 1/2 years earlier, the doctors told him it would take a year for the knee to regain full strength. No good, Carter told them. He still had work to do.

He came back on July 27, ten months earlier than prescribed. "I think I can help a team, hopefully this team, for a few more years," he said. "As far as rushing back, I didn't have much of a choice. There are just two months left in the season. Time was running out."

Time was indeed running out for him. In fact, it had probably already run out, at least in New York. His contract would expire at the end of the year, and Frank Cashen did not sound as if Carter fit into the team's plans for the nineties.

At first he sat on the bench while he worked to get the knee in some kind of shape to play. When he did get to hit, his efforts were puny, almost pitiful, and the fans booed even louder.

Finally, on August 9, manager Davey Johnson started him behind the plate. Just in case things didn't go well, Johnson started him on the road, in Philadelphia. Carter responded by going 4-for-4.

The next night, he pinch hit in each game of a doubleheader against St. Louis, driving in three runs with a single and a sacrifice fly. The next day he started again and had two more hits.

The Kid was playing again and loving it. During his long stint on the disabled list, he had done some thinking and come away with a new attitude. He realized that he no longer had any pressure to bear. "What do I have to prove?" he asked himself. "They can't take away what I've done."

But why did he come back so soon?

"Why do people climb Mount Everest? Why do people go to the moon? I don't want to give up just because I've had some adversity." He said it so cheerfully you'd think his injury had been a hangnail.

Davey Johnson was delighted at Carter's initial success. It was as if the Carter he had greeted at spring training in 1985 had returned. "One thing about managing and having any player that played for you and gave it everything he had—the memory you have is what he did for you in his time," Johnson said. "Nobody could have done more for this club than Gary did when he came over here."

So the manager wasn't surprised. "You gotta know Gary," Johnson said. "Me sitting him down or people writing him off, Gary's not going to believe that. Anyone would be a fool to ever write Gary off if you knew his heart."

Having said that, the Mets then wrote Carter off. He did not maintain the pace he had set in his first games back. Soon he wasn't playing at all as the Mets groomed Mackey Sasser and Barry Lyons as his successors. In Cashen's mind, both Gary Carter and Keith Hernandez (who was also in his last contract year) had been known by Mets fans as great ballplayers, and they could not exist in New York as less than great. "Whenever they would step onto the field, people would see them as the great players they were," Cashen said. "When they didn't perform to that level, they would be booed."

Carter finished the year hitting .183. He pinch hit in his last game at Shea Stadium and singled. The Mets were out of the race, and the crowd was small. What few fans there were, though, cheered heartily. They knew an era had ended.

Carter went home and cried. Then he went with the team on the season's last road trip. When the season ended a week later, Cashen made it official, and Carter and Hernandez had a final press conference together. Accepting his fate, Carter determined that there was a pot of gold over the next hill. "I'm not going to break down and cry now because it was something that was expected," he said. "I had a great five years here. I came with a mission to nurture a young pitching staff, and that was accomplished, and to win a world championship, and we accomplished that. In my time here, we had three seconds, two firsts, and one world championship. I'm very proud of that. But I feel when one door is closed, another one is going to open."

A lot of people groaned inwardly when they heard Carter say that. Didn't the guy know when it was time to quit?

Frankly, Carter said, no. "I guess they'll have to tear the uniform off me," he once said. "I've played this game of baseball since I was five. That's more than thirty years. That's almost my whole life. To all of a sudden say that's it and not put the uniform on anymore, that's a tough thing to deal with. My feeling is to play the game as much and as long as I can. I haven't gotten the Kid out of me yet. It's still there."

If the Mets didn't want him, Carter was sure that someone else would. And sure enough, the San Francisco Giants, coming off a trip to the World Series in 1989, invited him to training camp for 1990. But he wasn't guaranteed a job. He would have to earn it.

That was no problem in Carter's mind. He knew, even if no one else did, that he could still play. "I've had a good career," he admitted as he worked out in camp. "I've had the opportunity to make it into the Hall of Fame. I'd just like the opportunity to end my career on a high note. Every athlete would like to have that happen. I don't want it to finish the way it did last season. My only focus right now is my tunnel vision—to go straight forward and see what happens."

His contract guaranteed him $250,000. Whatever else he earned depended on whether he made the club and then on how many games he played. He made the club, and by the end of the year he had appeared in 92 games, quadrupling his base pay.

His role with the Giants was, for the first time in his career, to be a platoon catcher. Although he freely admitted he wanted to play every game, he threw himself into his new role with his customary enthusiasm.

On May 9 he returned to Shea Stadium for the first time since being released the October before. When Giants manager Roger Craig sent him out to give the lineup card to the umpires, the New York fans who had so recently booed him cheered warmly. When he came up for his first at-bat, they gave him a standing ovation.

That welcome helped salve the wounds from 1989 that were still not fully healed. "It was very tough," Carter told reporters of his last year as a Met. "I'd like to try to forget about it altogether. Here I was injured, and I was criticized for being injured. All I did was try to play and help the ballclub."

A week later the Mets traveled to Candlestick Park, and Carter was given another start. He responded by throwing out Howard Johnson trying to steal third in the tenth inning of a tie game. Then in the bottom of the inning, he hit a double that drove in the winning run. Giants' left fielder Kevin Mitchell, with whom Carter had played on the Mets, later said that he'd never seen Carter so pumped up over a hit.

In San Francisco, Carter was allowed to be a platoon catcher who hit .254 with 9 home runs and 27 RBIs. In some ways Carter, although still wearing his just-happy-to-be-here smile, seemed comfortable in that role. Late in the 1990 season, however, he was talking about playing at least another year, maybe even more. He had become more philosophical about the game he played and why he had insisted all his life on playing it no matter how he felt.

"It might be courage," he says when the word is suggested to him, but he is reluctant to ascribe that quality to himself. He sees himself more as a throwback to an earlier era, when playing the game—not how much money you made—was the important thing. "I consider myself, in baseball terms, a gamer," he says. "That means you go out there at all costs. If you're hurt or something's ailing you, you go out there every day anyway. There's a mutual respect among players and you say, 'That guy's a gamer. Look at him. He's all banged up and all and still he goes out and plays.' Some guys, if they've got a little hangnail, they may not play. They have to be one hundred percent to go out there. If I had sat out and waited until I was one hundred percent before I played, I would have missed half my career."

Carter almost enjoys talking about his injuries, but he doesn't consider himself extraordinary. "That's just the way it is with gamers," he says. "That's the way we are. We're guys who go out and play the game the way it's supposed to be played. With these big contracts, you have guys who want to be careful. There's a lot of money in this game. Some players may try to protect themselves a little bit more so that they can prolong their careers."

While Carter was with the Mets, making more than $2 million a year, he was one of the highest paid players in the game. If anyone had reason to protect himself, it was him. But instead he exposed himself—both to further injury and to criticism.

That's what a lot of people fail to understand about Gary Carter and other players like him. If their performance falls off, there's a reason. "That's why I was disappointed and kind of upset with the way it was all handled in New York," he says. "I was just trying to be part of the club, to help them. I should have had surgery in March," he says of his 1989 knee problems. "So I think some of the writers who wrote about me and my abilities were a little unjust. I think if somebody would have looked at it they would have seen that this guy was just trying to help. He was trying to go out and do the job and, look at him, he's on one leg."

The Giants had told him that they would probably only need him for one season. By the time it ended, he was only 30 hits and 21 runs shy of becoming only the fourth catcher in history to have 2,000 hits, 1,000 RBIs, 1,000 runs, and 300 home runs. (The other three are Yogi Berra, Johnny Bench, and Carlton Fisk.)

At this point, the money isn't important. All that's left is the game and the goal of joining those illustrious names. He's already the National League career leader in games, chances accepted, and putouts by a catcher.

When the Dodgers offered Carter a shot at their team in 1991, he jumped at the opportunity. "The goals are really academic," he says. "Whatever I achieve will help the ballclub. If I do achieve those milestones, it will be icing on the cake."

Meanwhile, he continues to raise money for the Leukemia Society of America, for which is he national sports chairman. In 1989 he was the society's volunteer of the year. For years he has run an annual golf tournament to benefit the charity and has raised more than $1.5 million for leukemia research. Some of that money and research went toward helping a teammate's child, and Carter is as proud of that fact as he is of any of his baseball records. When Gary Carter was twelve, he couldn't do anything to save his mother, but now he may be able to help save someone else's.

And so he plays on, this man called Kid. "I was blessed by the Lord with this ability and I've never taken it for granted," he says. "I'm very grateful to play. That's why I appreciate it so much, because it's not always going to be there. I'm almost thirty-seven years old, and I'm still playing a kid's game. I love it."

No wonder Tommy Lasorda, Dodger manager and Carter's equal in goodwill, wanted Carter around in 1991. You can't put a price on enthusiasm, and you can't underestimate desire. Gary Carter is proof of that.

Once, when things were at their worst, he said, "There's one thing I will never do. That's lose my enthusiasm and curl up and die."

It's the lesson he learned from his mother.

Playing Tall

I thank God every day that I stuck it out.

It is the eve of the start of the 1988 Olympic basketball tournament in Seoul, South Korea, and Anne Donovan is talking about her most cherished desires. There's an Olympic gold medal, of course, but there is something else just as dear to her, something most people wouldn't think that big a deal.

"All I really want is my own address labels," she says.

Having address labels would mean having an address, a home. Donovan has done a lot of things in her life. She made a good living for five years playing basketball in Japan. She won a gold medal in the 1984 Los Angeles Olympics. In 1986 she was on the first U.S. women's team to beat the Soviet Union in international competition in 29 years. She has won a world championship, an intercollegiate championship, and an armload of high school championships. In the nearly eleven years since she first went overseas as part of a U.S. junior team, she's logged more than a million miles of air travel and spent more time in locker rooms than some people spend in their living rooms. Now, in September of 1988, just six weeks shy of her twenty-seventh birthday, the one question she can't answer is one of the first asked in every interview: "Where do you live?"

"I have no permanent address," she has to say. "I don't even have a state." Most of the time, she hardly knows what country she's in.

She isn't complaining, and she even laughs at her situation, but that doesn't make it less poignant. She is nearing the end of a career in which she has been one of the greatest women basketball players in the world. If she had been born male, she'd have had a steady job and a year-round address in one of the best sections of a city that is home to an NBA team. But because she is a woman in a country that offers little opportunity for women athletes to compete after college, she became a basketball vagabond.

She enjoyed it, too—maybe not every minute, but most of it. Basketball had taken her places she never imagined she would visit. It had gained her—if not fortune—at least a tidy bank account. It had brought her fame.

Anne Donovan never really planned to play basketball. She started playing because it was something to do, and she became valuable early in life because she was tall—very tall. But she became great because she wouldn't settle for being ordinary.

Anne Donovan was born on November 1, 1961, in Ridgewood, New Jersey. She was the youngest of eight children and it wasn't as if her height came as a surprise. Her father was six feet six inches tall, her mother five feet ten, and not a child in the family stopped growing at less than six feet.

If Donovan had grown up fifteen years earlier, her childhood would certainly have been a trial, because being tall and female was thought to have been of no redeeming social value. But in 1972, when she was eleven, Title IX—the federal law requiring equal opportunities for women in educational institutions receiving federal aid—was adopted. Across America women's sports went varsity, and college scholarships for talented women athletes became available.

So being tall was at least a ticket to an education. And Anne had the support of her older sisters in coping with her height. "I can't imagine being an only child and having to go through that," she says. "Being part of a big family helped."

Even so, growing up was difficult. She was six feet tall in elementary school and six feet six by her sophomore year in high school. Most children want to be the same as everyone else, or at least not different enough to stand out in a crowd, and Donovan stood out in every crowd. She was one of a kind at an age when everyone was trying to be all of a kind.

She was called, among other things, geek, gawk, and tiny. Her "nice" nickname was Bean—short for Bean Pole. At every rite of childhood, from first communion to high school graduation, she brought up the back of the line—the tallest kid in the class.

She never could understand why people were so insensitive. "I remember being young enough to still go trick-or-treating, and people would tell me I was too old for that. 'You're not a little girl,' they said. I remember people calling me 'sir' or 'young man.' People didn't look at me. They looked at my size.

"In school it was not a problem, but outside of school, it was. And it was the adults who made the comments. You expect it from kids, but when an adult makes a comment, it totally blows your head away. 'How's the weather up there?'—I must have heard that a million times. Even now, on a bad day, I still want to snap back at people who are rude. People don't think. They stop me in malls and say, 'Can I ask you a question?' I just say, 'I'm six eight.' "

Anne was a shy girl, and living with the accident of being tall made her even more so. She could open up with her family and friends, but in a group of strangers she pulled inside herself. The combination of her shyness and her height pretty much eliminated a social life. "Boys didn't play a part of my life until I got out of high school," she says.

"It had to be very difficult for her," says her mother, Ann Matthews. "I'm amazed at the way she handled it. She never complained." And she never grew resentful, she never got mean.

That was because she looked at her size not as a curse but as a gift. "I never resented being tall," she says. "I grew up really believing it was a gift from my father." She was only five when her father died, so the gift was all the more precious. But the question at first was, to what purpose was this gift?

She began to find out in the fifth grade when she joined a CYO basketball program. She wasn't the most coordinated player on the floor, but her height made her successful. Even so, basketball was just something to do. She was not an aggressive child, and she was reluctant to try new things. (As a star in high school, for example, she resisted her coach's urging that she develop a hook shot.)

But when she was in the seventh grade she won a most valuable player award in a tournament. "That was what really got her going," says her mother.

It made her realize that maybe this was something at which she could excel, something for which her uncommon size was a precious gift.

Because she was taller than everyone else, the game was easy for her, and, like many other gifted athletes, she had trouble making herself work to get better. "She wasn't that hard a worker," her mother admits. So it was a long time before anyone knew whether she had the desire, the *will,* to win—the mark of a champion—or if she would become just another promising player who would go through life with the label *Potential* stuck to her back.

When Anne joined the Paramus Catholic Paladins in 1977, the girls still wore skirts on the court. She became a starter—and a star—as a sophomore. Her sister Mary was a senior on the team, and together they became the "Twin Towers of Paramus," with Anne already six feet six and Mary six feet four. Their coach was Rose Battaglia, one of the country's finest high school coaches.

From the very start, Battaglia, who had been coaching Donovan since seventh grade, urged Anne to greater achievement. She seldom talked about what Donovan had done, but rather about what she could yet do. Early in 1977, Battaglia told Mike Farber of *The Record* (Bergen County) that Anne and Mary "are both nice kids and sometimes just aren't as ferocious as they can be. Both are so tall that neither has had to jump for rebounds. They can get away with it at this level, but not further on. And both are capable of playing big-time college basketball."

That was the challenge from the beginning, and Battaglia never let up. Some coaches might have been happy to let such players rake in the championships. But Battaglia always looked to the future for her players. By the end of that season Mary was on her way to Penn State on a basketball scholarship, and Anne was on her way to Taiwan to play in a tournament with the U.S. Junior National Team. Not yet a junior, she made her first appearance on *Parade* magazine's annual high school All-American list.

The trip to Taiwan opened Donovan's eyes. "I wasn't aggressive enough when the trials started," she says. "I got pushed and shoved all over. But then I learned I had to give some back to survive. The third day there, I had some girl around five nine covering me. I took a shot, and before I came down she had pushed me off the court. That's when I really got mad and started playing more aggressively. I would have scratched her eyes out if I had to."

Donovan made the team, but she didn't play much, and the United States finished sixth out of eight teams in the tournament. "I was a pipsqueak," she remembers. "But it gave me a taste for what was out there. It convinced me that basketball was number one to me. I quit volleyball and high jumping. I quit playing the piano. All my goals now related to basketball."

In her junior season of high school ball, she started using the weight room, even though she admitted she didn't look forward to her sessions with the heavy metal. Still, she found herself playing to the level of the competition. Halfway through the season she said, "I really haven't played as aggressively as I did last summer. I know I should, but sometimes I just can't make myself."

"She's very kindhearted," Donovan's mother says, explaining why it was always difficult for her daughter to be fierce on a basketball court.

After her junior year, she went to the Colorado Sports Festival—the annual event has since become the U.S. Olympic Festival—and led the East squad to a gold medal.

What set Donovan apart was an understanding of herself and a desire to overcome her shortcomings. As a senior at Paramus Catholic, she once scored 31 points and had 16 rebounds in a game, but afterward she admitted that she hadn't played well.

By then she knew she wanted to make the 1980 Olympic Team. Battaglia nourished that ambition while at the same time letting Donovan know just how far she had to go to realize it. "She gets very little sympathy from me," Battaglia said at the time. "I want to prepare her for the future. College coaches will be even more demanding. Anne can be a success just by standing around on the floor because of her size. It's tough to convince her she she'll need to do more to succeed at the college level. As her competition becomes greater, I'm sure she'll respond to it.

"If she wants to, she can become great. She can become the women's equivalent of Bill Russell, Wilt Chamberlain, or Kareem Abdul-Jabbar, but she must also have their motivation. With that, there's no stopping her."

In her senior year of high school, there was no stopping her. She scored 58 points in one game and 61 in another. She shattered the New Jersey high school girls' scoring record with 2,582 points. She averaged 38 points a game and led the Paladins to 43 straight victories and a third straight state championship.

At the same time, she was being pursued by no fewer than two hundred colleges around the country, ranging from complete unknowns to Old Dominion, the reigning national powerhouse whose team was anchored by the great guard, Nancy Lieberman. Donovan wasn't offered cars or money, as male recruits sometimes were, but when she went to visit the campus of the University of Kentucky, where basketball is a religion, she was offered something even better. Joe B. Hall, the men's basketball coach at Kentucky, met with her personally to tell her that if she enrolled there, she could practice with the men's team almost anytime she wanted. The unprecedented offer only underlined how desperately she was wanted. No woman basketball player had ever been more heavily recruited.

Donovan took it all in stride, not even minding the phone calls that kept her family jumping every evening. "It's a good feeling," she said. "It's kind of nice to know that so many people want you."

The only problem she had was telling schools she wasn't interested. She was too kindhearted to say no. All the attention flattered her rather than giving her a swollen head. "These people are willing to spend a lot of money on my education," she said at the time. "It makes me feel kind of special." She never did turn the coin over and look at how much money the schools could make off her. It wasn't in her nature. So Battaglia handled the chore of saying no while Donovan decided to whom she would say yes.

In May, after the high school season was over, Donovan settled on Old Dominion in Norfolk, Virginia, the defending national champions. When she signed, her new coach, Marianne Stanley, said, "This is the first time I've felt speechless, totally excited."

That summer she went from a high school All-Star game in the Catskills to an AAU tournament in Kansas, to the Colorado Sports Festival, and to California for the Junior Pan American Games tryouts and tournament. Then she went off to college to team with Lieberman and All-American center Inge Nissen—who would soon move to forward to make room for Donovan—and try for another national championship.

Donovan didn't think she'd play much her freshman year, but others knew better. In Old Dominion's first game of the season (against Virginia Union), Donovan started and played 31 minutes. In that time she hit 12 of 17 shots and seven free throws for 31 points, hauled in 18 rebounds and blocked four shots.

"That was a shock," she said of her play.

To her maybe, but not to others who knew what she could do if she really wanted to. And in college, she showed that she wanted to.

"I've become a lot more aggressive," she said then, "but not anywhere near what I'll need in college. Fortunately, my high school coach was the best. Miss Battaglia would keep drilling it into me, telling me I wasn't living up to my potential."

By the end of the season, she was Old Dominion's leading scorer, shot blocker, and rebounder—with averages of 17.4 points and 13 boards, and a total of 297 blocks. She shot 63.8 percent from the field. In the tournament at the end of the year, she was even better. In a second-round game against Brigham Young, she scored 30, took down 19 rebounds, and blocked eight shots.

Old Dominion won the championship that year and also lost its entire starting team except for Donovan. If there was a sour note in her college years, it was that the team never won another championship. In her senior year, they lost in the Final Four to Old Dominion's perennial nemesis, Louisiana Tech.

In high school Anne Donovan was six feet six inches tall. At Old Dominion she grew to six eight. She also grew into the nation's leading spokeswoman for college basketball. The once-shy schoolgirl was now a confident woman who could step up to a lectern and address a roomful of executives as easily as she could sink a turnaround jumper.

The biggest disappointment of her collegiate career was President Jimmy Carter's decision to boycott the 1980 Moscow Olympics. "I was infuriated," Donovan says. "There's no place for politics in athletics. It should be just true competitors."

But Carter thought differently. The Soviet Union had invaded Afghanistan, and Carter's response was the boycott. Hundreds of athletes saw their only shot at Olympic glory evaporate. Donovan wanted to play, but she was only a sophomore in 1980, and she knew she'd have another shot at the Olympics in 1984. Some of her teammates would not be so fortunate.

"I felt incredibly sad," she says. "Not for myself but for some of the older players like Carol Blazejowski. I was shocked that I had made the team, and I knew that with a lot more hard work and experience I could be back in 1984. Every woman's dream was the Olympics. I couldn't imagine going through a career without it."

The American women had won a silver medal in 1976, finishing behind the Soviets. They believed they could win the gold in 1980, but with the boycott a generation of players lost the chance to try to do that.

For women, playing for the Olympic gold medal was everything; men could look forward to playing in the pros. For a brief time women could share that ambition, but the first women's professional league, the Women's Basketball League, died in 1982 after a brief and ignominious run.

When Donovan graduated in 1983, there was another alternative—foreign leagues. Although the U.S. market would not support women's professional basketball, Europe and Japan would.

After playing her usual international schedule with the U.S. National Team in the summer of 1983, Donovan received an offer to play in Japan for the Schanson Cosmetics Company in the city of Shizuoka, a provincial capital about two hours southwest of Tokyo. She had also received offers to go to Europe, but she chose Japan because, she said, "It's not very well organized in Europe. Forty percent of the women who play in Europe have problems, especially in getting their money."

Donovan was not prepared for what awaited her in Japan. Her very arrival was a sensation. "They had never seen a woman that tall," she recalls. "The first day I got there, my picture was on the front page of the paper. They were amazed."

Donovan had traveled to Japan before signing a contract, but her hosts kept her clear of the masses, and everyone she met was polite.

Her coach was polite, too: when she watched a practice of the team she would play for, he was on his best behavior. In other words, she explains, "He didn't hit anybody. Some of the girls on the team had bruises, but I didn't know how they got them."

When she returned to join the team, she saw a different side of the Japanese people. Ironically, Japanese society, which is built on social conventions of correct behavior and politeness, doesn't extend its rules to *gaijin*—foreigners. With *gaijin,* anything goes.

"Discretion is not a part of their vocabulary," Donovan says. She can laugh now, but at the time it wasn't funny. "It didn't faze them to walk up to me, press themselves against my chest, and see how tall I was." On the street, people poked her and pulled at her clothing as if to see if she were real.

She knew that physical abuse was part of the training regimen for women's sports in Japan and other Oriental countries, so she had had the foresight to have put in her contract a clause that prohibited the coach from hitting her. She also believed she had an agreement that the coach wouldn't hit her teammates. And at first he didn't. But old habits die hard, and it wasn't long before he resorted to his time-tested motivational techniques.

"He was unbelievable," she says. "He would hit them in the stomach, in the face. He would punch them, kick them, slap them—he did it all. They had told me it wasn't going to happen, but it did. The first time it happened in practice, I was so upset I just went through the motions the rest of the practice."

The woman he had hit was Donovan's best friend on the team. In the dormitory after practice, the woman came to Donovan's room and told Anne that she deserved to be hit because she had thrown the ball away. Donovan realized then that she wasn't going to be able to change an entire society overnight. But she made it clear to the coach that she could not be mentally strong and give her best if everyone around her was getting beaten for making mistakes. Once she got so furious with the coach that she purposely provoked him—daring him to hit her. He wanted nothing more than to oblige her, but he didn't. Gradually, not by making demands, but by her quiet strength and dignity, she got him to stop assaulting his players. "I'm real happy to say that by the time I left after five years, he wasn't doing it anymore."

The routine of practice was unchanging and unrelenting: the team left its dormitory at 7:30 A.M., practiced shooting for two or three hours, then returned to the dorm for lunch. After lunch the first day, the other women rolled out their futon mats and went to sleep. "I said, 'No way am I taking a nap,' " Donovan recalls, and she went out for a walk before the afternoon session.

The second practice of the day was the killer. For four to six hours, the players ran constantly until they were beyond exhaustion. By the second day in Japan, Donovan was taking an afternoon nap with everyone else.

For the Japanese players, there was no break. Although the season lasted six months, their training was year-round. They got one week off every year to go home. Other than that, they lived in the dormitory and practiced six or seven hours a day, every day—summer, fall, winter, and spring. They weren't allowed to date. Sports medicine was virtually nonexistent, and if a player wrenched a knee, she was expected to play anyway.

"I don't think it works," Donovan says. "They just aren't ready for that kind of work. They were just out of high school. Weight training has improved since I was there, but it was primitive back then. There were an incredible number of injuries. Kids would be playing on knees that were just blown out. For fundamentals and learning, I think teams played under such fatigue that they never knew how good they could be. You can't perform when you're that tired. But repetition is a part of their society. They do the same thing for the same amount of time every day whether they need to work on that skill or not."

American baseball players who have played in Japan repeat the same sort of stories. The *gaijin* who fight the system are labeled bad. The ones who go along with it are celebrated.

Donovan went along with it because she couldn't live with herself if she had privileges that her teammates did not. She had always been a star, but never a prima donna. Even so, when she went home for six months after the season was over, she felt guilty because she knew her teammates never stopped training, never went home.

Donovan's first year in Japan was made even more difficult by the fact that she had contracted viral hepatitis at the Pan American games in Caracas the preceding summer. The disease made her anemic, sapping her strength and making the long practices even more hellish. The team didn't investigate the illness. No blood tests were taken.

She had always fought homesickness, but by December she was miserable. "We didn't have a game all month and we were preparing for the All-Japan Tournament, which has thirty-six teams," she says. "The coach was worse than ever, and I wasn't able to go home for Christmas. It was the worst month I ever lived through." Still, she led her team to a league championship and was an all-star.

In February 1984, the Japanese season over, she returned to Old Dominion, where she hit the weight room to put back on the weight she had lost because of her illness in Japan. She also hit the basketball court to get her timing back. She tried out for and made the U.S. Olympic Team. Once again the women's basketball team hoped to meet the Soviets to decide the gold medal. And once again their hopes were dashed when the Soviets repaid the United States for boycotting Moscow in 1980 by boycotting Los Angeles in 1984.

The U.S. team had come close to beating the Soviets the previous summer and had been pointing toward the Olympics. Five members of the 1980 team, including Donovan, were on the 1984 team. Even Donovan thought that the 1984 Olympics would be her last hurrah. Going into the tournament, she said, "I've dreamed of this moment ever since I was a kid sitting in front of the TV watching the Olympics."

The U.S. team went through the tournament like a tornado through a trailer park, but Donovan was not the primary offensive tool. Already the game in the States was being taken over by smaller, quicker players. But she was the rebounding and shot-blocking force in the middle of the court, the intimidating presence that held the defense together. And when the U.S. beat Korea 85-55 in the gold medal game, Donovan declared herself satisfied with her career. "It's the end of a lifetime goal for me," she said. "Everything I've done in the last eight years led up to this moment."

She had signed to play one more year in Japan. After that, she would come home and go into coaching. But first there were some honors to collect. Her hometown of Ridgewood, New Jersey, held a day for her and renamed a street Anne Donovan Way.

Her second year in Japan wasn't much better than her first. She still didn't understand the language well enough to be comfortable in society, and the practices were just as grueling. "When I said I was going to go back, my sister said, 'Let me read your letters to you.' The entire first two years there, I didn't enjoy a day of it."

But it was basketball. For the second straight year, her team won the league championship, and she was again an all-star. When the season was over and she came home to play her normal international schedule, she discovered that she still hadn't had enough of basketball just yet. So she returned for a third season for Shizuoka in 1985–86. By now she could converse in Japanese, and she made friends with an American woman who had married a Japanese national. "From then on, it was a breeze," she says. "I loved Japan in years three, four, and five."

She was enormously popular in Japan. One day, while watching a Japanese version of "Jeopardy" on television, she was amazed to hear a description of herself given as the clue—and even more amazed when one of the contestants immediately knew the answer. She says that her quiet nature was a key to her acceptance by the public, especially women. "I really believe the reason I did so well in Japan was that there was a part of my personality that could empathize with the Japanese women," she says. "I don't stir up trouble. Their idea of what an ugly American was—they couldn't find it in me. I wasn't loud or overbearing. I didn't complain a lot."

She was a trooper. Always had been. And the older she got and the more the game changed, the more she found herself enjoying the challenge of staying among the best.

In the summer of 1986, she was on the U.S. team that went to the Goodwill Games and the World Championships. The Goodwill Games were in Moscow in July, and the United States team finally got its shot at the Soviets. Eight years of waiting culminated in an 83-60 victory, the first win by a U.S. women's team over the Soviet women since 1957. Donovan was given the assignment of stopping the Soviets' monstrous center, seven-foot-one Liliana Semenova. Donovan didn't just stop her; she freeze-dried her. She blocked one of Semenova's shots early on and simply took her out of the game. Semenova finished with four points and not a single rebound. After that victory, Donovan realized she wasn't quite through. There was still an important goal to achieve.

"In eighty-six, I wasn't sure I would ever wear the red, white, and blue again," she says. Then she helped beat the Soviets. "I realized how important it was to win the gold medal in an Olympics that haven't been boycotted. The fun came back."

However, the game that had once been so easy for the girl who was a foot taller than most of her peers got increasingly difficult. The constant play took a toll on her lanky frame, and she had to fight continuously to make herself useful in a game that no longer waited for the center to get down the court. "Every year it got more challenging instead of getting easier," she says. "Going into the 1988 Olympics, I was working harder than I had ever worked in my life."

In 1986–87 she led Shizuoka to its fourth straight Japanese championship and her fourth straight all-star berth. But in the 1987–88 season, she partially tore an Achilles tendon and, with her leg in a cast, missed all but a few games.

When she came back to the States in February, she was still healing, and the Olympic trials were getting closer. If there had ever been any lingering questions about her desire, they were now gone. The lessons of Rose Battaglia were still bringing dividends earned on an investment of sweat. Donovan made the 1988 Olympic team.

"At one time you would build a team around her," said Kay Yow, then-coach of the U.S. Olympic team when the team selections were announced. "Basketball is more of a transition game, and she's not a transition player. But she still makes a contribution."

A "transition game"—that's what basketball people call the style of play dominated by quick, do-everything players who score quick points by moving the ball up and down the court. In the men's game, the style is epitomized by Michael Jordan and Magic Johnson, players who can lead the fast break.

Donovan had grown up in an era dominated by the half-court game, in which a team moves the ball deliberately up the floor and runs set plays. A towering center is the centerpiece of such an offense, and he or she can take as long as needed to get from one end of the court to the other. The team will wait.

Donovan was made for that game: she was big. But although she was as slender as a deer, she was slow. She didn't fit in with the small, quick players who now made up the team—women like Olympic co-captain, five-foot-eleven Teresa Edwards of the University of Georgia; six-two Katrina McClain of Georgia; five-eight Teresa Witherspoon of Louisiana Tech; and six-four center Chana Perry of San Diego State.

"I look at this group as a bunch of strong, quick young women," Donovan said of the team. "None of those words describes me."

Yet Yow had said—and Donovan had believed—she could still contribute. That's why Yow chose her for the team. "Lord knows I know the ropes," Donovan said. "I look at myself as having a leadership role."

She said that months before the Olympics, when the team was in training, and she *had* been an important part of the team during the spring and summer leading up to the games. She didn't expect to be the whole show, but she never dreamed that when gold medal time rolled around, she would be a mere cheerleader.

As the gold medal game loomed, that's what she was—a cheerleader. She had started the first two games of the Olympic tournament, but it quickly became apparent that the team would rely on quickness, not height. After hitting one basket in ten shots in limited playing time, Donovan found herself on the bench in games three and four, as much a part of the sideline in Seoul's Chamsil Arena as the scorer's table.

The American women won every game without her, beating Czechoslovakia 87-81, Yugoslavia 101-74, and China 94-79 in the round-robin round. In the medal-round semifinals, they beat the Soviet Union 102-88, and they didn't need Donovan at all. The only hurdle remaining between the U.S. juggernaut and the gold medal was a rematch with the Yugoslavs, who had been so helplessly overmatched a week earlier.

Donovan had come to Seoul for a number of reasons. She didn't need the exposure or the fame; she already had that. She wanted a gold medal, but even more than that she wanted to help earn it.

She was playing in her third Olympics, and no one else on that twelve-woman team could say that. She had been denied her first shot at a gold medal in 1980 because of the Soviet boycott. In 1984 she had won her gold medal in Los Angeles, but the Soviets had boycotted those games. Now, 1988 was her last hurrah. The Soviets were there. The whole world (except Cuba and North Korea) was there. And she was on the bench.

Not that she wasn't willing to cheer. She had always been a team player. She even felt sorry for Yow. "Kay Yow, bless her heart, she didn't want to bench me. She just realized the team would be better with five good players."

The gold medal game between the United States and Yugoslavia was to be played the morning of September 30. The Americans had already trashed the Yugoslavs in a preliminary game with virtually no help from Donovan, so there was little reason to think that the team would need her to finish the job.

Donovan had known for some time that her days as a star were nearing an end. When she had first burst upon the national scene in a blizzard of points, rebounds, and blocked shots, she was the state-of-the-art woman basketball player. She was the Kareem Abdul-Jabbar of her sport—the tall, lean player who could reach above the common press of players to gobble rebounds and sweep away shots; a scoring machine who could put in a tap-in or loft a soft jumper from twenty feet with equal ease. Even if she wasn't the dominating player she had once been, it was nearly inconceivable that her team would take to the court for the big game without her.

Donovan didn't let the distress she felt affect her relationship with the team. When the team members were chosen six months earlier, Donovan had been named co-captain along with Teresa Edwards. Ever since her senior year at Old Dominion, she had been a second coach on the floor whenever she played. Even from the bench, she continued to offer help, and no one cheered more loudly for her teammates.

But now the gold medal game loomed, and Donovan desperately wanted to be part of it. It was what she had lived for, why she had put up with the indignities of being a stranger in a strange land, why she had worked so hard to recover from her Achilles tendon injury.

"I had so much that led up that team," Donovan says. "I had pretty much been out for a full year before the Olympic trials. I knew that to make the team I really had to play well. I felt good about making the team and being elected co-captain and then playing the first game."

Then came the benching. Looking back, Donovan says, "I don't think I've ever been tested as a person so much in my life."

Her mother, one brother (who had also been playing basketball in Japan), and one sister had come to Seoul to watch her play. Now, they took it upon themselves to keep her occupied and keep her from dwelling on what had happened. "We knew she was suffering," her mother says. "We talked to her a lot. She felt pretty bad, but she didn't criticize the coach or her teammates. She just sat it out."

Mrs. Matthews and Anne's siblings took her to other Olympic events and around the city. "My family was there for me," Donovan says. "It's always been that network that keeps me going."

The night before the game with Yugoslavia for the gold medal, three chaplains—all of them former Olympians—talked to the team about the importance not of winning but of doing their best and letting go of everything that would keep them from doing their jobs. One of the speakers, a woman, pointed at Anne Donovan. "I can see how dejected you are," she told Anne. "But you have a gold medal. You're here for the third time. It's out of your hands now."

The words washed over Donovan, and she let them pour into her soul, where they soothed the hurt, the doubt, the pain. "People who don't have faith don't understand," Donovan says of the effect those words had on her. For the first time since being benched, Donovan felt at peace. The chaplain was right: she had had her turn. She was there. If the team won, she would win as well, whether she was on the court or not. "That was the first night I slept the whole night," she says.

The game was played in the late morning (prime time the previous night in the New York television market). The day before, the U.S. men's team had been smothered by the Soviets in the gold medal game, so the women had the added incentive of avenging that defeat. Donovan pulled on her red, white, and blue uniform for the last time, went out on the court with her teammates, and went through pregame warmups and introductions. With appropriate Olympic fanfare, the starting units took the floor in front of a full house. Donovan took her place at the end of the bench, ready and eager to do anything she could to help—even if that meant leading the cheers.

Like everyone else, Donovan figured the U.S. women would blow out the Yugoslavs. They had done so once before, and the bigger and slower Yugoslavs had shown no sign of being able to cope with the quickness and daring of the Americans. If anything, Donovan figured that Yow would put her in at the end of the game when the U.S. had run up a big lead—a sentimental appearance so she could say that she played in the gold medal game.

The game didn't go according to plan, though. For the first fifteen minutes of the first twenty-minute half, the Yugoslavs gave the Americans all they could handle and more. The key to the Yugoslav attack was their center, a mountain of a woman who stood six feet seven, weighed 225 pounds, give or take a stuffed cabbage, and answered to the name Razija Mujanovic.

Quickness wasn't working for the Americans. Tenacious defense wasn't working. Yow ran in platoons of fresh troops and juggled her line-up, but to no avail. Razija was unstoppable. The best the Americans could do was hold their own.

From the end of the American bench, Donovan formulated battle plans. "I was praying coach Yow would go to me," Donovan says. "I was desperate to get in. I could see that the only way to deal with her was to keep her from catching the ball. I thought, 'God, if I could get the chance, I could do that.' "

With 4:04 left in the half and the score tied for the thirteenth time, 30-30, Katrina McClain, the American center who had replaced Donovan, picked up her fourth foul trying to stop Mount Mujanovic. With play stopped, Yow turned toward her bench, looked down to the far end, and said one word: "Anne!"

Donovan was up before the word disappeared into the din of the arena. She stripped off her warmups as she had thousands of times before, and walked with certain strides to the scorer's table, where she informed the appropriate bureaucrats that she wished to enter the game.

"I always felt there would come a time when she could help us," Yow said after the game. "Today was the day."

"I remember it all," says Donovan. "I remember the feelings in my stomach as I walked to the scorer's table. I can't put it into words."

But she could put it into action. After Mujanovik sank her two free throws to make the score 32-30 in favor of Yugoslavia, Teresa Edwards brought the ball up the court for the Americans and looked for her co-captain. She found Donovan at the free-throw line, fed her the ball, and watched as Donovan put up the jump shot.

"I knew the whole time running down the floor that it would turn into a basket," Donovan says. And it did. The ball hit nothing but net, and now the score was tied for the fourteenth time. It would not be tied again.

"Teresa knew," Donovan says. They were co-captains and they were teammates, the veterans of many wars together. When Donovan had been relegated to the bench, Edwards had not known what to say to her teammate. On the court she didn't have to say anything. She just gave Donovan the ball and watched. "I don't think there was anyone happier for me," Donovan says. "She found me immediately. It was very special."

To the Americans, yes. To the Yugoslavs, it was something else entirely.

After Donovan tied the score, the Yugoslavs set up their offense and fed the ball to Mujanovic. Donovan stole it, started the fast break the other way, and now the Americans were leading by two.

The Yugoslavs reloaded, tried another shot, and missed. Donovan hauled in the rebound and got another break going. Back on defense again, she blocked a shot and then ran downcourt and canned a baseline jumper.

Suddenly, Mujanovic no longer existed: Donovan simply wouldn't allow her to catch the ball. At the other end, she quickly attracted extra attention that freed up her guards and forwards. She added two free throws to give her six points in four minutes, and when the horn sounded on the first half, the U.S. team was ahead 42-36.

The Americans took to their locker room amid a blizzard of high fives. When they came back out, Donovan took the floor with the starting five for the second half. She didn't score again, but she didn't have to. The damage had been done. Mujanovic was reduced to a noncombatant, and the floor belonged to the slashing American guards again.

Donovan played the first six minutes of the second half. When she sat down—this time for good—her team was up 51-40 and on its way to a 77-70 victory that was not nearly as close as the score. She had played ten minutes, and during that time, the United States had outscored Yugoslavia 21-8.

After the game, the U.S. team swarmed all over one another, then mounted the victory stand, stood at attention as the American flag was hoisted to the rafters and "The Star-Spangled Banner" played, daubed at their eyes, and finally retired from the court to tell the microphones and notepads how they felt.

"I wanted to be a big part of this gold medal," Donovan said, holding the big round medal that hung by a ribbon around her neck. "I'm not used to being a bench player. It has not been easy for me. I reach for words, and I can't find any."

There was a party that night with her family. They went out on the town and didn't worry about curfews. They didn't even mind the usual crowds of gawkers or the inquiries about the atmospheric conditions. The weather was just fine up there, thank you very much. Says Donovan, "Nothing hurt that night."

Although the quest was over, Donovan's odyssey wasn't quite finished. Although she had said she wanted a set of address labels, when it came time to get them she decided instead to play one last year of professional ball in Italy. The money was twice what she had made in Japan, and instead of a dormitory she had her own three-story apartment, a luxury car, and only two hours of practice a day and one or two games a week for eight months. "Those eight months went by a lot quicker than any five months in Japan," she says. "It was the best move I ever made." Some would argue that the best move she ever made was the jumper she put up from the foul line against Yugoslavia.

There were a few odds and ends to wrap up over the next year. A shoe company put out a poster of her in her Olympic uniform with her two gold medals. Her high school retired her number. She was honored with a special citation by the governor of New Jersey.

After her season in Italy, she came home and got a job as an assistant coach at her alma mater, Old Dominion. She bought a house and got her address labels. It was difficult at first to adjust to coaching after having been a player for so many years, but she's enthusiastic about the future and about someday becoming a head coach. Whenever she can, she still plays pickup games in the gym.

She could have ended up with a lifetime of regrets, but she didn't allow it to happen. There's pride in that, but even more, there's the confidence that comes from facing the worst and overcoming it.

"It took a lot of strength to get through the Olympics in eighty-eight," she says. "The whole experience taught me so much about myself and about life. When things come easy all your life, you don't realize what it's like to be at the other end. I didn't know if I could do it. I thank God every day I stuck it out."

Return to Eden

I think Dante knew very well what Paradise is. He would approve very much of something whose first game was played in 1845 in the Elysian Fields in Hoboken, New Jersey.

The lords of baseball chose A. Bartlett Giamatti to be the steward and guardian of their game because of his unflinching moral standards. But they didn't know—no one knew—how severe the application of that moral code could be until August 24, 1989.

"The banishment for life of Pete Rose from baseball is the sad end of a sorry episode," were the first words Giamatti spoke that day for the consumption of camcorders and reporters. As he spoke—in a clear, strong voice and without the flourishes that decorated his normal speech—Giamatti clung with both hands to the lectern at which he stood.

The words landed with the heavy thud of artillery shells. It had been sixty-nine years since Shoeless Joe Jackson—another star of Rose's magnitude—had been banned for life for participating in the fixing of the 1919 World Series. Rose's crime, to which he never admitted (but neither did he contest the charges against him), was not as severe as Jackson's. He had not conspired to throw a World Series or even a game. He was accused of betting heavily on baseball games, including games played by the Cincinnati Reds, the team he had managed up until that year. The evidence indicated that he never bet on his team to lose, but he had bet on it just the same.

Ever since the Black Sox scandal of 1919, baseball's only mortal sin had been gambling on games. The game offered forgiveness—after suitable penance—for every other type of human error. Only gambling on games was fatal. The major leagues' absolute prohibition of the act was posted in large print in English and Spanish near the door of all fifty-two of the league's clubhouses in its twenty-six stadiums. It didn't take a lawyer to interpret the language. It was unequivocal: gamble on baseball, and you're gone forever. History, finito, adios, goodbye.

If the miscreant had been the bullpen catcher for the Seattle Mariners, no one would have questioned Giamatti's decision. Giamatti could have ordered him drawn and quartered in Times Square, and the public would have applauded. But this was Pete Rose—AKA Charlie Hustle—the man who had broken Ty Cobb's record for most hits. You just didn't go around banning Pete Rose from the game that he had helped define.

Before Giamatti ordered the banishment, the speculation had been that he would suspend Rose for a couple of years. Perhaps he would note that Rose's gambling was a disease that needed treatment. Surely, he would remember that Rose was not accused of betting on his team to lose and was not charged with attempting to fix a game. Besides, many argued, hadn't Babe Ruth been a womanizer and a drinker? Hadn't Cap Anson, the first three thousand-hit man, been a racist of the first order? Hadn't many other stars engaged in reprehensible behavior and not been punished?

Indeed they had, but that wasn't the issue. The issue was gambling, and to Giamatti, an absolute rule was just that—absolute. As much as he admired the way Rose had played baseball, he could make no exceptions. In a world that was becoming increasingly gray in the area of morals, Giamatti believed that some things were still black and white.

"I believe baseball is a beautiful and exciting game, loved by millions—I among them—and I believe baseball is an important, enduring American institution," Giamatti read from his two-page statement. "It must assert and aspire to the highest principles—of integrity, of professionalism of performance, of fair play within the rules. . . .

"I will be told that I am an idealist. I hope so. . . . Let there be no doubt or dissent about our goals for baseball or our dedication to it. Nor about our vigilance and vigor—and indeed our patience—in protecting the game from blemish or stain or disgrace.

"The matter of Mr. Rose is now closed. It will be debated and discussed. Let no one think that it did not hurt baseball. That hurt will pass, however, as the great glory of the game asserts itself and a resilient institution goes forward. Let it also be clear that no individual is superior to the game."

With those words, Giamatti fulfilled the most extreme duty of his office in the only way he saw possible. He banned Pete Rose forever, excommunicated him from the game that Giamatti held in sacred trust, forbade him from ever again setting foot on the playing fields where Rose had forged a career for the ages.

It was the last public act of Giamatti's life. Eight days later, at the age of fifty-one, he died of a heart attack. If he had been able to choose a last act, it certainly would not have been the banishment of Pete Rose. It would have been to go to a ballpark, sit in the stands in the sunshine, and partake one last time of the game that nourished his soul.

The end of Rose's baseball career—and ultimately his eligibility for baseball's shrine, the Hall of Fame in Cooperstown, New York—shocked the nation as only the downfall of an idol can. And beyond that shock was anger; anger at the short, rumpled man with the sunken eyes and the eccentric beard who dared to visit baseball's harshest punishment on one of its greatest heroes.

It was an act of the highest kind of courage—moral courage—yet few recognized it as such. Instead, those who never had liked Giamatti saw it as the final insult to the game committed by a man who talked too much about ideals, a man who was not of baseball. Others saw it as a pious overreaction by a man they had come to admire for the very warmth and humanity they thought he did not show in dealing with Rose.

Giamatti himself, answering questions after he read his statement, said that the decision involved none of the subtleties so many tried to find. "This is really not very complicated, friends," he said. He didn't say the task was pleasant, but it hadn't been difficult. The rule was clear, and the evidence was clear and uncontested. The conclusion, as Shakespeare put it, must follow as the night does the day. Any logical person could see that.

And Giamatti was extraordinarily logical, a characteristic many people had difficulty understanding when he was first introduced to the tightly knit world of baseball. The problem was not so much with anything he said, but with where he had come from. Before baseball, he had made his living as a scholar and educator, and few were as good at their bookish business as he.

On June 10, 1986, in a ballroom at the Waldorf-Astoria, A. Bartlett Giamatti was introduced to a part of the world that, when you speak of something being ivy-covered, thinks immediately of the outfield walls of Wrigley Field. Beneath the crystal chandeliers, one of the first things he told the audience of reporters and camera operators was that they needn't call him A. Bartlett Giamatti. Just Bart would be fine.

They were curious about this man whose previous life had been steeped in the cadences of medieval epic poetry. They knew he had been a professor of English, a specialist in Renaissance literature who had written books so learned that most people couldn't even understand their titles. His last job had been the presidency of Yale University—not the usual training ground for the job he had recently agreed to accept.

Even as "just Bart," he wasn't the sort of fellow the reporters were accustomed to associating with, not the type they instinctively liked. Yet, they would be dealing with him for some time to come. Three days earlier, the owners of the twelve National League baseball teams had unanimously elected him the new president of their league. He would replace Charles S. Feeney, a down-to-earth baseball man known to everyone as Chub. As far as anyone knew, Giamatti's principal qualification for succeeding Feeney was that, nine years earlier, when Giamatti was sworn in as president of Yale, he had said, "The only thing I ever wanted to be president of was the American League."

He was a fervid fan. As president of Yale, he amused the undergraduates by walking around campus wearing a Boston Red Sox cap. He had also written a number of articles on baseball, including a prize-winning one on Tom Seaver in *Harper's* in 1977, the year he was named president of Yale.

But were wearing a baseball cap, charming though that may be, and writing a few articles—even a prize winner—sufficient credentials to lead the National League? If so, then every person in the ballroom was just as qualified as Giamatti.

Not that being president of the National League appeared to be that difficult a job. His most visible task would be to have his autograph imprinted on every baseball used in the league. Other than that, he was responsible for reviewing player contracts (a chore that could be done by league lawyers), supervising the league's umpires, and disciplining an occasional player. No one was thinking of Pete Rose that day.

Everyone knew, however, Giamatti was being groomed for the office of Commissioner of Baseball, which would come open in another two years when commissioner Peter Ueberroth's term concluded. And even if the league president seemed a glorified bureaucrat, the commissioner had real power, and they didn't know if a former university president was the man to wield such authority. Ever since the days of baseball's first commissioner, Judge "Kennesaw Mountain" Landis, a white-haired thunderer of a man who was brought in to clean up the ugly debris of the 1919 Black Sox betting scandal, the caretakers of baseball's tradition had longed for another strong commissioner. These times particularly—with skyrocketing salaries, enormous television contracts, spreading fan violence, imminent expansion, and the neverending employer-employee battle over free agency—seemed to demand such a man.

Quite frankly, few people in that ballroom could conceive of Giamatti in such a role. First of all, he was an English professor. He had lived his life in an ivory tower, a philosopher-king strolling serenely through the gardens of academe. A nice life, to be sure, but when it came to being tough, English professors ranked somewhere below poached salmon.

The only weapons Giamatti could use to defend himself on that June day would be his words. And in the minds of most of his listeners, he had a lot of defending to do. He wasn't, after all, a *baseball* man. He was an—harumph—*academic.*

Then he started to speak, and with his first words there was no question but that this was not the speech of a "just Bart." This was an Angelo Bartlett Giamatti, Ph.D. A fountain of words shot into the air like a Grucci fireworks display, then cascaded down into a series of pools, where they were gathered together before tumbling off a precipice, and another, and another, burbling and lively, clear and fresh.

The audience gasped—not audibly, of course, because these were, after all, the ladies and gentlemen of the press. They had too much professional poise to swoon at the first hint of the pluperfect subjunctive. This was, rather, a gasp they felt rather than heard. As the metaphors washed over them and eddied dizzily about them, they scribbled furiously, the smoke rising from their pen points as they tried to get even the tenth part of it down on paper.

There are tricks journalists use to take notes during an interview. Speech is always faster than the pen, but by catching the patterns and rhythms of a speaker, it is possible to write down the key parts and fill in the rest later. Such tricks invariably worked with the people the journalists in that ballroom normally spoke to. Those people were athletes and managers and coaches, and it was sometimes possible to write down an interview even before it took place, so predictable were the pronouncements of the interviewees.

They'd sit around in their underwear, these men of baseball, with cheeks full of Skoal and tongues full of sturdy, Anglo-Saxon obscenities, which they sprinkled over their speech like sugar on doughnuts.

They would say: "I got a [naughty word] fastball up in his [naughty word] wheelhouse and he was sitting on the [very naughty word]."

Or: "I got thirteen [naughty word] years in the [naughty word] bigs and the [very naughty collective noun] are treating me like [barnyard epithet]. Sure, the [naughty word] kid is hitting three-ninety, but he's barely out of [naughty word] Tidewater. He's going to come back to earth. And you know I ain't no [naughty word] buck-ninety-five hitter. I just gotta get the [naughty word] at-bats, and if it ain't here, then I want a [naughty word] trade. But not to Cleveland, Minnesota, Texas, Atlanta, Seattle, San Diego, Houston, Montreal, Toronto, or Dee-troit. There's gotta be a team out there that can use my talents. Says so in my [naughty word] contract."

Those were the kinds of speeches the men and women in the

Waldorf ballroom were accustomed to putting down on paper. Trouble was, this "just Bart" fellow didn't talk with a mouth full of snuff and he didn't give interviews in his underwear. And although the words all sounded familiar, he wasn't speaking any brand of English they had ever heard from anyone remotely connected to baseball. Or newspapers, for that matter.

Once, legend has it, journalists wrote in a similarly ornate fashion. Once they were allowed to use words of more than three syllables. But modern journalist had long since been broken of any aspirations to scholarly discourse by editors who told them daily that their readers could barely get through "See Spot run" without a dictionary. They were taught the value of simple, declarative sentences composed of words that even a survivor of an American public school could understand.

And now here was a man who could drag Spenser, Dante, and Shakespeare into a discussion of baseball. Who was this Spenser fellow anyway? Didn't he play first base for the Yankees? And Dante? Is that the guy who played end for the Browns—or was it the Packers?

The writers could deal with it for a day. What distressed them was that this wasn't going to be just a one-shot deal. This guy was going to be with them for a long time. As of that day, A. Bartlett Giamatti was the president of the National League. This wasn't some ivy-clad university. This was the [naughty word] national pastime. What was a professor of English doing here? Why hadn't the owners of the twelve National League franchises chosen a baseball man?

Looked at objectively, the ascension of a reformed university president and English professor to the throne of the National League shouldn't have been that strange. After all, many of the same people who were now questioning Giamatti's credentials for running a baseball league accepted without flinching the fact that Ronald Reagan, a reformed actor, could be president of the world's most powerful democracy. For that matter, Peter Ueberroth, then the commissioner of baseball, was a reformed travel agent.

Roger Angell, writing for *The New Yorker,* put the dilemma this way: "Baseball, for all its ordered paths, is a game of constant surprises, but its choice of a bearded Ivy League scholar-prexy, easily capable of turning the full mid-title colon, as the twelfth president of the senior circuit, was a startler unmatched in the pastime since Al Weis's home run for the Mets in the fifth game of the 1969 World Series."

Or, to put it in the vernacular: So what about it, Bart? What's a cultured guy like you doing in a place like baseball?

"Men of letters have always gravitated to sports," Giamatti intoned. "I've been a lover of baseball. I always found it the most satisfying and nourishing of games outside of literature."

Uh, right. Now what about interleague play?

"I favor the fundamental grid, the geometrical beauty, the fundamental structure of the history of baseball," he began, gathering momentum as he went. "And I think it ought to be tampered with very gingerly. I support the current autonomy of leagues, except, of course, for the All-Star game and World Series play, as exciting and meaningful."

Gotcha. How about the designated hitter?

"I have very strong and subtle feelings on the DH, which I will try to soften for you," he replied. "I think it's appalling."

Good one, Bart. Wanna try artificial turf?

"I am sure it is a distinguished composition," he said graciously. "But grass is wonderful."

With that, he declared himself firmly on the side of tradition. He also gave notice that he would not apologize for who he was. He would not gush about what a lucky guy he was, and he would not change his language or his delivery to please his audience any more than he would compromise his beliefs.

His adherence to his beliefs made him unusual. No one could be sure of it at that first meeting, but he would prove to have that rarest of qualities—intellectual honesty. Coupled with that was emotional ardor for a game that he was introduced to by his own father when he was a boy growing up in South Hadley, Massachusetts.

He had thought about why he was a fan and why the game he loved was so captivating. He was captivated by the idea of paradise and the park—a concept, he pointed out, that was born in ancient

Persia. Clearly, the two were connected—the park an attempt to recapture and confine the paradise that had been lost, a green and ordered place where one could escape the chaos and care of the workaday world.

"The word *paradise* is originally an old Persian word meaning an enclosed park or green," he once said. "Anything that's closed is fundamentally artificial. Nature doesn't enclose things perfectly. You fly over a great city at night and you look down and you see lit up this green in the middle of the city and you realize that the reason they're in the middle of cities is that there is in us a fundamental, vestigial memory of an enclosed green space as the place of freedom or play."

This was where he differed from the traditional breed known as baseball people: while they merely loved the game of baseball, Giamatti loved the *idea* of baseball.

A. Bartlett Giamatti was born in Boston on April 14, 1938. His father was Valentine Giamatti, a Yale graduate and professor of Italian at Mount Holyoke College in South Hadley. His mother, Mary Claybough Walton, was a graduate of Smith College.

In 1946, when Giamatti was eight years old, his father took him to Fenway Park to see the Red Sox, who were driving toward the American League pennant and, ultimately, an October appointment with the St. Louis Cardinals. It was at that time that the young Giamatti got his first lesson in the terrible heartbreak that is the birthright of every Red Sox fan. The Sox lost in the eighth inning of the seventh game when shortstop Johnny Pesky held a relay throw too long, and Enos Slaughter raced from first to home on a double.

In 1947, Valentine Giamatti took his family on sabbatical with him to Italy. While there, the father bought a baseball glove from a soldier who was returning to the States and gave it to his son. "I remember my father teaching me to play baseball," Giamatti said. "I guess one reason I love the game is because I loved him."

Back home in South Hadley, Giamatti mixed an early interest in literature with his passion for baseball. Dinner table conversation at the Giamatti home ranged from Dante to Bobby Doerr, the Red Sox second baseman who became Giamatti's hero. Doerr was an unusual man to pick as hero. The Red Sox, after all, was the team of Ted Williams, the "Splendid Splinter," the greatest hitter of his day and maybe all days. But Giamatti, who had no illusions about his own talents as a ballplayer, didn't think it appropriate to aspire to be like the mighty Williams. So he picked the steady and far less spectacular Doerr, who himself became a Hall of Famer.

Giamatti listened to baseball on the radio in those pretelevision days, and he found radio to be perfect for the sport. "You thought about it, you saw it in your head," he said. "You'd get a mental image of it, and any kid could go out and reproduce it."

Giamatti was not one who could reproduce it well. In fact, as a baseball player, he made a swell student manager, which is what he was for the South Hadley High School team. That, he joked, was where he got his taste for the front office. Although it was disappointing that he couldn't be another Bobby Doerr, that didn't diminish his affection for the game. "Baseball doesn't demand that you be very good at it to enjoy it," he said.

He told Roger Angell about hanging out at a gas station in South Hadley during the summer listening to the Red Sox. One day, he remembered, a driver with New Hampshire plates pulled up to the pump and was roundly ignored. "He got out and stomped around and stared at us—ten or twenty men and boys, just standing there in the service bay. He thought he'd come to a place where he could get gas, but he was wrong. The purpose was to let us stand in the shade of the bay and listen to the Red Sox. It was like that all over New England then, of course. The Red Sox were the lingua franca."

With the years, Giamatti's passion for baseball grew, and his understanding of the nature of being a fan grew, as well. "You're never, at the beginning, a baseball fan," he once told writer Charles Siebert. "You come to it through the love of a locale. You don't love baseball in the abstract before you love it in its particularities. When I got to high school, I wasn't good enough to star on the team so I became the team manager. Maybe I love baseball so much because I wasn't very good at it."

Like his father, Giamatti attended Yale, graduating magna cum laude in 1960 with a degree in English. He continued in graduate school and obtained a doctorate in comparative literature in 1964.

Thus began his meteoric academic career. In the fall of 1964 he took a job teaching Italian and comparative literature at Princeton University. The next year, he was promoted to assistant professor. In 1966, he published his first book, *The Early Paradise and the Renaissance Epoch.* His second book was *Play of Double Senses: Spenser's Faerie Queene.* By 1967, he was back at Yale, as an assistant professor of English. Within three years he was promoted to associate professor, and by 1971—just seven years after he began teaching—he was a full professor and the master of Ezra Stiles College, one of the twelve residential colleges for undergraduates that make up Yale University.

"He's the best English teacher I've ever had," a student once said of him. "He makes you excited about the subject, even if you're not."

He was, in short, a marvelous teacher, the rare person who not only knew his subject, but felt it deep in his bones. As it lived for him, he made it live for his students. But he had one flaw in the eyes of students: he was a tough grader. For that reason, although his courses were popular, many students chose to audit them—that is, attend the classes but not for grades or credit—rather than risk the effect of his stern standards on their precious grade-point averages. Grades are academic currency, and Giamatti would not pay more than the worth of the work. It was a matter of intellectual honesty, the same rigid standards he would bring to baseball.

In 1977 the New York Mets, angry with Cy Young Award winner Tom Seaver's desire to make more money, traded him to the Cincinnati Reds. Giamatti was moved to write about this banishment of a hero. The article, which appeared in *Harper's,* was entitled "Tom Seaver's Farewell." Giamatti did not think highly of the Mets' ownership's decision: "Among all the men who play baseball there is, very occasionally, a man of such qualities of heart and mind and body that he transcends even the great and glorious game, and such a man is to be cherished, not sold."

The same year, in November, the Yale *Alumni Magazine and Journal* printed another article by Giamatti, this one a valedictory to a baseball season just past. It was entitled "The Green Fields of the Mind."

"It breaks your heart," Giamatti wrote. "It is designed to break your heart. The game begins in the spring, when everything else begins again, and it blossoms in the summer, filling the afternoons and evenings, and then as soon as the chill rains come, it stops and leaves you to face the fall alone. . . . Today, October 2, a Sunday of rain and broken branches and leaf-clogged drains and slick streets, it stopped, and summer was gone."

October 2 was not the end of the World Series. It was merely the end of the Red Sox season, another season of heartbreak, with the home team losing the game, and a chance to go into a playoff against the Yankees.

He wrote about how, done properly, baseball was listened to on the radio, in "the enclosed, green field of the mind," and not watched on "the all-seeing, all-falsifying television." He recreated the game, the late-inning rally by the Sox, the old hopes resurrected that this time, this one time, the Red Sox would prevail. He relived the elation and then bared the deep agony that descended when the Sox fell short once more.

"Of course," he concluded, "there are those who learn after the first few times. They grow out of sports. And there are others who were born with the wisdom to know that nothing lasts. These are the truly tough among us, the ones who can live without illusion, or without even the hope of illusion. I am not that grown-up or up-to-date. I am a simpler creature, tied to more primitive patterns and cycles. I need to think something lasts forever, and it might as well be that state of being that is a game; it might as well be that, in a green field, in the sun."

The caretakers of baseball took note of these writings and marked down the name of A. Bartlett Giamatti. Then, late in the year, when he was named the next president of Yale and said his famous line about wanting to be president of the American League, they put a star next to it. Most of the world hadn't noticed, but those who mattered had.

By 1978 he was director of Yale's Division of Humanities and, at thirty-nine years of age, one of the brightest stars in the glowing firmament of his profession. But when he agreed to become president, his fellow professors were more disappointed than they would be when he became president of the National League.

Taking a job in baseball, he told Roger Angell, "caused much less of a shock and seemed much less of a sellout to the academic community than my previous move, from teaching to administration—to being a college president. That was considered infinitely worse—it was as if I'd joined the Vietcong."

At forty, when he took over the leadership of Yale, he was the youngest president the university had had since before the American Revolution. He replaced Kingman Brewster, a tall patrician with a name as Ivy League as Oxford cloth shirts and button-down collars. Next to Brewster, Giamatti—the grandson of an immigrant—seemed as unlikely a choice to head Yale as he would to head the National League.

In the late 1970s, the venerable university was foundering in red ink. The physical plant was disintegrating, and fund raising was not keeping up with spending. Putting the institution back on firm financial footing would be Giamatti's main task. It wasn't glamorous, and he didn't particularly enjoy it, but he did it well. Giamatti may have loved the literature of the past and the fantasy world of the ballfield, but he was a pragmatist who understood the virtues of a healthy bank balance. By the time he left Yale in 1985, the university was in better shape than ever.

He also found time to use the bully pulpit of his post to attack societal changes he saw around him. In his first major address, to the 1978 freshman class, he urged the students to become involved in the community: "I sense in our country a growing mood of withdrawal and isolationism, a retreat from obligations stated and unstated, a desire to redefine everything in terms that only serve the self, rather than defining the self with a civic sense for others."

Two years into his term, he riled up the alumni when he decried a growing emphasis on sports in the Ivy League and called for a reduction of the length of seasons and the elimination of post-season league play. He also suggested that coaches might better serve the academic community by teaching as well as running athletic teams.

The following year, he took on the Moral Majority, the political organization founded by the Reverend Jerry Falwell whose goal it was to fight what it called the growth of "secular humanism." The organization fought for the teaching of "creationism" instead of—or in addition to—evolution in science classes. It used anti-Communism in the same ways that Senator McCarthy had thirty years earlier, as a cudgel with which to bash in the brains of liberals.

Few dared to brook the wrath of this group, which was of questionable morality and was never a majority of anything. But Giamatti did. "What nonsense," he told the 1981 incoming class of freshman. "What disgusts me so much about the 'morality' seeping out of the ground around our feet is that it would deny the legitimacy of differentness. We should all be dismayed with the shredding of the spiritual fabric of our society."

"Spiritual violence," he called the tactics of Falwell's minions. "The 'Moral Majority' is a cry of exhaustion, a longing for surcease from the strain of managing complexity."

It seemed he questioned everything and accepted no one's opinions until he had thought them through for himself. In an article in *The Washington Post,* he warned of the dangers of the popular notion that if only enough computers were installed in classrooms, the American crisis in education would be solved. More balderdash, he said, taking the unpopular view that while computers might be a tool, they were not a cure.

He also found time to comment on baseball. When players and owners engaged in a bitter, midseason strike in 1981, *The New York Times* asked him to write an Op-Ed piece about the strike. Giamatti minced no words in declaring his abhorrence of it:

"Call it a symptom of the plague of distrust and divisiveness that afflicts our land. Call it the triumph of greed over the spirit of the garden. Call it what you will, the strike is utter foolishness. . . . O. Sovereign Owners and Princely Players, masters of amortization, tax shelters, bonuses and deferred compensation, go back to work. You have been entrusted with the serious work of play, and your season of responsibility has come. Be at it. There is no general sympathy for either of your sides. Nor will there be. The people of America care about baseball, not about your squalid little squabbles."

Three years later, in 1984, he found himself in the middle of a strike closer to home when Yale's clerical and technical workers walked off the job. This "squalid little squabble" did not yield any better than baseball's strike had, and Giamatti was roundly criticized for not giving in to the strikers' demands, but in the end he forged a new agreement.

After the strike, he told the board of trustees that he had served long enough. At the end of the 1985–86 academic year he would take a year off. Maybe he'd go back to teaching. Maybe he'd run for the U.S. Senate as a Republican. Certainly, he would travel and catch up on his studies.

The year off never came. Instead, the National League called.

He ran the league like he ran the university. Indeed, he said, the jobs were more similar than anyone would think. Both organizations were medieval in structure, resistant to change, jealous of parochial interests, wary of consensus. The owners were like department heads, the players like professors. Both university and baseball league, he said, "have very traditional values rooted in history that are a great source of strength."

He entertained no illusions about how the world would receive him. "I knew I'd be viewed as an outsider. I was aware the first time I did something people didn't agree with, I'd be called an academic who didn't know anything about baseball and would be told to go back where I came from. The surprise was that it took so long—at least half an hour."

He could laugh at himself that way, a trait more and more people noticed as they took the time to talk to him. For that was another thing he brought to the job—a willingness to talk to anyone on any subject at the drop of an adverb. And if talk is cheap, a conversation with him was priceless.

One approached him gingerly at first. If experience teaches us anything, it is that some men of accomplishment do not willingly engage in conversation with their intellectual inferiors. But he was different, a great man who was also humble. Baseball might have had something to do with that. For he had aspired to play the game but had not the skills to play even at a high-school level. No matter what he did later in life, he had no cause to boast, for what does it profit a man if he masters the medieval meter of Dante and the magical metaphors of "The Faerie Queene" if he can't turn the double play?

Unlike other great talkers, he took as much pleasure in listening and batting around ideas as he did in his own words. In an age of sound bites and electronic images that flash on the glowing screen and then vanish into the ether, listening is nearly a lost art.

You couldn't buy a conversation with Peter Ueberroth, the commissioner of baseball before Giamatti. Ueberroth, who gave the impression of always being on his way to someplace important (perhaps the bathroom), was too busy to exchange ideas. He was the sort of man who checked your credentials to see if you were important enough to talk *at*. A child of the modern age, Ueberroth didn't want discussion. He wanted information.

Giamatti was never like that. He loved the verbal thrust and parry of a good conversation. And because he loved discourse, he loved people. He was full of thoughts, not himself.

Once, while taking in a game between the Mets and Reds at Shea Stadium, several young men struck up a conversation with him. After a few pleasantries, the fans told Giamatti that they were old high school classmates of John Franco, who was then the ace reliever for the Reds. Giamatti observed that Sandy Koufax and Mets' co-owner Fred Wilpon had gone to the same school—Lafayette High in Brooklyn. Soon, he was talking about the Italian neighborhood they had grown up in.

One of the men, struck by revelation, said, "You're a fan."

"Thank you, sir," the league president replied.

This was Giamatti at his best, watching a ballgame, exchanging views. In his head, all the ideas and knowledge from the ancient world to the present came together in his passion—baseball. For him, it was more than a sport, more than a way to pass an afternoon or evening. It was a vital part of a vital country.

"Baseball is one of the few things that holds this increasingly diverse and fragmented country together," he once told Michael Bauman of *The Milwaukee Journal.* "Somehow, this is part of the rhythm that America has set for itself. And you violate things like that at your peril, because what you're dealing with is something much larger than the business of baseball. It is much more part of the country than sometimes the very people who are engaged in it fully realize, because they are so close to it."

To him, there was a sanctity—which he defined as integrity and consistency—to the game. But he distinguished between sanctity and traditionalism. The umpire is sacred, as is the idea that a rule is a rule, even if that rule was the maddeningly nebulous "discernible stop" clause of the balk rule. The source of the light shining on Wrigley Field, on the other hand, was a tradition. Traditions could be broken. Rules could not.

He said these things in May 1988, over a cocktail and half a dozen cigarettes (his primary vice, he called them) with a reporter. In his second year as league president, he was already in hot water up to his carefully combed goatee.

In 1987 he had given the first real demonstration of the kind of leader he was when he slapped a ten-day suspension on Phillies pitcher Kevin Gross, who had been caught with a bit of sandpaper wedged in the laces of his glove, apparently to be used to scuff baseballs for the purpose of making them dance in ways that baseballs don't ordinarily dance.

Such chicanery had long been part of the game. Gaylord Perry had won more than three hundred games and Cy Young awards in both leagues by artfully applying foreign substances to baseballs. Don Sutton, another three hundred-game winner, had more ways to scuff a baseball than the government had ways to levy taxes. On the receiving end of the ball, Norm Cash of the Tigers had led the league in hitting in 1961 while swinging a bat that was drilled out and filled with cork, a subterfuge that continued to Giamatti's day. Some teams sloped the foul lines on their fields to help bunts roll fair or foul depending on how well the team bunted. And in the sixties, the Dodgers, among others, raised and lowered the pitching mound from game to game depending on who the starting pitcher was.

Tricks were accepted by players, management, and even umpires as part of the game. If you were caught, you were out of the game, but if you could get away with it, more power to you.

Giamatti didn't agree, and he served notice of that fact with Gross's ten-day suspension. Ten days was twice as long as Giants pitcher Juan Marichal had gotten two decades earlier for beating Dodger catcher John Roseboro over the head with a bat. It was also much longer than the four-day suspension Giamatti himself had given to Pedro Guerrero for throwing his bat at Met pitcher David Cone.

Giamatti's formal ruling on the Gross suspension consumed ten pages of text. "Acts of cheating," he wrote, "are . . . secretive, covert acts that strike at and seek to undermine the basic foundation of any contest declaring . . . that all participants play under identical rules and conditions. . . . They destroy faith in the game's integrity and fairness; if participants and spectators alike cannot assume integrity and fairness, and proceed from there, the contest cannot in its essence exist."

To which baseball people replied, "Say what?"

But Giamatti was firm. "The fans have to believe that what they see conforms to the reality that is," he explained. They had to be assured that the rules in the rulebook were the rules the game was played by.

In 1988, he came under fire again when the league began enforcing the textbook definition of a balk. The book said the pitcher, after taking his stretch with a runner on base, had to come to a "discernible stop" before delivering the ball to the plate. In practice, a discernible stop had become barely a hesitation. The previous winter, an entire committee had discussed the enforcement of the rule, but when the season began and umpires suddenly began calling balks at fire-sale rates, the heat was applied to Giamatti.

Balks were nothing compared to what happened at the end of April 1988, when Giamatti first went nose-to-nose with Pete Rose, then-manager of the Cincinnati Reds. During a game with the Mets before a packed stadium in Cincinnati, Rose took issue with a call by first-base umpire Dave Pallone. The game was heated and the fans rabid toward the Mets, who were on their way to an annihilation of the National League's Eastern division. When Rose began arguing, the home crowd roared encouragement.

In the course of the argument, Rose jabbed himself in the face with Pallone's finger. In the heat of the moment, Rose shoved Pallone—an absolute no-no—and Pallone shoved back. By the time Rose was escorted off the field, the fans had turned uglier than a bucket of toads. Objects were being thrown from the stands, and the situation was an eyelash away from being a full-scale riot of the sort that hadn't been seen since the day years earlier when the Cleveland Indians had made the tactical error of holding a nickel-beer promotion. The only thing that prevented the final explosion was Pallone's exit from the field of battle, a move taken for his own survival.

Giamatti belted Rose with a thirty-day suspension—one-sixth of the season. In return he was crucified on the cross of public opinion.

Giamatti stood up under the pressure. "The number of Pete Rose letters didn't approach what came to me in New Haven in 1981 after I made a speech laying into the Moral Majority," he said, "and the level of bitterness didn't come close to what I heard after I once refused to let the Yale Glee Club sing the solidarity anthem in a broadcast for the Voice of America. George Will [conservative columnist and sometime writer about baseball] practically stripped me of my citizenship. . . . The student press began to compare me with General Franco and some other epigones of the right."

But Giamatti did admit that "for sheer noise, the Rose thing was probably bigger." He knew why, too. "Everybody feels that he or she owns baseball, right across the country," he observed, "which is one of its incomparable assets."

The people who thought they owned baseball felt that the Rose suspension was far too long. A punishment that harsh had never been levied before, they argued. Giamatti, a fierce protector of his umpires, answered that he had taken the situation into account in making his decision. Among the factors aggravating the case were the fact that Rose had shoved Pallone and the effect that had on an angry hometown crowd.

As for the argument that there was no precedent for a suspension of such length, Giamatti went back to his ideas of the traditional versus the sacred. "You can't be enslaved by precedent," he said. "Every time someone does something differently, the traditionalists argue that it has never been done before. In the fourteenth Century, athletes fought to the death. Is that what we want?"

Increasingly, that seemed to be the case with the breed of fan that Giamatti found in his ballparks. Crowds which thirty years earlier had demonstrated their passions within the unwritten rules of civil behavior had gotten increasingly unruly. By 1986, it was not uncommon to see a half dozen fights a night in Shea Stadium as the Mets romped through the schedule. Besides the fights, the language in the stands had become so foul and behavior so uninhibited that some ballparks—that enclosed refuge that harkened back to Paradise—were no longer a fit place to take a family.

The stands were being taken over by a crowd that had been weaned on rock concerts and beer. At the ballpark they found giant video boards telling them when to cheer and sophisticated sound systems blaring rock music between innings. They came to the ballpark to drink large amounts of beer and engage in what Giamatti called "recreational violence," a term that conjured up images of Anthony Burgess's frightening glimpse into a possible future, *A Clockwork Orange.*

Giamatti worried a great deal about recapturing the ballparks for families and making them a refuge once more. Some wondered why he was concerned: baseball attendance was rising every year. But Giamatti knew that attendance could rise while fans were lost. He didn't want that to happen.

"I'm not sure you can take for granted that people will want to go out to the ballpark if it's hard to get there and if simple, fundamental needs aren't met," he said. Among those needs he counted convenient parking, clean restrooms, courteous ushers, and confidence-inspiring security. They sounded so simple, yet it was amazing how many ball clubs neglected them.

Giamatti disliked the video boards. He particularly disliked instant replay. Once, while watching a game with Joe Garagiola, somebody executed a phenomenal play. "Wow! I'd like to see that again," Garagiola exclaimed, looking up for the video replay. Giamatti barked at him, wanting to know what was wrong with seeing the play live.

"Replays make us analytically lazy. It puts no pressure on one to pay close attention, because if a fine play occurs, it will be shown again. It's like a laugh track," he said of the big prompter in the outfield, telling everyone what was worth looking at. He was particularly amazed at people who bring portable televisions to the park, as if an event isn't really happening unless it's on television.

He believed that constant replays, instead of heightening the experience of watching a game, detract from it. The play that looked so marvelous on the field becomes banal after half a dozen super-slow-motion repeats from an equal number of camera angles.

Giamatti was particularly opposed to the use of instant replays to review umpire decisions, a growing trend in sports. The game is played by men and officiated by men, none of them perfect. That is how it should be, he felt. Then in June 1988 one of his umpires, Paul Runge, during a game that again involved the Mets, was behind home plate when Dwight Gooden threw what Runge thought was a wild pitch that allowed a runner to advance. When the replay was shown on the video board, Runge happened to look up and see that the ball had actually been fouled off and thus was not a wild pitch. He reversed his call based on what he had seen, saying it was "a moral issue." He couldn't allow a wrong call to stand.

The call affected the outcome of the game, and a controversy naturally followed. Giamatti, hater of replays though he was, refused to criticize his umpire. Rather, he congratulated him. "There are no grounds for reprimanding a guy for trying to do his job right," Giamatti concluded. "My God, I commend him for it."

It was this practical streak that made all the philosophy and cosmic pronouncements acceptable. For among Giamatti's many beliefs was the belief that few things can be carved in stone and lived with forever.

Thus, he did not side with those who wanted to clean up ballparks by banning the sale of beer. He himself liked a beer now and then and knew that it was possible to drink without getting drunk and without turning into a maniac. "Order without freedom is repression, and freedom without order is anarchy," he reminded people.

His outlook, the obvious thought he put into his opinions, his willingness to talk with anyone and everyone, and his sheer love of the game—it seemed he was always at a ballgame—won him respect and admiration.

One of the things that endeared him to the masses was his confession of what it had been like in 1986, his first year on the job, when he had to sit in the National League President's box at Shea Stadium and watch his beloved Red Sox blow a two-run lead with two out in the bottom of the tenth inning and lose both the World Series and the game when Mookie Wilson's famous ground ball rolled through Bill Buckner's legs.

"I told my son I planned to root for the Mets," he said. "He said he was confident I'd be able to rise above my duty. Sure enough, when things got close, an atavistic demon far more ancient than I took over. Before long, I was advising Mr. Buckner how to field his position, and Mr. McNamara [the Red Sox manager] what to do with his lineup. Naturally, they paid me as much heed as they did any other nut."

Whitey Herzog, the garrulous and profane manager of the St. Louis Cardinals, said about Giamatti: "For being book smart, I thought he had a lot of street smarts, which is tough to find sometimes."

Even Rose liked him. "I get along damn good with him," Rose said. "I think he's great for the National League. I think my suspension was too long, but that's my opinion." And then, in one of the great ironic statements, Rose added, "I think he'd make a great commissioner."

Many people say he did make a great commissioner. They say that in the five months he spent in that office, he was the greatest commissioner the game had ever seen. But the short time he spent in the office—from April 1 to September 1, 1989, was spent under the dark cloud of the Rose controversy.

The accusations that Rose had gambled began before Giamatti took office. Firm allegations that he had bet on baseball were received by Commissioner Ueberroth in February 1989. Ueberroth did the only sensible thing for a man who planned to leave office in two months. He rounded up an investigator and handed the mess over to his successor.

Thus, Giamatti became commissioner with the Rose investigation in full swing and occupying the nation. The principal witnesses against Rose were former friends of his, an unsavory cast of characters who didn't appear to have made an honest nickel in years. Slowly, the allegations leaked out to the press. Betting slips from Rose—with games involving the Reds—had been uncovered. The Internal Revenue Service was after Rose (who was replaced as manager after the 1988 season) for evading taxes. It was said that he had placed bets on games from his office in the clubhouse and had lost huge amounts of money gambling.

To baseball fans, this was akin to a child being told that Bambi had trampled Thumper to death. He didn't mean to do it. It was an accident. He didn't see him. He was temporarily insane.

Rose was given an appointment to meet with Giamatti to defend himself against the evidence that Giamatti's investigator, John Dowd, had gathered. Rose instead went to the courts to prevent Giamatti from holding the hearing. The commissioner, Rose argued, was prejudiced against him, and therefore he could not get a fair hearing. The courts ultimately sided with Giamatti.

Rose continued to fight a hearing. Then, just as matters were reaching a head, Rose's lawyers called Giamatti's lawyers and proposed a deal.

No deal, Giamatti told them, then he laid out the articles of surrender. Rose accepted them on the condition that no formal finding be made that he had gambled on baseball games. Giamatti said fine.

That's how matters stood on August 24, 1989, when Giamatti, like a medieval pope, declared Peter Edward Rose to be anathema and excommunicated him forever from the sacrament of baseball. As promised, Giamatti's formal decision contained no finding of guilt.

But do you think he did it? Giamatti was asked.

"Yes. I have concluded that he bet on baseball."

On the Reds, too?

"Yes."

The decision crushed Rose, who would soon be off to jail after being found guilty on the tax charges. The decision also outraged millions of baseball fans. But it was done.

Giamatti stayed in New York for a few days, cleaning up the debris of the case and getting things in order. Then he went to his summer home on Martha's Vineyard. The day after he arrived, September 1, he dropped dead of a massive heart attack. He was 51.

With the shock of his passing, the inevitable conclusion was drawn that the strain of the Rose case had killed him, and how unjust it was that Rose had survived and Giamatti hadn't. But the man who wanted to be "just Bart" wouldn't have bought that. He was simply a heart attack waiting to happen—a somewhat overweight, out-of-shape man with a sedentary job, and an enthusiastic smoker of cigarettes to boot. He understood better than most that even the longest life is but a moment in the enormous stretch of history. It is the lot of all mortals to die, some sooner and some later. It's what you do with the time you have that matters.

Giamatti did a lot. He made lasting contributions to the study of literature, to journalism, to a university, and to baseball. During his time as president of the National League, he had even in a moment of whimsy appointed an old teaching colleague "Physicist to the National League" and charged him with explaining how a curveball curves, discovering whether a fastball can really rise, and determining the ideal angle at which to strike a ball to get the maximum carry.

He made friends wherever he went. Not everyone agreed with him, but few could actively dislike him.

"He was a magnificent human being," said Bud Selig, owner of the Milwaukee Brewers, who had a particularly close relationship with him. "He was our captain, and now our captain is gone."

"His life on earth was far too short, but certainly no one made better use of his time," said Dr. Bobby Brown, President of the American League.

"In my nineteen years as a National League umpire," said Bruce

Froemming, "we never had a man in the position who commanded the respect he did and gave the respect he did."

Baseball dedicated the 1989 World Series—the Series that was interrupted by the San Francisco earthquake—to Giamatti. And then, when the season was well over, baseball held a tribute to him: It was called a "Celebration of Bart Giamatti in Baseball."

It took place in Carnegie Hall—the Fenway Park of auditoriums—on October 31. Ralph Branca was there, sitting next to Eddie Lopat. Willie Mays and Hank Aaron, Joe DiMaggio and Bobby Doerr, Yogi Berra and Bill White—they all came to New York that day to pay tribute.

Doerr was the surviving link, the man who had inspired the young Giamatti to love the game he served so well. And, as pictures from Giamatti's life in baseball—pictures of him obviously enjoying the heck out of life—flashed on a giant screen, you had to think how fortunate it was that Giamatti hadn't been able to play ball as well as Doerr, or even as well as Marv Throneberry. He had, it turned out, something greater to give to the game than base hits. He had his leadership to give.

On the stage at Carnegie Hall, beneath the mighty proscenium arch, were two lecterns and eleven chairs. The people chosen to sit in those chairs were a cross-section of the sport and society: the new commissioner and Giamatti's good friend, Fay Vincent; league presidents Bobby Brown and Bill White; Yale president Benno Schmidt; Hall of Famers Doerr and DiMaggio; broadcaster Joe Garagiola; writers Claire Smith and Roger Angell; owner Selig; and Giamatti's eldest son, Marcus. There were men and women, white and black—America as Giamatti saw it should be.

Once Giamatti had been asked to select an all-Italian-American baseball team. When he completed the task, he was asked who he wanted to sing the National Anthem. Julius LaRosa, he said, and so that day at Carnegie Hall LaRosa walked on stage and sang "The Star-Spangled Banner." The Yale Glee Club followed with a medieval student song, "Gaudeamus Igitur." If anyone in the audience understood Latin, they would have heard the song begin with the sentiment: "Therefore let us rejoice, for we are young."

There was much to celebrate about the rumpled little man who had radiated childlike delight at having a free front-row seat at every baseball game.

"He went to the ballpark when he didn't have to," said Garagiola. "That's important." He told the story about the instant replay. He told of how Giamatti had once told him that "talking baseball with Yogi Berra was like talking to Homer about the Gods." Garagiola concluded, "You'll never hear anybody say, 'I know a guy just like Bart Giamatti.' "

"He wrote and spoke about the game in a way none of us had ever heard before," said Selig. "He was not encumbered by evil in any way."

Rose's name never came up during the ninety-minute program. It wasn't a day for clouds.

Claire Smith recalled how Giamatti had answered his brethren educators when they expressed horror at his abandonment of the university for the ballpark. "I love teaching, but the world will survive if I don't write another book about Edmund Spenser," he had said.

Then his image, in a film clip, was playing on the screen behind the dignitaries. And his voice rang out through a hall so quiet you could hear a tear drop. "We have fallen from Paradise," the voice of Bart said. "Paradise is lost to us. So we will always try to approximate this perfect state, but we will never get back to it." The closest we could get was baseball, the game which to him was "part of America's plot."

His son Marcus, a Yale graduate and an actor, told of going with his father just that year to a Red Sox–Yankees game at Yankee Stadium. His father had gestured grandly toward the vast field and said, "You see, Marcus, this is the last pure place where Americans can dream. This is the last great arena, the last green arena, where everybody—*everybody*—can learn the lessons of life."

"This was no ordinary grader of papers," Vincent said in his turn. "If I were to choose one word Bart stood for, it was civility. Bart attacked uncivil behavior." Giamatti wanted ballparks to be refuges where adults and children could dream, not asylums where they walked in fear. He did a lot to make that come true. He was fond of the word *noble,*" Vincent said. "To me, he was the noblest of them all.

"Bravo, noble Bart. And goodbye."